RED MARKERS

Close Air Support
for the Vietnamese Airborne
1962–1975

Gary N. Willis
Red Marker 18
1969–70

In Memoriam

Lt. Colonel Eugene R. McCutchan, USAF Retired
1919 - 2012

Veteran of WWII, Korea and Vietnam
Red Marker 01

NOTICE
All rights reserved.
Copyright © 2013 by Gary N. Willis.
Reproduction in any manner of the text and/or photographs in this document, in whole or in part, in English or in any other language, without the prior written consent of the author is prohibited.
Questions regarding this document should be addressed to the author at 2911 Keagan Falls Drive, Manvel, TX 77578, USA. He can also be contacted through the Red Marker website at www.redmarkerfacs.com

PUBLISHING HISTORY
Published by Gary N. Willis, 2013.
Library of Congress Control Number: 201390531
ISBN: 978-0-9859231-1-2

BOOK ORDERS
Books may be ordered at: http://www.lulu.com/search for "Red Markers."

PHOTOGRAPHS
Front Cover	Red Marker Bird Dog at Bien Hoa. Collection of Gary Willis.
Section I	Inside Hue Citadel. Collection of Mike Morea.
Section II	Airborne Drop in IV Corps. Collection of Jack Cebe-Habersky.
Section III	O-1 Bird Dog Over IV Corps. Collection of Bruce Freeman.
Section IV	Red Marker Compound at Tay Ninh. Collection of Jim Hoppe.
Section V	FAC's Side Arm. Collection of Dave Langas.
Section VI	Tay Ninh West–Abandoned. Collection of Jim Yeonopolus.
Section VII	Freedom Bird. Collection of Gary Willis.
Page 210	Vietnam Memories. Collection of Gary Willis.
Back Cover	Lieutenant Willis at Song Be City. Collection of Gary Willis.

MAPS
Page 12	South Vietnam, Tactical Air Control System. Ryan Willis
Page 30	South Vietnam, Airborne Operations, 1962-1964. Ryan Willis
Page 56	South Vietnam, Airborne Operations, 1965-1968. Ryan Willis
Page 124	South Vietnam, Airborne Operations, 1969-1970. Ryan Willis
Page 155	Cambodia Fishhook, Combined Operations, 1970. Peter Condon.
Page 178	South Vietnam, Airborne Operations, 1971-1972. Ryan Willis
Page 196	South Vietnam, The Final Invasion, 1974-1975. Ryan Willis

DESIGN
Book design and layout by Australian FAC Peter Condon using Bookman Old Style font for text and Orwell for Headings.
Cover design by Ryan Willis.

CONTENTS

Preface – Gary N. Willis, Red Marker 18	7
Foreword – Lt Col Eugene R. McCutchan, USAF (Ret)	9
SECTION I – BACKGROUND	11
Chapter 1 – Introduction	13
Chapter 2 – United States Air Force Structure	17
Chapter 3 – Vietnamese Airborne, Red Hats and Red Markers	25
SECTION II – THE ADVISORY YEARS	29
Chapter 4 – 1962 – Major Gene McCutchan	31
Chapter 5 – 1963 – Major Gene McCutchan, Lt Col James Martin	37
Chapter 6 – 1964 – Lt Col James Martin, Lt Col Carleton Casteel	43
SECTION III – THE BUILD UP	55
Chapter 7 – 1965 – Lt Col Carleton Casteel, Major Gene McCutchan	57
Chapter 8 – 1966 – Lt Col Gene McCutchan	77
Chapter 9 – 1967 – Lt Col Gene McCutchan, Lt Col Pete Almquist	93
Chapter 10 – 1968 – Lt Col Pete Almquist, Lt Col Don Glenn	105
SECTION IV – VIETNAMIZATION	123
Chapter 11 – 1969 – Major Bill Fulton, Major Michael Branz	125
Chapter 12 – 1970 – Major Bob Drawbaugh, Lt Col Robert Daugherty, Major Jack Koppin	147
SECTION V – RETURN TO ADVISORY STATUS	177
Chapter 13 – 1971 – Major Dean Haeusler, Major Chuck Waterman	179
Chapter 14 – 1972 – Major Bob Johnson, Lt Col Jack Bryant	183

SECTION VI – GOING IT ALONE — 195
Chapter 15 – 1973-1975 – VNAF FACs, B-130s, Xuan Loc, Newport Bridge — 197

SECTION VII – BACK IN THE WORLD — 203
Chapter 16 – Red Markers Revisited — 205

EPILOGUE — 211

APPENDICES
I	Glossary	213
II	Reconstructed Red Marker Roster – Chronological	215
III	Reconstructed Red Marker Roster – Alphabetical	221
IV	Red Hats who became Generals	227
V	Individual Medals Awarded Red Markers	229

BIBLIOGRAPHY — 231

PREFACE

GARY N. WILLIS, RED MARKER 18

For about seven months during the Vietnam War, I served with the Red Marker Forward Air Controllers. This unit supported the Vietnamese Airborne Division from 1962 to 1973. Forty years later, I began contacting others from the unit. I found that the Forward Air Controllers Association had a database including many former Red Markers, but that no complete roster existed. Thus began the "Red Marker Roster Project." Each person I contacted recalled additional names to add to the list. Furthermore, each had interesting stories to tell or photographs to share. Over a six-month period, the roster project morphed into a history project.

Researching unit histories, personal diaries and stories already published confirmed that the Red Marker detachment was unique. It was the only FAC unit that operated in all four Corps areas of Vietnam. As this history began to take shape, I saw that I could easily fall into the trap of writing nostalgia. The generally outstanding performance of the Red Marker FACs and of the Airborne might support or even deserve that approach. However, that would be fantasy. This history opts for accuracy, trusting that the total picture is realistic.

For example, highly qualified fighter pilots initially staffed the unit. These were Majors and senior Captains who were experts in tactical air support. Over the years, however, the Air Force ran out of experienced personnel and began sending FACs newly graduated from pilot training. Most of these young pilots performed exceptionally well, but their lack of flying experience is reflected in the accident record. Low-time Lieutenants piloted each of the Red Marker aircraft that were in-volved in accidents. One died in a mid-air collision.

In later years, the unit also reflected the disparate views of an American population grown tired of a long and ultimately fruitless war. Some pilots and ground crewmen were eager participants. Others were more reluctant, questioning the value of their contributions and the long separations from their families. Regardless of background, experience or motivation, however, Red Markers performed their mission with skill and courage. This history tracks the evolution of the unit from the beginning to the end.

I greatly appreciate all who contributed to this effort both for their service in the unit

PREFACE

and for sharing their memories and stories. I especially thank my wife, Robin Rankin Willis, for her love and support during my Vietnam tour, during the completion of this book and for the forty years in between. She edited the entire book and is responsible for its readability. Any errors, grammatical or otherwise, are mine.

Gary N. Willis
Red Marker 18
Dec 69 – Jul 70

FORWARD

LT COLONEL EUGENE R. McCUTCHAN
USAF (RETIRED), RED MARKER 01

Red Markers were a part of the earliest efforts to establish a serious Air Force presence in Southeast Asia, an effort that quickly evolved into the use and control of Tactical Air Power. In this environment, the Forward Air Controller played a critical role. The first FACs and Air Liaison Officers came from fighter squadrons and probably had three months temporary duty with Army units, training as ground FACs in simulated close air support missions after attending the Air-Ground Operations School. They were familiar with most forms of ordnance, its delivery and results.

Early on, high-level thinking was that the Air Force was not really needed in Southeast Asia in a combat role. The Air Force strongly disagreed, and, in 1962, began the first serious introduction into SEA of FACs and of advisors to Vietnamese fighter squadrons. The disagreement among the services about the Air Force role led to a turbulent beginning in inter-service cooperation. Initially, Air Force personnel were not allowed to live in Army facilities, the only ones available. In many cases the ALO/FAC had to tell his Army counterpart that he did not work for him and remained under Air Force control.

Fortunately, this confusion and awkwardness soon changed in the course of operations where each side earned the respect of the other with courage, dedication and professional performance under live fire in combat. In fact, many close friendships were formed in the brotherhood that battle produces.

Working with the Vietnamese Airborne was a unique experience. The Airborne had very high unit esprit, which was reflected in the conduct of their operations. Red Markers equaled this standard of conduct in an environment that was completely new and strange to them. Red Markers operated from remote locations, in many cases using small, unimproved landing strips. On occasion, they made a landing strip from a wide spot in the road. They maintained a complete inventory of field equipment associated more with an Army than an Air Force unit—tents for living quarters and a command post, runway night lighting, a generator, mobile radios, cots, air mattresses and sleeping bags along with tables and chairs, rations and ammo. All of this was necessary to accompany the Airborne on deployments which on short notice could be sent anywhere in the country.

FORWARD

Many times a Red Marker was in an isolated location where all manner of situations developed. There was no one to help him. He made his own decisions, planned his own course of action and gained the aura of self-confidence that became a trademark of the Red Markers.

Early on, night FAC missions were done without flares. The control of an air strike at night with troops in contact, without flares, is the granddaddy of all FAC missions. In my view, it is the FAC's most demanding mission. On occasion, recovery after a mission was required in total darkness using only the headlights of a couple of jeeps to help the pilot find the landing strip.

Although Red Markers assigned with the highly mobile Airborne missed some of the comforts enjoyed by FACs with American units or with other ARVN forces, such as rooms with beds, dining facilities and other FACs for company, we had some good moments. The last FAC mission of the day might end with a landing at the closest facility to load the empty back seat with cases of coke and beer for a quick flight back to the remote location. This particularly endeared us to the Army advisors with whom we worked.

The Airborne celebrated its anniversary with a variety of ceremonies. One such ceremony was to place a ten-foot square platform in the Saigon River in front of the Majestic Hotel in downtown Saigon and use this as a target for sky-divers. I was asked to participate in the practice parachute jump before the actual ceremony. In the jump, I was the first out and laughingly named myself the "Wind Dummy" after I missed the platform and landed in the river.

The Red Markers were highly decorated for their service and their courage by both the Vietnamese and American governments. There were numerous awards of Vietnamese Crosses of Gallantry, some with palms and gold stars, and one award of the VNAF's Air Gallantry Cross with Silver Wings. There was one award of the highest Vietnamese medal, the National Order of Vietnam Knight. In addition to uncountable Air Medals, the American medals included many Bronze Stars and Distinguished Flying Crosses, plus a few Bronze Stars with V, numerous Air Force Commendation Medals, an Army Commendation Medal with V, an Army Air Medal with V and several Silver Stars. The highest US award earned by a Red Marker was the Air Force Cross presented to Captain Delbert W. Fleener for extraordinary heroism in action on 17 December 1965. The Red Markers were some of the finest people I have ever served with.

In closing, I cannot accept the fact that we lost the war, or that our country reneged on its pledge to a people, or that our leaving caused millions of Asian deaths. The Red Markers fought and died for a different outcome.

Gene McCutchan
Lt Colonel, USAF (Ret)
Red Marker 62-63, 65-67

SECTION 1 - BACKGROUND

- Introduction
- United States Air Force Structure
- Vietnamese Airborne, Red Hats and Red Markers

TACTICAL AIR CONTROL SYSTEM

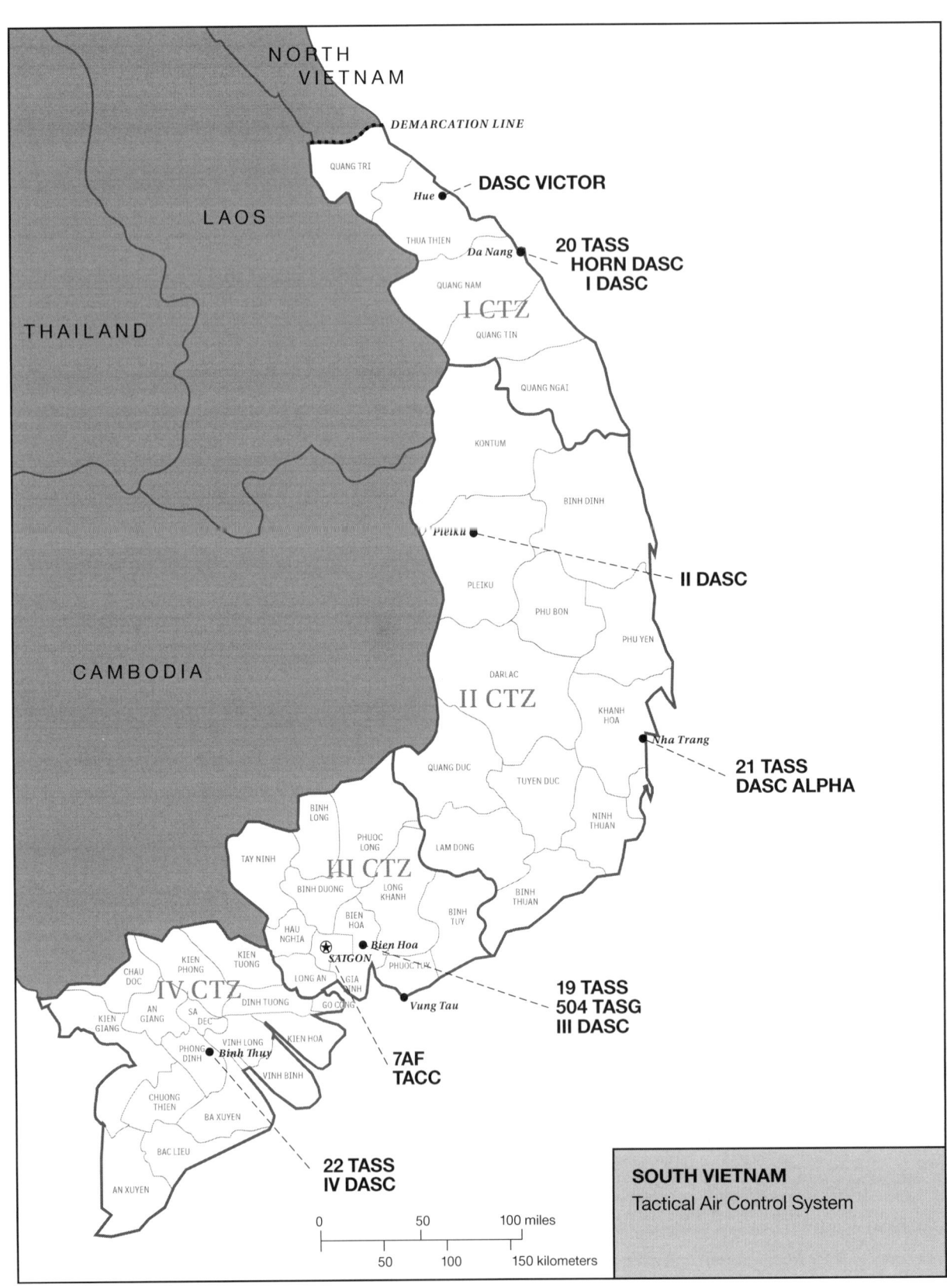

CHAPTER 1

INTRODUCTION

From 1962 until early 1973, a small unit of United States Air Force FACs (Forward Air Controllers), ROMADs (Radio Operators, Maintainers and Drivers) and crew chiefs supported the Airborne troops of the Army of the Republic of Vietnam (ARVN) in its battles throughout Southeast Asia. The FACs served alongside Advisory Team 162, a team of American Army advisors working with the Airborne. These Army advisors and the Air Force unit each adopted the Airborne's distinctive camouflage uniform and red beret. The Army advisors were known as "Red Hats" and the FACs as "Red Markers," which they took as their radio call sign.

The Red Marker unit began and ended as a single Air Liaison Officer (ALO) providing advice and coordinating air power for the Vietnamese Airborne. The unit grew to peak manpower of thirty-six officers and enlisted personnel in 1969, with a dozen aircraft and support equipment and operated simultaneously from several forward locations. The unit rapidly shrank from its peak manpower to a single ALO as the VNAF reassumed the role of coordinating air power support for Vietnamese ground forces in February 1971. Two years later the Americans withdrew from Vietnam.

At one time or another, the unit operated from locations in each of the four military regions in Vietnam from the Demilitarized Zone (DMZ) to the Mekong Delta and into Cambodia. An incomplete Red Marker roster (Appendix II) reconstructed during research for this book includes 163 Americans—88 officers and 75 enlisted men—who served during the decade of its existence. In addition to these American servicemen, there were two Vietnamese Airborne troopers who provided support to the unit for many years. The roster also includes a VNAF officer who served the Airborne as G-3 Air and flew many missions with Red Markers between 1966 and 1971. Of these brave men, three FACs and one ROMAD died in combat. An additional Red Marker FAC was killed in action after he had transferred to another unit.

In order to set the stage for describing the history of the Red Markers, it is helpful to look at the framework in which the unit operated.

• First, the USAF imposed a command structure and a Tactical Air Control System (TACS) applicable to all air power employed in Southeast Asia. The command structure provided administrative and logistical support to the FAC organizations while the TACS ran the daily operations. The TACS determined target selection, approval and the control of all strikes against those targets. The Red Markers were dependent upon both the logistical support and operational arm to accomplish their mission.

- Second, early in the conflict the Military Assistance Command–Vietnam (MACV) began embedding advisory teams with Vietnamese units. These teams of officers and senior non-coms assisted their Vietnamese counterparts in command and staff functions and helped the units coordinate with American ground, artillery and air forces. The Red Marker ALOs dealt directly with the Vietnamese Airborne commanders and senior staff. The more junior Red Markers' communications with the Airborne were focused on the Red Hats of Advisory Team 162.

- Last, the Vietnamese Airborne Division was one of the elite fighting units of the South Vietnamese army. It was used as the nation's tactical reserve, thrust into every hot spot in the country. The Red Markers had to match both the mobility and the esprit of the Airborne to provide the support needed.

The next chapter summarizes the Air Force command structure related to the forward air controller mission and the control system implemented for close air support. Some readers comfortable with their own understanding of this material will find the summary unnecessary. If so, skip it. Following that chapter is a brief summary of the Airborne, the Red Hats and Red Markers. Following this Background, the book turns to a chronology of the Red Markers and of the air support provided to the Vietnamese Airborne up to their final stand at Xuan Loc and at the Newport Bridge in April 1975.

I struggled with the treatment of the alphabet soup of acronyms, as does every writer on military subjects. Should each term be defined, and, if so, should the definition be in the text or in a footnote? And should the footnotes be endnotes? Or should this all be relegated to a glossary of terms in the Appendix? I opted for a combination. The terms are defined in the text. Some are defined more than once, as a reminder, and sometimes the full name is used rather than the acronym for ease of reading. Additionally, a Glossary is included as Appendix I, adopted in part from the glossary that appears in the Tactical Air Support Squadrons official histories. Finally, I chose to use footnotes rather than endnotes for sources and explanatory or supplemental information in the hope that that they will be less distracting to the reader than having to flip to the back of the book.

Dedication

This history is dedicated to the Vietnamese Airborne and their American advisors, the Red Hats of Advisory Team 162 and to all Red Markers, especially to those who lost their lives in this conflict—Airman Second Class James C. Henneberry, Captain Paul R. Windle, First Lieutenant Robert M. Carn, Captain Donald R. Hawley and Major F. Dale Dickens.

Special recognition is due two other Red Markers. The first is Lieutenant Colonel Eugene R. McCutchan, the first and longest serving Red Marker, who was ALO of the Airborne for more than thirty-six months. Gene reviewed and commented on the final draft of *Red Markers*. He died in June 2012, a month before its publication. The second is Major Joseph S. Granducci, II, Red Marker 02, 1965-66, who began this history project in 2000 but died in 2005 before its completion. A salute to both and thanks to all who contributed their memories to this history.

The Second Indochina War, known by the Americans as the Vietnam War and by the Vietnamese as the American War, like wars of all ages, revealed some of the worst and the best of humankind. The worst, in the destruction of property and the slaughter of life, innocent or otherwise; the best, in the selfless courage of some participants.

In that regard, the Red Markers were typical. The vast majority exhibited bravery and courage. Most were of high moral character. However, they were humans, not saints, doing their best under trying circumstances. Ironically, one of the most highly decorated was also found guilty of drug smuggling. Regardless, Red Markers share a bond with all who have gone to war, a relationship that is indescribable to those who have not experienced it and indestructible to those who have.

CHAPTER 2

UNITED STATES AIR FORCE STRUCTURE

The history of the Red Markers is a microcosm of the evolution of Close Air Support in Vietnam. The unit began in an advisory capacity then paralleled the buildup of the American forces into the late 1960s. That period was followed by the subsequent drawdown and ultimate withdrawal of those forces from Vietnam in 1973.

In late 1961, the USAF sent five officers to Bien Hoa Air Base, South Vietnam to train VNAF pilots and FACs to control airstrikes in O-1 Bird Dog aircraft.[1] The training program followed the guidelines of the Air-Ground Operations School based at Keesler AFB. There were some major differences, however, between the American and Vietnamese approach. American FACs both piloted the plane and controlled airstrikes. The VNAF, however, required that a separate pilot fly the plane and a FAC rode in back communicating with ground troops and fighter aircraft. These VNAF FACs in fact did not need to be pilot-qualified and most were not. One consequence was that during training the USAF pilots often piloted the Bird Dogs as the VNAF FACs learned to direct air attacks. During this early period, the USAF also assigned an Air Liaison Officer (ALO) to work with Vietnamese division commanders providing advice on the use of air power. These ALOs accompanied the Vietnamese forces on the ground during deployments to give direction to the VNAF FACs controlling airstrikes. Sometimes the ALOs would pilot the VNAF Bird Dogs.

O-1 Bird Dog of the Vietnamese Air Force from the internet www.aviastar.org.

When the need arose for additional FACs, the USAF brought in more instructors and aircraft in September 1963 and activated the 19th Tactical Air Support Squadron (TASS) at Bien Hoa as a larger organization to train pilots and FACs. The original plan was to run the school for a year and then turn it over to the VNAF in August 1964. The USAF executed the plan and deactivate the 19th TASS. How-

---

[1] "A Dangerous Business: Forward Air Control in SEA," online article of the Air Force Museum, www.nationalmuseum.af.mil/factsheets, 2010.

CHAPTER 2 - UNITED STATES AIR FORCE STRUCTURE

ever, it quickly reversed course after the Gulf of Tonkin Incident occurred later that same month. United States' involvement in the war soon became both more straightforward and more intense, with American ground and air forces committed to more than an advisory and training role. Tactical fighter wings began deploying to Southeast Asia along with other support forces, all under the aegis of the 2nd Air Division, which was part of the Thirteenth Air Force.[2]

The 2nd Air Division grew over the years to become the 7th Air Force. Eventually, it had operational control over nine tactical fighter wings in Vietnam and Thailand, four special operations wings, three reconnaissance wings, a tactical airlift wing, several combat support groups and the 504th Tactical Air Support Group (TASG). This last organization provided personnel, administrative and other support to the USAF FACs in the war.[3] At its largest in 1968, the 7th Air Force commanded 1,768 aircraft and more than 90,000 personnel operating within Southeast Asia (SEA) from twelve main operating bases (MOBs) and numerous forward operating locations (FOLs).[4] Additional air assets not reporting to the 7th Air Force included aircraft from Navy carriers offshore Vietnam and Strategic Air Command bombers and tankers from Guam.

As the American Air Force began its training program of Vietnamese FACs, it also installed a Tactical Air Control System (TACS). This system structured the approval, command and control of air attacks throughout the country.[5] As the allied air and ground forces increased during the 1960s, the tactical air control system also evolved, with modification tailored to meet the military and political reality in Vietnam. The TACS ensured governmental control of the targeting and use of air power.

The country was divided into four combat tactical zones (CTZs) numbered from I Corps in the north through IV Corps in the south. Each Corps commander controlled all the Vietnamese divisions stationed within his region and also occupied a position of political power. Requests for and approval of targets began at the battalion level Tactical Air Control Party (TACP), an Air Force team working with each battalion. A request proceeded through the chain of command to the Tactical Operations Center (TOC) at the Corps, which was co-located with a Direct Air Support Center (DASC) staffed jointly by the VNAF and USAF (see diagram opposite).

Target requests had to be approved at each level. If the Corps granted its approval, the request was sent for final clearance to the Tactical Air Control Center (TACC) and the Vietnamese Joint General Staff, which reported directly to the Vietnamese President. Requests for air support from civil defense sources proceeded up a similar chain to the Province Chief, who passed approved requests into the military system at the Corps TOC.

The four DASCs (one in each Corps) reported to the TACC, a direct arm of 2nd

---

2 *Id.* at 13, originally called the Advanced Echelon, Thirteenth Air Force; for anonymity the organization was renamed 2ND ADVON; in October 1962 it was designated the 2nd Air Division and after 1965, the 7th Air Force.

3 John T. Correll, The Air Force in the Vietnam War, Aerospace Education Foundation, Arlington, VA, 2004, P. 7.

4 *Id.* at 5, 9.

5 Major Ralph A. Rowley, "USAF FAC Operations in Southeast Asia, 1961-1965," Office of Air Force History, 1972, p. 16.

TACTICAL AIR REQUEST SYSTEM

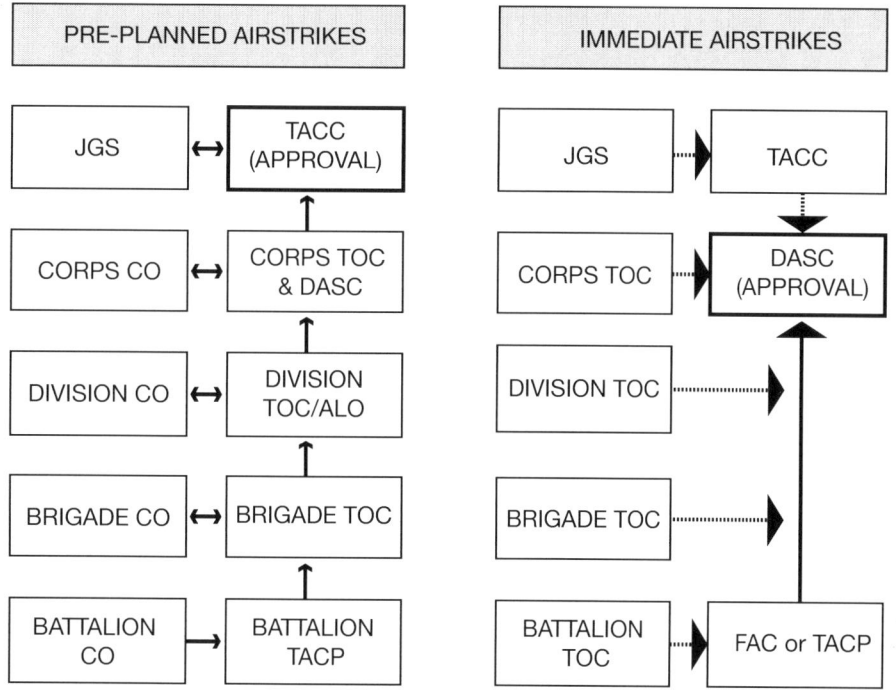

ADVON.[6] The TACC had responsibility for operations and planning, issuing daily orders designating the targets and ordnance by fighter-bomber unit, and indicating the FAC unit to control each strike. The appropriate portion, or "fragment," of this daily order–called a Frag Order–was sent to each unit informing the unit of its preplanned missions for the day.

Getting a mission "Fragged" for a target took a long time under this system, which provided numerous opportunities for requests to be denied or delayed. Further, the system did not lend itself to rapid response when troops in contact with hostile forces needed immediate air support or if a significant target of opportunity was sighted. Because of such shortcomings, a variation of the system for dealing with immediate air support was put in place by 1964. Under the revised system, a TACP at the direction of a FAC or ALO could submit a request directly to the DASC. All the sequential approval levels between (or above) the FAC and the DASC were responsible for monitoring the request, and silence would signify approval.[7] As intended, the new system allowed rapid response. When a call went in for airstrikes to support friendly troops in contact, the DASC could divert fighter bombers from a lower priority target or scramble a flight from an alert pad. With some modification, this system for requesting and approving both in-country preplanned and immediate airstrikes remained in place throughout the war.

During the years of escalation, the number of American FACs assigned to SEA increased dramatically. As each Ameri-

---

6 Major R. Scott Jobe, "Snake, 'Nape and Rockets at Dawn! Modern Joint Close Air Support and the Vietnam War," Air Command and Staff College, Air University, Maxwell AFB, AL, April 2006. DASCs and TACC were originally called Air Support Operations Centers (ASOCs) and the Air Operations Center (AOC), respectively, but were renamed in a reorganization in 1965.

7 Jobe

CHAPTER 2 - UNITED STATES AIR FORCE STRUCTURE

can or allied ground unit deployed to Vietnam, a new American FAC unit was formed to provide support. Additionally, American FACs were assigned to work for the ALOs advising each Vietnamese division. Furthermore, from this point forward the USAF FAC units had aircraft assigned. First, O-1 Bird Dogs were used and then augmented by O-2A Skymasters and finally OV-10 Broncos. For the rest of the war, American FACs would operate from the air rather than the ground. These changes had the effect of reducing the role of the VNAF FACs.

The basic battalion level control team evolved to include, with some variation, an ALO, a FAC, two radio operators, a crew chief and two aircraft. The control party would be headquartered with the battalion TOC and the FAC planes would fly from a local or nearby forward location. Thus, the TACP could provide all aspects of air support, including advice and planning as to the use of air power, visual reconnaissance of the area of operations, communications for requesting air support and control of any airstrikes. The ALOs built a close working relationship with the battalion staff in the American units and with the US Army advisors assigned to the ARVN units. The manpower and equipment requirements for this expanded USAF FAC role were enormous, leading to a reorganization of the units supporting the mission.

Initially, the 19th Tactical Air Support Squadron, which had been formed to provide training for Vietnamese FACs, became responsible for supporting the new USAF FAC units being assigned to locations throughout Vietnam. One immediate new task for the TASS was the reassembly and flight-testing of additional O-1 aircraft. These planes were shipped to Vietnam crated, with the wings off, in the cargo bays of transport aircraft. There were typically seven O-1s per shipment.[8] Further, the TASS had the task of handling the influx of pilots, crew chiefs and mechanics and getting them housed, checked out in the war zone and assigned to FAC units. This proved to be an overwhelming assignment for a single squadron.

Consequently, within a year of the Gulf of Tonkin Incident, four new support squadrons were activated. This resulted in one TASS within each Corps area of Vietnam, plus one in Thailand supporting the FAC activities in Laos and Cambodia. The 19th TASS remained at its location at Bien Hoa AB. Under a special order dated 6 May 1965, the 20th TASS was activated in I Corps at DaNang AB and became operational 4 Sep 1965.[9] Similarly, the 21st TASS became operational at Pleiku AB in II Corps (later moved to Nha Trang AB and later Phan Rang).[10] The 22nd TASS was created and based at Binh Thuy AB in IV Corps. Later, the 23rd TASS was activated and became operational at Nakhon Phanom Royal Thai AB, Thailand, controlling the "out-country" FAC program. With the exception of the 23rd TASS, the Red Markers dealt with each of these squadrons and with each DASC as they accompanied the Airborne on deployments throughout the country.

Upon activation, these new squadrons and the older 19th TASS reported to the 505th Tactical Air Control Group. This organization had responsibility for installation, operation and maintenance of radio systems, radar, radio navigation systems and power generation within the country. The reorganization marked the first time

---

8 The follow-on FAC aircraft, O-2As, were ferried into the war zone years later.
9 20th TASS History.
10 21st TASS History, Jan – Mar 1968, Foreword.

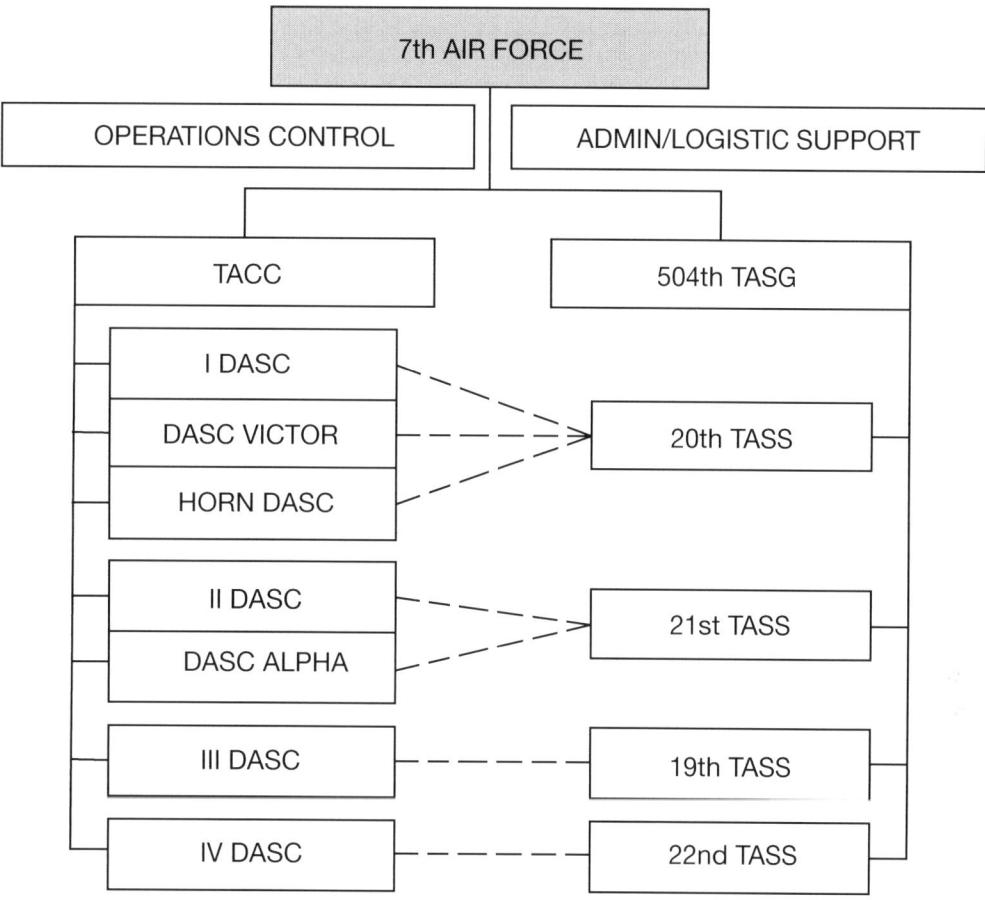

all the personnel and equipment required for the ALO/FAC mission were contained under the same operational umbrella.

Problems remained, however. Notably, all ROMADs belonged to one of the subordinate units of the 505th, the so-called Pack Rat Detachment. When ALOs needed a ROMAD for field operations, the 505th sent one on temporary duty (TDY). This was a holdover from the system in place during the advisory period of the war. The vast expansion of the tactical air war, however, required a more decentralized and self-reliant approach. The radio operators and maintenance personnel needed to work at the TASS level and to be assigned to individual ALOs. Another command issue was that the ALO/FAC mission had nothing in common with the rest of the mission of the 505th, i.e., electronic and power equipment installation and support (although both required personnel and equipment to be scattered all over the country).

In light of the distinct missions, Seventh Air Force reorganized again. In December 1966, it created the 504th Tactical Air Support Group (TASG) as the new umbrella organization for the five squadrons.[11] The 504th took over support of the physical assets and human resources committed to the FAC role, while the non-FAC squadrons remained under the 505th. This realignment did not solve all the problems inherent in such a far-flung

---

11 The 6250th TASG was initially the new umbrella organization. The 504th took over the role in December.

operation, but was a step in the right direction.[12]

One issue through most of the war was the bifurcated reporting inherent in the TASS-DASC setup (depicted on the above chart). Although the TASS owned the assets employed in the ALO/FAC mission, the commander of the TASS was not in the operational chain of command. Rather, the day-to-day operation of each ALO/FAC unit was dictated by the Direct Air Support Center. The TASS squadron commander and his staff had no control over target selection and approval or Frag Orders issued for airstrikes. Commanders and staff of the DASC and TACC controlled intelligence, planning and operations functions, while the TASS provided administrative control of ALO/FAC personnel. The Director of the TACC was the immediate supervisor of the Assistant Director in charge at each DASC. The structure worked well in some regions, but not so well in others. There was a natural tendency for the TASS hierarchy to try to become involved in operations, which was outside their bailiwick. This structure only changed as the VNAF began to control the DASCs.[13]

The command and coordination of tactical air power was further complicated when the Marine Corps deployed to Southeast Asia. Their integrated air arm required the creation of a separate DASC in I Corps, i.e., DASC Victor. Later, another DASC was added in both I Corps and II Corps to support the many U.S. Army and allied ground forces in those regions. This left the original DASC to support only the ARVN forces.[14] For example, II DASC located at Pleiku AB had operational control of the American and Vietnamese ALOs and FACs who supported the Vietnamese divisions. Meanwhile, DASC Alpha located at Nha Trang controlled American ALOs and FACs who supported the Free World Forces. Further, II DASC and DASC Alpha were under the operational control of Seventh Air Force Tactical Air Control Center. Nonetheless, 21st TASS supported all the ALO/FAC personnel in II Corps administratively and provided maintenance for all FAC aircraft in II Corps. The TASS was also responsible for administrative and logistical support of radio operators, intelligence personnel and electronic maintenance personnel within the Combat Tactical Zone.[15]

The coordination issues resulting from the multiple DASCs were illustrated most strikingly during the TET Offensive in 1968. For more than two weeks after the beginning of the offensive, the weather was so bad in I Corps that the allies could employ no tactical air. In mid-February weather conditions improved enough to launch tactical airstrikes. Vietnamese and American units near Hue asked for immediate strikes, but no one coordinated the response among the three operative control agencies. Aircraft under separate directions from I DASC, DASC Victor and Horn DASC were sent to targets so close to each other that FACs and fighters flew through artillery fire missions of adjacent ground forces. Their flight paths were dangerously close to each other. The lack of coordination meant that the airmen were put in unnecessarily unsafe conditions and that some meaningful targets were missed.[16]

---

12 22nd TASS History, Jan – Mar 1968, noted that it still had no permanent ground Communication and Electronics Maintenance (CEM) personnel assigned. Instead, TDY personnel from the Pack Rat Detachment handled the function. The TASS deemed this unacceptable.
13 20th TASS History, Jul-Sep 1971, as of 1 September all ALOs report to the TASS Squadron commander.

---

14 Jobe.
15 21st TASS History, Jan-Mar 1968.
16 20st TASS History, Jan-Mar 1968, p. 30.

504TH PERSONNEL AND AIRCRAFT AT MARCH 31, 1970								
UNIT	OFFICERS	ENLISTED	TOTAL	O-1	O-2	OV-10	TOTAL	DATE
19th	180	783	963		30	40	70	est Mar 70
20th	240	690	930		72	30	102	Mar 70
21st	187	596	783	22	68		90	Mar 70
22nd	165	374	539	57	39		96	Mar 70
23rd	101	238	339		12	30	42	Mar 70
TASS	873	2681	3554	79	221	100	400	
504th			75				2	est Mar 70
TOTAL			**3629**				**402**	

This split authority between the TASS and the DASC was confusing and uncoordinated, particularly in light of the multiple DASCs within a single Corps area. The arrangement also hindered the training of the Vietnamese in properly controlling tactical air resources.

Despite these operational coordination problems, the ALO/FAC forces continued their build up, becoming a significant part of the war effort. The FACs of the 504th logged about 357,000 hours of flying time during 1968. Those hours represented more than 32% of the total flying time for the 7th Air Force.[17] The 504th reached a peak of more than 400 aircraft and 3,600 personnel in early 1970. The table above shows the number of assigned personnel and aircraft at March 31, 1970.[18]

American policy changed after the TET offensive to focus on withdrawing Americans from combat and "Vietnamizing" the war. As a result, the number of in-country forces began to decline by 1970. For the FAC squadrons, gradual withdrawal and Vietnamization had two results. First, the Americans increased the training of Vietnamese pilots and support personnel in the ALO and FAC roles. Second, the Americans began turning over to the Vietnamese Air Force all close air support for Vietnamese ground forces. The withdrawal of American ground forces also reduced the need for USAF FACs. As each ground unit returned home, the supporting American FAC unit disbanded.[19] The FACs, ROMADs and crew chiefs from the disbanded units were reassigned or were sent home early. Their equipment was transferred to the VNAF or other allies, shipped to Korea, redeployed to the growing FAC effort in Thailand or sent to National Guard units in the States.

The Vietnamization plan initially focused on IV Corps. No U.S. Army units were stationed there, which meant the DASC and the FACs in the region had solely supported ARVN units. In essence, the war in IV Corps had never been completely Americanized. Consequently, the 22nd TASS completed the "Vietnamization" rapidly. By year-end 1969 it turned over its last O-1 aircraft, the FAC forward operating locations and all close air support responsibilities in IV Corps to the VNAF.

---

17 History of the 504th TASG, Oct–Dec 1968.
18 Based on tabulation of data in the unit histories of the 19th, 20th, 21st, 22nd, 23rd TASS for Jan-Mar 1970.
19 A similar reduction occurred for Australian and New Zealand FACs when their nation's ground units withdrew.

CHAPTER 2 - UNITED STATES AIR FORCE STRUCTURE

With that experience under its belt, the 22nd then moved from Binh Thuy AB to Bien Hoa AB to repeat the process. In January 1970, it took control from the 19th TASS of all FAC units and forward operating locations supporting the Vietnamese Army in III Corps. The 19th TASS retained responsibility for supporting the American ground forces in the region. The Red Markers were among those organizations transferred to the 22nd TASS.

The 22nd soon duplicated its transfer mission in III Corps (by then called Military Region 3, or MR 3). On 15 February 1971, the Vietnamese Air Force took over support of all ARVN forces in MR 3, including control of close air support for the Vietnamese Airborne Division. Now out of a job, the 22nd relocated to Wheeler AFB, Hawaii.

Not long thereafter, the 19th TASS also ceased operations in South Vietnam. As American and allied combat units withdrew from Vietnam, the 19th TASS increasingly focused on Cambodia. In August 1971, the 19th moved to Phan Rang AB in MR 2. Its remaining operations supporting the out-country war transferred to 21st TASS. On 15 January 1972, the 19th TASS relocated to the Republic of Korea and the 504th TASG was deactivated. By that time, the aircraft in the Tactical Air Support Squadrons totaled 106 O-2A Skymasters and 84 OV-10 Broncos. All the Bird Dogs had been previously transferred to allied forces.[20] The 20th TASS moved back to the continental United States on 15 January 1973. Consistent with the requirements of the Vietnam Peace Accords, 21st TASS (the last in-country unit) became inactive on 23 February 1973 as the final Free World Forces withdrew. The remaining Tactical Air Support Squadron in Southeast Asia, the 23rd TASS in Thailand, operated until 1975.

---

20 History of the 504th TASG, Jan –Mar 1972.

CHAPTER 3

VIETNAMESE AIRBORNE, RED HATS AND RED MARKERS

The Vietnamese Airborne was among the elite fighting units of the Republic of Vietnam. The Airborne began in 1951 as a battalion organized by the French Army in the First Indochina War. Until 1954, several battalions of Vietnamese paratroopers fought alongside French airborne troops against the insurgent forces of Ho Chi Minh and the Viet Minh. At Dien Bien Phu—the decisive battle of that war—several battalions of Vietnamese and French Airborne parachuted in to reinforce the garrison, which was ultimately overcome by General Giap's crushing siege. When hostilities ceased and Vietnam was partitioned at the DMZ, the surviving airborne units (including those that had been formed from volunteers in Hanoi) relocated to the southern capital at Saigon. Reconstituted as a Group (later known as a Brigade) of four battalions, the Airborne soon engaged the southern Viet Cong and earned a reputation as a loyal and fierce fighting force.

The American government had provided materiel support to the French and loyalist Vietnamese prior to Dien Bien Phu. Thereafter, the U.S. focused its aid on the new government of South Vietnam. In 1955, the U.S. assigned advisors to the Airborne and other Vietnamese units. The "Vietnamese Airborne Advisory Detachment," later named MACV Advisory Team 162, was staffed with veterans of the 82nd and 101st Airborne Divisions. Along with wearing U.S. insignia on their camouflage uniforms, Team 162 wore the patches of the Vietnamese Airborne and, notably, the Airborne's red beret. The advisors were thereafter known as Red Hats. At the outset Advisory Team 162 was small and only had advisors assigned at the Brigade level. The team was composed of an American "counterpart" for the Vietnamese commander and the head of each major staff function. By 1964, the entire detachment had increased to 26 personnel.[1] With the buildup of U.S. forces beginning in 1965, the advisory team expanded further. Staffing increased to provide an American counterpart to the Vietnamese command and staff hierarchy at the brigade and battalion level, and occasionally at the company level.

The Airborne itself also expanded, cre-

---

[1] Martin, Command Sergeant Major Michael, USA (Ret), *Angels in Red Hats, Paratroopers of the Second Indochina War,* Harmony House, Louisville, KY, 1995, 4 Dec 1964 photo at p. 20, which includes 26 US Army advisors and 2 USAF personnel, Lt. Colonel Casteel and Captain Bob Paradis, ALO and FAC, respectively.

ating the need for more advisors. Over the years, five more Airborne maneuver battalions and three artillery battalions were raised. In 1965, the Brigade was designated a Division, reflecting its larger size and capability. At its maximum strength, Team 162 had advisors in key positions from division through company level. It was the largest advisory team in Vietnam, numbering more than 100 personnel at its peak.[2] More than twelve hundred men served with Team 162 over its life, all of them volunteers; twenty-four of them died in combat fighting alongside their Airborne brothers. This was a greater loss of life than any other Advisory Team sustained. Hundreds were wounded. Estimates are that half the Red Hats were wounded at least once.[3] The last two losses occurred when two Red Hats died in a chopper crash 8 January 1973. Notable former Red Hats include Generals Jim Lindsay, Joe Kinzer, Barry McCaffrey, Pete Dawkins, Norman Schwarzkopf, Herb Lloyd, Guy Meloy and Edward Crowley. At least twenty-two Red Hats achieved flag rank.[4]

After 1963, the Airborne assumed the duties of official palace guard, a position of extreme trust in the governmental and military hierarchy. The Division also served as the nation's tactical reserve, on call to be deployed where most needed. During the early years of US involvement, the Airborne Brigade kept a battalion on alert at Tan Son Nhut AB, along with several C-123 aircraft, for airlift and parachute insertion into any hot spot. The Airborne were fierce combatants. At full strength the division totaled 12,000 troopers; during the course of the war they suffered more than 20,000 killed.

The Red Hats and during the early years, the Red Marker FACs, jumped with the Airborne or went in with them via helicopter and lived in the field during their operations. The Airborne operations evolved over the years from short-term battalion-sized forays into brigade-size deployments maneuvering in conjunction with U.S. formations. After the U.S. withdrawal, the bulk of the Airborne strength was permanently stationed away from Saigon to bolster the regional defense forces in Military Regions 1, 2 and 3.

Red Markers

Red Marker history paralleled the course of America's involvement in the war. In 1962, a single US Air Force officer, without an aircraft, was assigned as Air Liaison Officer to the Vietnamese Airborne Brigade to provide advice on the use of air power. This ALO reported directly to the 2nd ADVON; his boss was the Director of the Tactical Air Control Center. He accompanied the Brigade on field operations, coordinating the use of air power via backpack radios. A Vietnamese FAC flying overhead in an O-1 Bird Dog controlled the airstrikes requested by the ALO.

During the next two years, an American FAC was assigned to the ALO to assist in supporting the Airborne's operations. Sometimes these FACs flew borrowed VNAF aircraft, but usually they controlled airstrikes from the ground. By 1965, the USAF deployed more FACs along with aircraft, and controlling airstrikes was

---

2 The standard organization chart included in *Chien Su, Su Doan Nhay Du*, (War History, Airborne Division), published 2010 by the Veterans of the Airborne Division, p. 446, shows 2 division advisors, 9 advisors divided among the three brigades, 27 among the 9 maneuver battalions, 6 specialty advisors, 11 staff advisors G-1 through G-5, plus 4 Advisory Team staff. This would total 54 advisors down to the battalion level for three brigades and 66 for four brigades. Company level advisors could double that total.
3 Major John J. Martin, USA (Ret), email May 2012.
4 See Appendix IV. Data provided by Major John J. Martin, USA (Ret).

MRC-108 Radio Jeep ready for action in the field. Walter Stepaniak Collection.

no longer dependent upon the VNAF. The Red Markers were assigned O-1E Bird Dog aircraft and M-107/108 radio jeeps. Each jeep contained a radio pallet having four types of radios wired to run off the jeep's generator or from a separate trailer-hauled generator.[5] These radios enabled a deployed Red Marker ROMAD to contact all the elements on the battlefield: the Red Hat advisors (via FM), American or VNAF aircraft (via UHF), U.S. Army helicopters (via VHF), the Direct Air Support Center and Red Marker headquarters (both via HF), and the Red Marker FACs in the air (usually via UHF).[6]

By 1965, the Red Markers were listed for the first time as a subordinate unit to the 19th TASS. Regardless, the ALO continued to report directly to the TACC. By 1965, the Red Markers also had permanently assigned ROMADs and crew chiefs rather than having to depend on temporary assignment of personnel from a central organization. With the additional staff and equipment, the Red Markers could deploy to the field with a complete Tactical Air Control Party (TACP). The FAC flew to a field near the deployment site with the crew chief in the back seat. Meanwhile, the ROMADs, jeep and generator were airlifted to the location selected for the battalion Tactical Operations Center (TOC). Sometimes, a ROMAD would drive in convoy to the deployment location. However, that practice had tragic consequences on one occasion.[7] Once on

---
5 See Rowley, pp. 38-40, Availability and compatibility of radio equipment was an early and continuing problem for the FAC until about 1966. Although some early FAC units had access to M-94 six passenger pickup trucks equipped with UHF, VHF and FM radios, the Red Markers did not.

6 Within range Red Marker Control could also contact the FACs via FM or VHF since the Bird Dog carried all three types of radio.

7 See discussion of Airman Henneberry, Section 3 – The Build Up, 1965.

CHAPTER 3 - VIETNAMESE AIRBORNE, RED HATS AND RED MARKERS

site, the radio jeep was often backed into a depression carved out by a dozer to protect the equipment from incoming mortars and rockets. On lengthy operations, the radio pallet might be unloaded from the jeep and installed inside the Airborne TOC bunker. Typical TACP manpower doubled in size later in the war as the deployments of the Airborne increased in duration from a couple of weeks to several months at each remote location.

After the fleet expanded to add O-2A Skymasters to the existing Bird Dogs in 1969, the Red Marker unit achieved its largest size with about a dozen aircraft, 14 FACs and 22 enlisted men. In January 1970, the unit transferred from the 19th TASS to the 22nd TASS as the latter organization took over all American FAC operations supporting the Vietnamese Army in MR 3. In April 1970, the unit roster included 11 officers (seven O-1 FACs and four O-2 FACs) and 23 enlisted men.[8] As the unit began to shrink with Vietnamization, one ALO and three Bird Dog pilots transferred to the Raven FACs in Cambodia and Laos. In August 1970, the organization's O-2 aircraft and FACs moved back to the 19th TASS and were reassigned to other units, leaving the Red Markers with only Bird Dogs.

During the last half of 1970, the 22nd TASS periodically handed over to the Vietnamese Air Force responsibility for operating individual forward operating locations (FOLs) in MR 3 and for providing air support for the Vietnamese Army in those areas. In mid-January 1971, the remnants of the 22nd TASS merged into the 19th TASS and the remaining Red Markers were part of that transfer. Thirty days later, the Vietnamese Air Force took over the Red Marker mission, and the final Red Marker TACP closed. Following that closure, the Red Marker operation resembled the earliest years. A single Red Marker ALO operated in a purely advisory capacity to the Airborne, rather than heading a combat unit.

There were some new twists, however. First, reflecting its new responsibility, the Vietnamese Air Force provided a division ALO, a counterpart to the lone Red Marker. Further, the VNAF staffed a TACP for each deployed brigade of the Airborne Division, which they had not previously done. However, the VNAF FACs who provided coverage for the Airborne were not part of the TACP. Instead, those FACs belonged to one of eight liaison squadrons. They deployed TDY to fly support missions from forward locations for short periods of time before returning to the squadron. After supporting the Airborne a Vietnamese FAC might deploy next to a different area and in support of a different division. Familiarity with the Airborne personnel and advisors, experience in the Airborne operating area, and continuity in general diminished significantly under this approach.

The Red Markers continued its existence as a single officer, without an aircraft, attached to the Air Force Advisory Group (AFGP) until February 1973 when the U.S. withdrew from Vietnam. Having come full circle, from a single ALO advisor in 1962 to a robust combat unit in 1965-70 and back again to a single ALO by 1971, the Red Markers left an enduring legacy with those they served. They were a small but nevertheless significant part of the Vietnamese Airborne story.

---
8 504th TASG Special Order TD-9, 1 April 1970. The order was authority for Red Markers to move anywhere in the country TDY.

SECTION II - THE ADVISORY YEARS

- 1962 – Major Gene McCutchan
- 1963 – Major Gene McCutchan, Lt Col James Martin
- 1964 – Lt Col James Martin, Lt Col Carleton Casteel

1962–64 AIRBORNE OPERATIONS

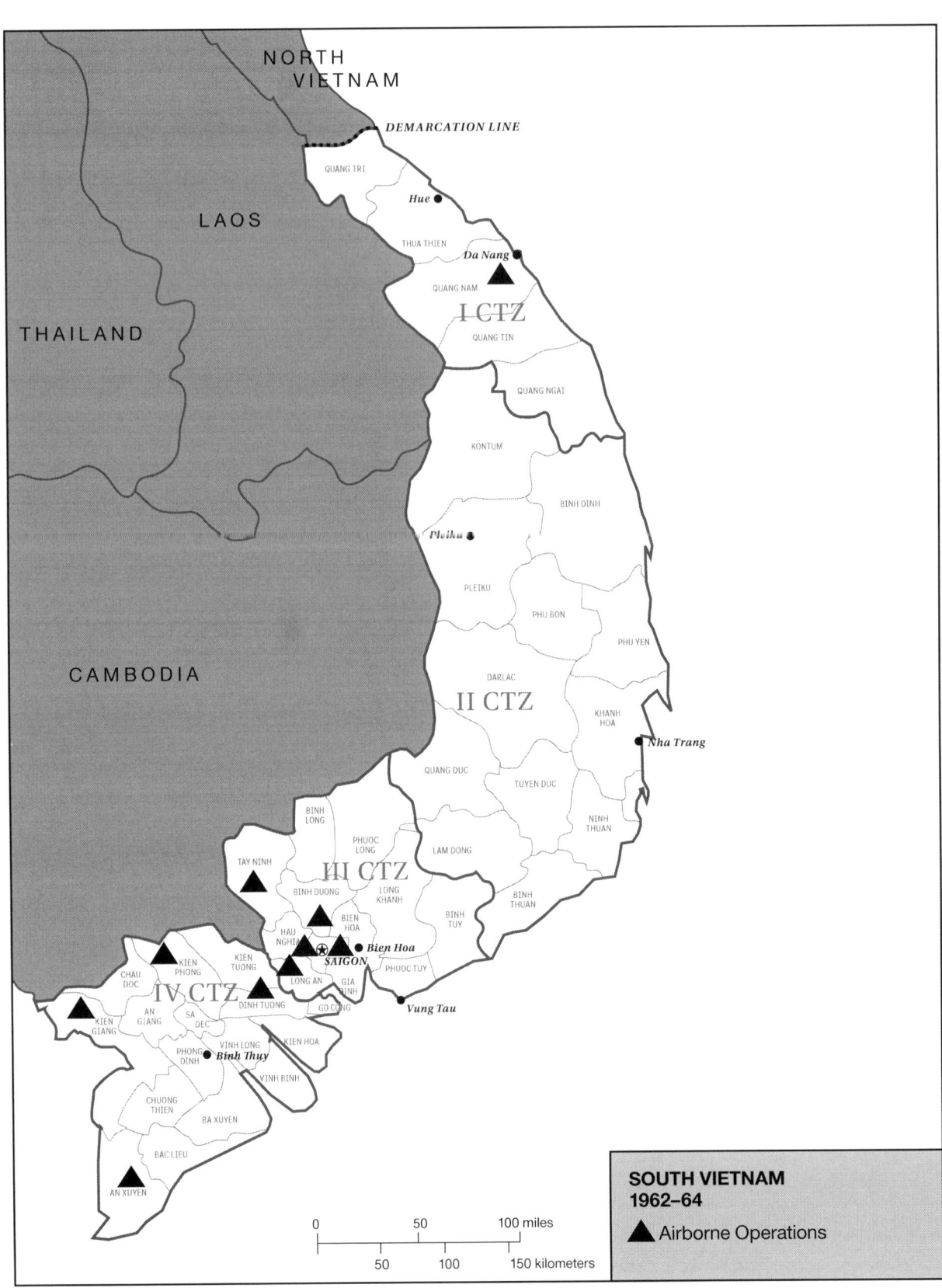

CHAPTER 4

1962 - MAJOR GENE McCUTCHAN

Major Gene McCutchan, the original Red Marker, from his collection.

Unless otherwise indicated, the material about Gene McCutchan is from his book *A Mark Too High*, edited, published and distributed by Colonel Alva L. Matheson, USAF (Ret), Cedar City, UT, 2004. The proceeds from its publication are for the benefit of the Forward Air Controller Association. Use of this material is with the permission of the author.

In 1962, Major Gene McCutchan was posted to Southeast Asia along with nine other highly experienced Air Force officers. Gene had flown B-17s in World War II and fighters in Korea. He had been an F-100 squadron commander at George Air Force Base prior to his assignment to SEA. The other nine officers were similarly well qualified. These men were the first permanently assigned Air Liaison Officers serving various South Vietnamese army units. At the time, the ARVN units were receiving training from U.S. Army advisors regarding combat weapons and tactics, planning and logistics. The new Air Liaison Officers' task would be to train the Vietnamese in the proper use of tactical air power to support their mission. McCutchan elected from various possible unit assignments to join the Vietnamese Airborne Brigade.

Red Markers 1962

Major Gene McCutchan
Sgt Tran Dinh Luong

The U.S. Army advisors with the Airborne were working under the auspices of the Military Assistance Group as Advisory

31

CHAPTER 4 - 1963 - MAJOR GENE McCUTCHEN

Team 162 and were under the command of MACV, the Military Assistance Command–Vietnam. They were known as Red Hats, having adopted the red berets and other uniform elements worn by the Vietnamese unit they advised.

When McCutchan arrived at the Airborne, he immediately had to resolve a couple of issues. The senior Red Hat, a colonel, greeted Gene, "Welcome to Advisory Team 162." Gene responded that although the colonel outranked him, Gene did not work for him. He reported directly to Lt. Colonel Charles Bowers, Director of the Tactical Air Control Center, the agency that controlled all air operations in country. Indeed, McCutchan pointed out that his advisory role regarding air power was equal and parallel to the Army's role regarding army operations. Gene had, however, expected to be housed with the Army advisors, but MACV refused to provide accommodations at the Red Hat resident quarters in Saigon. Gene, therefore, rented his own apartment in the city and began operations with the Airborne as an independent Air Force representative.

The Airborne Brigade was the national tactical reserve force for the South Vietnamese Army. During this time period, one of its battalions was always on alert at a hangar on Tan Son Nhut Air Base in Saigon ready for an immediate airborne deployment anywhere in the country.[1] As ALO, McCutchan was responsible for both advising the brigade commander about air power and for employing that power in the field. Since he would be joining the Airborne in the field, Major McCutchan went through the ARVN paratrooper school to become jump qualified. McCutchan then accompanied the brigade on deployments. He coordinated air strikes through a Vietnamese Air Force forward air controller flying above the battlefield in an O-1 Bird Dog aircraft. On Gene's first deployment, the battalion commander reacted to McCutchan's air force uniform, a sage green flight suit, stating he made himself a target by standing out from the crowd. In response, McCutchan then adopted the uniform of the Airborne, including the red beret, and took the call sign "Red Marker."

As a ground-bound ALO, Gene had neither an aircraft nor effective radio equipment, which limited his effectiveness considerably. Coordination of an airstrike in those early days was rudimentary. First, the Airborne commanders provided target information to the FAC using FM radios. Then, the Airborne marked friendly positions with colored panels or smoke grenades. Sometimes the color of the smoke changed by pre-agreement to prevent the Viet Cong from popping decoys to confuse the air attack. The FAC then dropped a smoke grenade on the target and directed attack aircraft, usually T-28s of B-26s, communicating over UHF or VHF radios.

If the FAC spoke English, the Airborne commander often asked Gene to talk to him directly using the Airborne's FM radios, and the FAC then put strikes in at the desired location. Gene could only talk directly to the attack fighters if the aircraft carried an FM set. However, the only aircraft so equipped was the A-1E Skyraider.[2] Occasionally, on deployment Gene brought a HF single side band radio, which was not very portable. Two Airborne troopers were needed in order to carry the radio and the battery. Further, the antenna was a 25-foot long wire that had to be strung from the radio to a tall tree. Thus, the ALO could only use the

---

1 With a capacity of 50 troopers per C-123, it would take eight or more sorties to lift an entire battalion.

2 USAF A-1E Skyraiders first appeared in May 1964 during Gene's second tour.

radio from a stationary position. Moreover, even when operated in this stationary mode, the HF set would only provide a communication link back to the DASC since it was incompatible with any aircraft-installed equipment. It took years before the USAF addressed the ALO's inability to communicate directly with attack aircraft and the limited view of the battlefield from being confined to the ground.

According to *Angels in Red Hats*,[3] the Airborne made three combat jumps in 1962 and early 1963:

• 5 March 1962 at Bo Tuc to reinforce a garrison under attack near the Cambodian border in Tay Ninh Province;

• 14 July 1962 north of Saigon to reinforce a unit under ambush (in this action, the Red Hats lost their first advisor in combat when Captain Don J. York was killed in the ambushed convoy);[4] and

• 2 January 1963 at Ap Bac to reinforce the 7th Infantry Division and Civil Guards.

Major McCutchan made thirteen jumps during his time with the Airborne, and while some of them were in full combat gear into uncontrolled areas, none were considered combat jumps.[5] When the Director of the TACC learned that Gene was planning to make a combat jump, he forbade it, not wanting a fighter pilot and a former squadron commander to take such a risk. Consequently, Gene's deployments with the Airborne were all by helicopter.

As the American presence in Vietnam grew, the Airborne adopted helicopter insertion in lieu of parachuting as the standard for their operations.[6] Gene vividly remembers the mad dashes to the tree line in hot landing zones with bullets buzzing like bees overhead. Gene soon got himself checked out in a VNAF O-1. He then provided air support more effectively. With a better view of the battlefield he could relay his impressions to the Red Hats on the ground. When Gene flew combat missions, he followed the VNAF policy requiring a two-man crew for the Bird Dog. Gene flew the plane while the backseat Vietnamese Observer/FAC communicated with the ground troops and directed the NVAF fighters. On more than one occasion, Gene piloted Lieutenant Truc Van Tran who served as a FAC with the VNAF 112th L-19 Squadron from 1961–1965.

Often, an American pilot flew in the flight of VNAF attack aircraft as an advisor to the Vietnamese fighter squadron. In those cases, Gene could communicate directly with the strike flight, although he was not authorized to control the strike. Regardless, Gene was far more effective in the air than on the ground.

Selecting a good drop zone or landing zone was an important part of a successful operation. Typically the Airborne Commander, his Operations Officer, the Red Hat Senior Advisor and McCutchan previewed the area from a helicopter provided by the Army. This reconnaissance was usually done on a single straight fly-by to prevent tipping off the VC. A Huey helicopter was usually sufficient for the size of the selection party. On one occasion, a larger party was assembled and Gene arranged for an Air Force helicopter rather than an Army Huey. The Airborne

---

[3] Martin, pp. 39, 182.
[4] *Id.* at 18.
[5] "Pacific Stars and Stripes," Monday, Jan 14, 1963, p 7, for example, notes that the Airborne jumped into an unsecure area near Cu Chi hoping to surprise the VC.

[6] Martin, p. 182 documents only two combat jumps in 1965, two in 1966, and one each in 1968 and 1972. This compares with 47 jumps during the eight years of the First Indochina War.

CHAPTER 4 - 1963 - MAJOR GENE McCUTCHEN

Sergeant Tran Dinh Luong. Gene McCutchan Collection.

Commander saw possible anti-paratrooper stakes in an otherwise promising drop zone and asked to descend for a closer look. The pilot initially refused to go below 1,500 feet until McCutchan convinced him otherwise. The end result was the team got a good close look at the field, and Gene never asked the Air Force to fly another helicopter recon mission for them.

When McCutchan first arrived at the Brigade, the Airborne assigned Sergeant Tran Dinh Luong as his permanent driver and aide. Luong accompanied Gene everywhere. On operations, Luong cooked for him and stood guard at night or after days in the field while Gene bathed in a nearby stream. Sergeant Luong served in that capacity for subsequent ALOs and as a supply liaison between the FACs and the Airborne at least through 1970. He helped build bunkers, outfit hootches, convoy radio jeeps, scrounge and transport supplies, and many other tasks, including cookouts for the Red Markers. When not in the field, Sergeant Luong was an able chauffeur and bodyguard, shuttling McCutchan from his apartment on Vo Thanh Street in Saigon to the Airborne Headquarters on Tan Son Nhut AB, or to social engagements that were part of the ALO function.

McCutchan's renting a Saigon apartment was not unusual. Prior to the American withdrawal, many American personnel lived in civilian housing in Saigon because of overcrowding at nearby military installations. Saigon was initially relatively secure and peaceful. During the early years of the war, some officers assigned to the Saigon area served 24-month tours if accompanied by their families. If unaccompanied, tours were fifteen months in Saigon and twelve months elsewhere in the country.[7] By 1966, the Air Force standardized its policy of a twelve-month, unaccompanied tour for all personnel in Vietnam. The U.S. Army policy went through a similar evolution.

In time, Saigon became more dangerous. Several Red Hats barely escaped serious injury when a Viet Cong bomb exploded at the Tan Son Nhut soccer stadium in 1964. One officer on an accompanied tour missed that explosion only because he had driven back into Saigon to get his pregnant wife.[8] In 1965, a Red Hat died in the bombing of the My Canh Restaurant,[9] and in 1966 there was a grenade assassination attempt on a Red Marker.[10]

---

7 Donald D. Little and Barry L. Spink, "USAF Personnel Rotation in Southeast Asia (A Chronology)," Air Force Historical Research Agency, Maxwell AFB, AL, April 2008, p. 4.
8 "Airborne Brigade Newsletter," Headquarters Airborne Brigade Advisory Detachment, APO San Francisco, 10 Apr 1965, p. 2.
9 "Airborne Division Newsletter," Headquarters Airborne Division Advisory Detachment, APO San Francisco, 5 Apr 1966, p. 11, Red Hat SFC Al Combs was killed in the restaurant bombing. Red Marker Captain Mike Morea had a grenade thrown at his jeep, per his personal memoir.
10 "Pacific Stars and Stripes," Monday 23 Jun 1965, p. 24, reported 42 persons killed in the bombing of the My Canh Restaurant.

By executive order, after February 1965, dependents no longer accompanied military personnel during their tours. Per that order from President Johnson:[11]

"I have directed the orderly withdrawal of American dependents from South Viet-Nam. It has become clear that Hanoi has undertaken a more aggressive course of action against both South Vietnamese and American installations, and against Americans who are in South Vietnam assisting the people of that country to defend their freedom."

In April of the same year, the President declared Vietnam and the adjacent waters a combat zone retroactive to January 1, 1964.[12]

By 1969, the USAF installed heavy mesh screen over the windows of buses shuttling troops among various locations in the Saigon area to prevent grenades being tossed inside.

[11] http://www.presidency.ucsb.edu/ws/index.php?pid=27252 - Lyndon B. Johnson, 7 Feb 1965, The order states further, "In addition to this action, I have ordered the deployment to South Vietnam of a Hawk air defense battalion. Other reinforcements, in units and individuals, may follow."

[12] Presidential Executive Order 11216, Designation of Vietnam and Adjacent Waters as a Combat Zone for Purposes of Section 112 of the Internal Revenue Code of 1954, 24 April 1965.

CH-37 Mohave Extraction. Cebe-Habersky Collection.

VNAF pilot and FAC. Cebe-Habersky Collection.

CHAPTER 5

1963 - MAJOR GENE McCUTCHAN
LT COL JAMES MARTIN

In early 1963, Colonel Bowers, Director of the Tactical Air Control Center, invited Major McCutchan to take over the Strike Plans section of the TACC. Gene tried to decline to no avail. His knowledge of aircraft capabilities and weapons applications plus his prior experience as a fighter squadron commander made him a perfect fit for the job. Although he preferred to be either in the field or go home on time, Gene agreed to a tour extension of a couple of months and took over issuing Frag Orders for the air war. The TACC, like the subordinate DASCs in each Corps, was a joint operation: an American and a Vietnamese counterpart staffed each position. Consequently the Tactical Air Control System served two purposes. It controlled the tactical air power in Vietnam and simultaneously trained the Vietnamese in the American system. Having had his tour extended because of his specialized knowledge and skill, Gene was understandably speechless when his replacement in Strike Plans came from Air Training Command and had no prior experience with fighters or weapons!

The Air Force next assigned Gene stateside to the headquarters of the Tactical Air Command. He did not know at the time that he would soon return to the ALO slot at the Airborne Brigade, and that he would see the brigade grow into a division and the Red Markers develop into a fully functioning combat unit.

When Gene had moved to Strike Plans at TACC, Lt. Colonel James F. Martin replaced him as ALO of the Vietnamese Airborne. Colonel Martin, like Gene, was a veteran of both WWII and Korea. Martin had flown F-86s with the 334th Fighter Interceptor Squadron in Korea and served as their squadron commander for several months in 1952. He was awarded the Silver Star for one engagement involving thirty MiG-15s versus the dozen Sabre jets he was leading.[1]

Captain Jack V. Cebe-Habersky joined Martin in the spring as the first Brigade FAC assigned to the unit. Cebe-Haber-

---

Red Markers 1963
Major Gene McCutchan 01
Lt Col Jim Martin 01
Capt Jack Cebe-Habersky 02

---

[1] Per George Willik: http://www.gcwillick.com/482ndFIS/Scrapbook/MartinSStar.html.

CHAPTER 5 - MAJOR GENE McCUTCHAN & LT COL JAMES MARTIN

First published without personnel identification in "Angels in Red Hats."

sky, a senior captain and an experienced F-100 pilot, served until April 1964.[2] Jack was born in Czechoslovakia and had seen WWII as a child before coming to the United States. In Vietnam, he saw a lot of combat from a very different angle. He flew 211 missions for 270 combat hours and made thirty parachute jumps with the Airborne, including several combat jumps. Apparently, the TACC Director no longer objected to ALO/FACs making combat jumps. Jack was awarded two Bronze Stars, eight Air Medals and two Vietnamese Crosses of Gallantry. The number of flight hours and missions are remarkable because the Red Markers still did not have assigned aircraft. Instead, they flew borrowed VNAF Bird Dogs with a Vietnamese FAC in the back.

The Airborne's six battalions were extremely mobile during 1963 conducting helicopter assaults or parachute jumps in each Corps area. Notwithstanding the intense activity and number of field operations, the Airborne claimed only 163 KIA, 123 POWs and thirty-two captured weapons. The Airborne suffered eighty-two troopers killed, 290 wounded and 1 missing in action during the year.[3] A typical operation deployed one or two battalions to an area of reported Viet Cong concentration. Despite the fact that such sweeps often lasted ten days to two weeks, they rarely resulted in significant contact, notwithstanding intelligence reports of VC presence. The Viet Cong were

---

2 "Airborne Brigade Newsletter," Headquarters Airborne Brigade Advisory Detachment, APO San Francisco, 18 Dec 1963, p 9, Roster at December 1963 notes DEROS of 8 Apr 1964 for Cebe-Habersky.

3 Airborne Newsletter, 5 Apr 1966, p. 16.

Captain Jack Cebe-Habersky and Lt Col James Martin. Cebe-Habersky Collection.

skilled at avoiding contact except on their own terms, usually an ambush with overwhelming force. They were seldom surprised, which led to obvious questions regarding security of the Airborne's plans. More on that later.

Following each operation, the battalions returned to Tan Son Nhut to rest and refit before being called out to fight the next fire. Later in the war, Airborne forces deployed on extended duty for months at a time, staging repeated sweeps from major base camps in I, II and III Corps. In 1963, however, the Airborne provided only short duration tactical response. Usually, the Red Marker ALO or brigade FAC supported the forces for as long as they were in the field. Back at Tan Son Nhut, the ALO and FAC completed after action reports and evaluated with the Red Hats plans and intelligence for the next operation.

Near the end of the year the military overthrew President Diem in a coup involving combat with the Presidential Guard. The 6th Airborne Battalion actively participated in that fight.

Living Conditions

The Red Markers continued to rent their own quarters in Saigon. During Cap-

tain Cebe-Habersky's tour, he shared an apartment for six months with Captain Don MacKellar, a pilot assigned to a different unit. During the last six months of his tour, Jack rented space from Dave Quinet, a Frenchman, and his Vietnamese wife. Jack celebrated both Vietnamese and American holidays with this couple and their two children.

Ap Bac I & II, Kien Giang Province, IV Corps

The year 1963 began with the previously mentioned combat jump at Ap Bac in IV Corps to reinforce elements of the 7th Division and the Civil Guard. The 8th Battalion, serving as the "Airborne Alert," parachuted two companies and a small command post into the fight at dusk. After a long night both sides were bloodied. Two Red Hats, Captain Fletcher Ware and Sergeant First Class Russell Kopti were wounded but recovered and returned to duty. Many of the Airborne's casualties came during the jump because the parachuting troopers were easy targets against the sky. This first Battle of Ap Bac was reported later as a significant victory for the Viet Cong, which held off a superior force supported by helicopters and APC's[4] (although there were no airstrikes since the opposing forces were too close together). The Viet Cong retreated during the night, leaving fewer dead and wounded than the attacking South Vietnamese forces. The VC also returned shortly thereafter. Ten days later, the 5th Battalion swept the same area in a ground operation. The battalion took its objective, however, the Airborne casualties included a company commander killed and the battalion commander wounded.

A few days later, an Airborne battalion

---
4 Armored Personnel Carriers.

jumped into Cu Chi hoping to catch the Viet Cong napping. As reported by the Pacific Stars and Stripes:

"Five C-123 Providers from Tan Son Nhut Airfield Saigon dropped 50 paratroopers each from the ARVN Airborne Brigade on a drop zone near Cu Chi 20 miles northwest of Saigon. The drop zone for this practice drop was left unsecured before the airborne arrived from the sky hoping that the exercise would flush some Viet Cong guerillas in the area. Such was not the case, however, and the training runs were made without any contact with the enemy. A second run of the Providers completed the days' effort with a total of 500 Airborne troopers taking part in the practice."[5]

Jack Cebe-Habersky and Red Hat John Ault. Cebe-Habersky Collection.

During the next two months, the Airborne conducted two more operations into the Ap Bac area. The 3rd Battalion and then a Task Force of the 5th and 6th Battalions assisted the 7th Division seize and hold strategic hamlets.

Tay Ninh, Tay Ninh Province, III Corps

In April, the 6th Battalion deployed for a long sweep near the Cambodian border in Tay Ninh Province. Five days into the operation on the day before Easter, seven companies of the Viet Cong Phu Loi Regiment attacked them. The battle lasted four and a half hours that day and into the next morning. The Airborne killed at least thirty-six VC and captured two. This was the troopers' first engagement using newly supplied M-79, 40mm grenade launchers, a highly effective weapon in the hands of the Airborne. Red Hat Captain John Ault was wounded in the forearm during this battle and received the Silver Star for his actions. Sergeant First Class Herbert J. Lloyd[6] and Staff Sergeant Willie Mack each received the Bronze Star.[7] The air support coordinated by Red Marker Cebe-Habersky was a deciding factor in the Airborne success in a very close fight. This deployment lasted another 40 days before the battalion returned to Tan Son Nhut for rest.[8]

Training At Da Ria, Vung Tau Province, III Corps

During most of March and April, the 8th Battalion went through formal refresher training at the Phuoc Le Training Center near Ba Ria north of Vung Tau. The 3rd Battalion followed the 8th for the two-month formal course. The Brigade intended to send each battalion through the course during the next several months, but political events interrupted that schedule

Tay Ninh, Tay Ninh Province, III Corps

In June, the 8th and 6th Battalions conducted a joint operation in Tay Ninh. The 8th jumped and according to the Red Hat Newsletter,

"As usual, the C-47s dropped us on the DZ

---

5 "Pacific Stars and Stripes," Monday, Jan 14, 1963, p 7.

6 Herbert Lloyd went to OCS in Jan 1964 and ultimately retired from the Army as a Brigadier General.

7 Airborne Newsletter, 18 December 1963, p. 2.

8 Brig. General Herbert Lloyd, USA (Ret), email 26 August 2011.

and the C-123s put most of the people in the jungle."

The 6th Battalion went in by chopper into a blocking position, although there was little to block. This operation engaged very few enemy.

DaNang, DaNang Province, I Corps

In July, the 6th and 7th Battalions moved north of DaNang as part of the 2nd Task Force in I Corps, with similar results.

The Vietnamese government instituted martial law in August in response to political unrest and repeated rumors of an attempted coup. Consequently, all battalions were ordered to remain close to Saigon, interrupting the proposed training of battalions scheduled to cycle through Ba Ria.

Cai Ngoc, Ca Mau Province, IV Corps

On 10 September, the 5th Battalion, serving Airborne Alert, parachuted into Ca Mau Province near Cai Ngoc to counter a Viet Cong attack on the village. The troopers arrived late in the afternoon and scattered the VC who were diligently searching for the village Regional Force garrison. Many of these local defenders were hiding underwater in the nearby river. Most of the Viet Cong escaped by sampan down the river as the troopers attacked.

November Coup, Capital Military District

On 1 November 1963, a military coup deposed President Diem, and replaced him with a military junta headed by General Minh. A period of instability at the top levels of the South Vietnamese government ensued. A series of leaders headed the country over the next several years. The disposition of the six Airborne battalions immediately prior to the coup was as follows:[9]

- 1st Battalion was in Duc Lap on a routine security mission
- 3rd Battalion was at Tan Son Nhut on Alert status
- 5th Battalion was near Trang Bang 35 kilometers northwest of Saigon, part of a III Corps operation
- 6th Battalion was preparing to go to Ba Ria for eight weeks of training that had been delayed
- 7th Battalion was with the 5th near Trang Bang
- 8th Battalion was in Ca Mau Province on an emergency mission to search for three American advisors captured by the VC.

When the 5th and 7th arrived at Trang Bang, they relieved two Marine battalions that immediately departed for the Gia-Long palace. Early on 1 November, the 6th was ordered to Ba Ria, supposedly for an emergency security mission. Upon arrival, the 6th was put under the command of the training center commander, Lt. Colonel Loc, and dispatched to Saigon with an infantry battalion and the school's armor force.

Red Hats Captain Joseph M. Spears, Jr., Lieutenant Charles M. Titus, and Sergeant First Class Winfred B. Niles were with the battalion on this deployment. As the troops crossed the bridge from Bien Hoa to Saigon, they came under fire from the Presidential Guard Barracks. The battalion was ordered to attack the barracks and the fight was on. At this point, Captain Spears and his team left the battalion and retired to the Brigade Headquarters along with the other non-deployed advi-

---

9 Airborne Newsletter, 18 December 1963, pp. 4-5.

sors, including the Red Markers Colonel Martin and Captain Cebe-Habersky.[10]

An assault by the combined Airborne and armor at 2130 overcame Diem's guards at the barracks. Meanwhile, the Marines attacked the Gia-Long palace. By Saturday morning the coup was complete. While Acting Airborne Commander Major Ho Tieu had promised the support of the entire Airborne Brigade to the coup, only the 6th Battalion was committed to the battle.

Major Tieu had been among the coup organizers. Colonel Cao Van Vien, the Brigade Commander, was a known supporter of President Diem. Colonel Vien and other senior officers not involved in the plot were invited by the Joint General Staff to a luncheon on the day of the coup, and were informed of the day's events while at that meeting. Each had to choose between the president or the coup organizers. Colonel Vien resigned on the spot and was arrested. He escaped execution, which befell other Diem loyalists, and before the end of the year returned to the command of the Airborne Brigade.

Shortly after his return to the Airborne, Colonel Vien was promoted to General and made Chief of Staff of the JGS before being made III Corps Commander. Ironically, the Airborne became the official palace guard in the years to come.

---
[10] Major General Edward M. Crowley, USA (Ret), email 2 February 2011. As a lieutenant in 1963, Crowley was deputy battalion advisor to the 5th Battalion.

Cebe-Habersky Certificate. Cebe-Habersky Collection.

Colonel Vien & Cebe-Habersky. Cebe-Habersky Collection.

CHAPTER 6

1964 - LT COL JAMES MARTIN
LT COL CARLETON CASTEEL

In the spring of 1964, Captain Robert L. Paradis arrived to replace Jack Cebe-Habersky as Brigade FAC. In July 1964, Lt. Colonel Carleton N. "Cas" Casteel took over the ALO job at the Airborne as Lt. Colonel Martin went to Headquarters Pacific Air Forces.[1] Casteel was a fighter pilot who served as deputy director of operations for the Twelfth Air Force at Waco, Texas, prior to his Vietnam tour.[2]

While Casteel was at Waco, the Air Force issued a request for fighter pilots willing to take parachute training. Casteel volunteered and went to jump school at Fort Benning, Georgia. Shortly thereafter, he received orders for Vietnam as a Forward Air Controller, about which he "knew nothing."[3] After arriving in Vietnam, Casteel qualified in a VNAF Bird Dog but rarely flew, logging less than 20 hours of combat time.[4]

Red Hat Captain James J. Lindsay, who served as the 1st Battalion S-3/S-4 advisor through much of 1964, remembers Bob Paradis.[5] Jim recalls going on a couple of operations with Bob but most vividly remembers Paradis as a skydiver.[6] This, of course, made Bob a natural for assignment to the Airborne. In fact, Paradis helped Jim design and conduct free fall (high altitude, low opening, or HALO) training for the other advisors in September. If possible though, Casteel was even more gung ho for jumping than Paradis. Casteel logged more than 100 jumps during his tour.[7]

Red Markers 1964

Lt Col Jim Martin 01
Capt Jack Cebe-Habersky 02

Lt Col Carleton Casteel 01
Captain Bob Paradis 02

Sgt Tran Dinh Luong

---

1 Airborne Newsletter, 10 Apr 1965, p 5.
2 "Twelfth Air Force History," online, http://www.globalsecurity.org/military/agency/usaf/12af.html, The 12th Air Force focused on training tactical aircrews to a state of combat readiness. During the war in Vietnam, the Twelfth was a primary source for tactical fighter, reconnaissance and airlift forces in the theater.
3 Colonel Carleton N. Casteel, USAF (Ret), audio notes March 2011.
4 Colonel Carleton N. Casteel, USAF (Ret), questionnaire February 2011.
5 S-3/S-4, Intelligence and Operations.
6 General James J. Lindsay, US Army (Ret), interview November 2010.
7 Headquarters, 2nd Air Division, Thirteenth Air Force, Order placing Captain Robert L. Paradis on jump status effective 20 April 1964, and Lt Col Carleton N.Casteel effective 1 Aug 1964, dated 21 October 1964.

CHAPTER 6 - 1964 - LT COL JAMES MARTIN & LT COL CARLETON CASTEEL

Team 162 at Tan Son Nhut Headquarters, including Lt Colonel Carlton Casteel and Captain Bob Paradis from "Angels in Red Hats" published with permission.

Casteel, Paradis and Lindsay are all pictured in a December 1964 photograph of the Airborne Advisory Detachment in front of the Tan Son Nhut AB headquarters of the Airborne.[8] Lt. Colonel Casteel is on the front row, second from the left, Captain Paradis is on the back row, third from the left, and Captain Lindsay is on the second row at the left end just behind Casteel. Casteel and Paradis are each wearing US and Vietnamese parachutist wings as well as US pilot wings.

Meanwhile, Major McCutchan was involved stateside in operations at Tactical Air Command Headquarters, but actively sought a return to Vietnam. He was rewarded with an assignment in August 1964 as ALO to the 23rd Vietnamese Division flying out of Ban Me Thuot, as "Baron 01."

Before McCutchan left the Airborne on his first tour, the Vietnamese brigade commander approached him one night asking if Gene would be willing to fly an immediate mission in support of a unit under attack. The VNAF would not launch a FAC because of either darkness or bad weather.[9] Gene agreed to fly but could not convince the Vietnamese to lend an aircraft to him, even after the Airborne commander intervened. Gene believed this and similar incidents pressured the Air Force to permanently assign American FACs and aircraft to support the close air support mission for Vietnamese forces like the Airborne.[10] He was pleased when he returned to SEA to find that he

---
8 Martin, p. 20.

9 McCutchan cannot recall which reason they cited for the refusal.

10 Given the relative lack of experience of the pilots assigned to the Liaison Squadrons and the difficulty of flying the O-1 on instruments, it is no wonder that the VNAF declined to fly this mission.

had an assigned aircraft and did not have to borrow one.

Although Gene had his own Bird Dog, he had no crew chief. Consequently, he performed all the necessary minor care on his airplane, including refueling, replenishing oil, and reloading rockets and smoke grenades. The plane was relatively simple to maintain day to day, and he took it back to Bien Hoa for periodic inspection or other specialized servicing as required. Gene also had an assigned FAC, Lieutenant Kenneth R. Lape. Ken flew out of Tuy Hoa in support of another regiment of the division.

One of Gene's duties as ALO was to identify potential targets for airstrikes and to submit about five to ten requests per week. He or Ken would control the preplanned airstrikes on the approved targets. On one occasion McCutchan received a Frag Order targeting a village, although Gene had not requested that target. The target was in Lieutenant Lape's area of operations. Being very familiar with the area, Ken knew that women and children were in the village. When the fighters showed up with napalm, he marked a nearby hillside instead of the village and had the fighters drop their payloads in the forest. When word of this got back to the TACC, some of the brass wanted to court martial Lape. Instead, Gene defended him successfully for refusing to kill innocent people. As McCutchan points out, the Province Chiefs' and the Corps Commanders' dominion over activity in their realms was occasionally suspect. Gene wondered if the Vietnamese requested some strikes as reprisals for disobedience by the peasant population. Often both the Vietnamese government and the Viet Cong taxed the villagers. Either force might punish the village for failure to pay. The peasants were clearly caught in the middle.

The Bird Dogs Gene and Ken flew included major improvements over the VNAF planes. The American planes were fitted with two rocket tubes under each wing, so each plane could carry four smoke rockets. The FACs were able to mark targets with rockets instead of smoke grenades. The rockets were much more accurate than grenades and also provided a safety advantage since the FAC did not have to fly directly over a target just prior to an airstrike. Such an overflight might draw ground fire, as well as tip off the enemy that the area was a potential target. Furthermore, the American aircraft had improved UHF, VHF and FM radios installed, allowing them to talk to both the ground forces and any type of aircraft.

After several months with the 23rd Division, Gene was again assigned to the TACC in charge of Strike Plans, coordinating the disposition of the growing USAF tactical air being introduced to SEA. The rate of growth increased markedly after the August 1964 Gulf of Tonkin Incident led to broader American involvement in the conflict.

One of the practical problems Gene addressed while he was at the TACC was the fact that normally fused bombs would penetrate several feet into the soft earth of rice paddies before exploding, muffling the force of the explosion and limiting the effectiveness of the weapon. A team working with Gene came up with the idea of attaching several feet of pipe to the nose of the bomb. This extension impacted and penetrated the soft earth, triggering the fuse and causing the bomb to explode before it got to ground level. These so-called "Daisy Cutters" became standard additions to ordnance in certain areas of the country.[11] These extensions were also adapted to the massive 15,000 pound

---
11 McCutchan, p. 123.

bombs known as Commando Vault that were used to clear LZ's in forested areas. C-130 aircraft deployed these bombs on a pallet from the cargo bay. The Commando Vault exploded a few feet above the ground, leaving a radius containing nothing but stumps and fallen tree trunks.

While Gene was with the 23rd Division and the TACC, the Airborne was busy trying to draw the VC into a fight. The Viet Cong remained elusive. The Airborne posted greater success than the prior year, with 180 hostile KIA, 53 POWs and 85 captured weapons. This was at a cost of 103 troopers killed, 362 wounded and 1 missing in action.[12] Five of the six Airborne battalions were deployed to the field for most of the year.

Long An Province, III Corps

In January, the 3rd Battalion conducted five so-called "Eagle Flights" into Long An Province; the 5th Battalion led one. During each such mission, the Airborne made contact with Viet Cong and had favorable results. An Eagle Flight was a small unit helicopter operation usually consisting of four choppers, each carrying a squad of soldiers. Armed escort helicopters and tactical air support accompanied the troop carriers. This highly mobile force deployed into an area of reported Viet Cong activity to attack targets of opportunity or to take a blocking position while a larger force engaged the VC. Given its flat terrain, lack of roads and numerous sites where helicopters could land, the region southwest of Saigon was a prime area for using these tactics.

In a larger scale operation on 5 and 6 June, the 2nd Task Force (1st and 8th Battalions) engaged the 514th VC Battalion south of Tan An, inflicting significant

APC engaging the enemy south of Tan An. Cebe-Habersky Collection.

casualties. The Viet Cong sustained an unconfirmed 68 KIA and 91 WIA. Captain Jack Cebe-Habersky volunteered to accompany the 8th Battalion on that operation. During the battle, Jack climbed atop an armored personnel carrier to get better visibility to control airstrikes from the ground. He remained in that exposed position for more than eight hours.[13] In recognition of his actions, Jack was awarded a Bronze Star.

Cao Lanh, Kien Phong Province, IV Corps

On 3 March, a Task Force of the 1st and 8th Battalions and a Brigade Command Group, supported by a blocking force of tanks and APCs, engaged in a brief but fierce fight in Kien Phong Province.[14] Intelligence reports indicated a large North Vietnamese Army (NVA) force located just inside the border with Cambodia near the Mekong River. The Airborne planned to trap the hostile force by going up river during the hours of darkness, disembarking in Cambodia and moving southward to prevent the NVA's escape across the border. The reinstated Brigade Commander Colonel Cao Van Vien led the

---

12 Airborne Newsletter, 5 Apr 1966, p. 16.

13 Phoenix Gazette, 22 Dec 1964, from Lt Colonel Jack V. Cebe-Habersky scrapbook.

14 Its modern name is Dong Thap Province.

Task Force; the command group included Red Marker Lt. Colonel Jim Martin.[15] After landing about midnight and trekking southward with the 1st Battalion in the lead, the group paused at dawn to check its position. The lead elements were in an open area about 100 yards west of a well concealed NVA position. The enemy opened fire shortly after the Airborne paused catching the troopers by surprise. Lieutenant John G. Campbell, assistant advisor to the 1st Battalion, was with the lead company. The company had sent security to the front and to both flanks when the group paused. Unfortunately, the scouts who had gone toward the NVA position had been killed silently.[16] The Task Force headquarters was immediately behind the 1st Battalion and was caught in the open when the firing began. Colonel Vien was among those wounded. The Task Force operations officer, Major Le Van Ngoc, was also seriously wounded.

Caught in the open, Captain Thomas McCarthy, the 1st Battalion Senior Advisor, helped organize an immediate frontal assault into the NVA in the tree line. McCarthy was killed in that attack. After reaching the tree line, the close quarters fight lasted about 45 minutes. During the fight, an NVA threw a Chinese made hand grenade that landed a few feet away from Campbell. The grenade was similar to a German "potato masher" of WW II fame, a tin can with a wooden handle protruding from the bottom. To activate it, one pulled a string from the can portion and threw it using the wooden handle; it exploded about four to six seconds after the string was pulled. The one that landed close to Campbell did not explode because the NVA soldier failed to pull the string! While the Airborne engaged in hand to hand fighting, the tanks and APCs intended as the blocking force arrived. Those units got into the battle but withdrew after losing one of their tracked flamethrowers to an RPG round. With the blocking force out of position, the NVA withdrew northward across the border.

Campbell remembers the Airborne suffered five dead and fifteen wounded seriously enough to be evacuated, while he counted about thirty NVA bodies. The enemy casualties may have been greater. The Airborne captured a fair quantity of small arms, a machine gun, ammunition and mines, especially Chinese made water mines. No artillery or airstrikes could be used during the battle since the forces were too closely engaged. However, Martin directed airstrikes to good effect as the NVA withdrew toward the border.

Captain McCarthy was awarded posthumously the Distinguished Service Cross —the second to be awarded in Vietnam— for his gallantry and leadership. He was also the first American to be awarded the Vietnamese Medal of Honor 1st Class.[17] Red Marker Lt. Colonel Jim Martin was awarded the Vietnamese Cross of Gallantry with Gold Star for his actions on the ground at Kien Phong.[18]

About two weeks later, a unit of South Vietnamese infantry ran into enemy forces in the same vicinity, demonstrating the ease with which the VC and NVA moved back and forth across the Cambodian border. Lieutenant Truc Van Tran, a FAC with the VNAF 112th L-19 Squadron, was scheduled to provide air cover for the operation. Truc and his pilot took off from Can Tho at 0700 and were enroute to the AO when he checked in with the infantry and learned heavy contact with VC had

---

15 See p. 42 regarding Colonel Vien's arrest during the November 1963 coup.
16 Colonel John G. Campbell, USA (Ret), letter 6 February 2011.
17 Airborne Newsletter, 10 April 1965, p. 2.
18 *Id.* at p. 5.

CHAPTER 6 - 1964 - LT COL JAMES MARTIN & LT COL CARLETON CASTEEL

Captain Bob Paradis from the Air Force Magazine, published with permission.

Captain Bob Paradis. Casteel Collection.

just begun. Truc immediately called IV DASC requesting they scramble a flight of fighters. When the fighters arrived over the battlefield, Truc identified VC moving along trench lines heading toward Cambodia and directed the flight of VNAF A-1Es onto the target. He used a second set of fighters to inflict further damage on the enemy. Truc and his pilot remained on station until shortly before noon when they had to leave the area to refuel. Lieutenant Khue and an American pilot from the 112th arrived to continue the air coverage. About an hour later, Truc learned that the replacement Bird Dog had been shot down, killing his good friend Lieutenant Khue and seriously wounding the USAF pilot.[19]

Lieutenants Truc and Khue and many other young VNAF officers graduated from the Observer/FAC program conducted at Nha Trang. This course, as part of the military assistance program, provided training in communications, weapons capabilities, coordination of air/ground operations and in the procedures needed to control an airstrike.

In April, Cebe-Habersky left for an assignment at Luke AFB and was replaced by Captain Robert L. Paradis. Bob arrived before Jack left so that Paradis, Cebe-Habersky and Martin were all present at a party honoring the promotion of Colonel Vien to General.[20]

Captain Cebe-Habersky received a Bronze Star for Meritorious Service prior to his departure from Vietnam.[21] Jack's career later intersected with some former Red Hats. In 1975, Jack was a Lt. Colonel stationed at Ft. Bragg as ALO of the 82nd Airborne, and former Red Hats Jim Lindsay and Mike Flynn were both with the 82nd at the time.[22] Jack was diagnosed with a brain tumor in 1977 and died late that year.

A photo of Captain Paradis in Airborne beret and camouflage fatigues appeared in the 2006 almanac *The Air Force in the Vietnam War*.[23] He is acting as a ground FAC handling what appears to be an AN-PRC 25 FM radio. Bob is pictured with an unidentified Airman who is carrying a UHF radio on a backpack frame. The Airman is in non-camouflage fatigues and

---

19 Major Truc Van Tran, emails Oct 2011.

20 Lt Colonel Jack V. Cebe-Habersky, scrapbook photo.

21 Airborne Newsletter, 10 Apr 1965, p. 3.

22 Per Red Hat Colonel Michael J. Flynn, USA (Ret), who served as assistant G-2 with the 82nd during Cebe-Habersky's tenure as ALO, email dated 25 Aug 2011.

23 Correll, p. 6. Photo reproduced with permission of "Air Force Magazine," published by the Air Force Association.

is likely a radio operator from the 33rd Air Base Squadron, the central organization from which radio operators were dispatched at that time. The third person in the photo is also unidentified but may be an Australian or New Zealander in light of his khaki uniform and flop hat. It also appears the man has winged insignia above his right pocket, perhaps airborne wings. Given the ribbons on the khaki uniform, as well as the beret and Air Commando style hats rather than steel pots, this might have been a "photo op" picture instead of one taken during an actual operation.

Bang Lang, Dinh Tuong Province, IV Corps

In June, the 1st Task Force under Lt. Colonel Dong with senior advisor Major East took the 1st and 3rd Battalions on a search and destroy mission near Bang Lang.[24] Each battalion clashed head on with a hard-core VC battalion, the 261st and the 514th. The fighting was fierce. The VC were routed, leaving behind 58 dead and 26 prisoners along with 20 captured weapons. The Airborne lost 29 killed and 89 wounded, including all nine platoon leaders (5 KIA, 4 WIA) from the three 1st Battalion companies that led the assault. Nonetheless, the troopers never wavered; they waded in and slugged it out. Forty troopers and advisors were decorated for gallantry after this action, and the Task Force commander was promoted to full colonel. Captain James Lindsay and Sergeant Combs each received the Silver Star and Lieutenant Fred A. Dilkes the Bronze Star with V for their actions that day.[25]

On 4 July at a victory parade in My Tho, Gallantry Crosses were presented to the

---
24 Modern province name is Tien Giang.
25 Airborne Newsletter, 10 April 1965, p. 4.

Lt. Colonel Casteel on deployment. Casteel Collection.

newly promoted Major Lindsay, Lieutenant Dilkes and Master Sergeant Colvin. Red Marker Lt. Colonel Martin was awarded the Gallantry Cross with Gold Star prior to his rotation to PACAF.

Rach Gia, Kien Giang Province, IV Corps

In July, Lt. Colonel Carleton Casteel arrived in Vietnam on a rainy afternoon typical of the summer monsoon season. He caught a taxi to the Airborne Brigade Headquarters on Tan Son Nhut AB and reported for duty. The Airborne commanders and advisors were just completing the plans for a jump scheduled for that evening. They remarked to him, "Of course, you'll want to come along!" Later that evening, even before being assigned quarters or retrieving his clothing,

Casteel found himself aboard a C-47 with about twenty-one Vietnamese paratroopers. He noted the weather was abysmal, a low ceiling and misty rain. Expecting that the mission would be scrubbed, he poked his head into the flight deck and asked the pilots whether they were go or no go. To his surprise, the mission was definitely on.

The aircraft soon reached the general vicinity of the drop zone and began to circle, a clear signal the pilots were not really sure of their location. While he had started at the end of the stick, Casteel was soon motioned to the head of the line by the jumpmaster. With a queasy feeling in his stomach about what was coming next, the lights over the door glowed red, then amber, then green, and he was out. His parachute opened, he swung once and immediately hit the ground, indicating he had jumped from 500 feet or less. It was pitch black on the ground, but soon a Red Hat with a flashlight joined him. The Red Hat shot a flare into the air, letting the circling C-47 know it was safe to drop the rest of the troopers. Casteel remembers that a number of them were injured during the drop. They spent the next few days walking without making contact with any hostile forces. Trucks picked up the troopers and hauled them back to Saigon. Welcome to Vietnam.[26]

Casteel asked two questions during that operation that would never be answered to his satisfaction during his entire tour. Where are we going? And what are we going to do when we get there? The Newsletter indicates that this jump was probably related to an attempt by the 5th Battalion to secure a POW camp reportedly holding 1,000 Vietnamese soldiers and 12 American advisors. The combined parachute

Slick Huey used for insertion and pickup of troops, resupply and Medevac. Casteel Collection.

drop and helicopter insertion of troops went well, but yielded no results.[27]

When he arrived back at Saigon, Casteel retrieved his clothing and went to investigate his assigned quarters. Finding them not to his liking, he set out to rent a place for himself. This was not a particularly easy task in Saigon at that time. After some frustrating dead ends, he stopped in at a local bar and soon his problem was solved. A young Vietnamese woman who worked at the bar had recently lost her American boyfriend, a young pilot who had been shot down. She was in need of rent money, and a trade was made. Her apartment would be Casteel's home when not deployed in the field.

Long An Province, III Corps

Casteel did not remain in Saigon very long before another operation began, this time a helicopter insertion in Long An Province with the 3rd Battalion. Helicopter insertions were sometimes more harrowing than parachute drops. In some areas of IV Corps, the helicopters would come to a hover a foot or so above a grass field that looked as smooth as a mown lawn.

---

26 Colonel Carleton N. Casteel, USAF (Ret), audio notes, March 2011.

27 Airborne Newsletter, 10 April 1965, p 5.

Casteel and the troopers soon found that the grass was six feet tall. When they exited the choppers, they were swallowed and blind to their surroundings. Using whistles and bugles, the Airborne reassembled their troops and pressed forward.

In other parts of the country, the jungle was so thick that there were few landing zones suitable for helicopters. In those areas, the Viet Cong often had pre-sighted the clearings and would begin a mortar attack when helicopters approached touchdown. Regardless of the incoming fire, the helicopter pilots never balked or backed off a landing. They always came in and dropped their passengers, and they always came back and picked them up. They were some of the bravest people Casteel had ever seen.

Ben Cat, Binh Duong Province, III Corps

During August, the Airborne 1st and 5th Battalions teamed up with the 5th Division near Ben Cat. This was reportedly the largest helicopter operation to date in the war. However, the combined force conducted an 86-kilometer ground sweep in four days with very little VC contact. One result of the operation was that the Army was convinced that a ground FAC could adequately control airstrikes. According to the Newsletter:

"The Air Force insisted that our qualified FAC, Captain Paradis, who was with the ground troops, could not see to direct the strikes. This fallacy was soon exposed and Bob directed many subsequent strikes."[28]

Notwithstanding the Newsletter's assertion, this controversy was not resolved except possibly in the eyes of the Army. In reality, the decision to increase the Army and Air Force presence in Vietnam following the Gulf of Tonkin incident ushered in once and for all the era of the airborne FAC. Within a year, the ALO successfully resisted attempts by Red Hat advisors to keep the FACs on the ground. Manpower was one argument. If FACs remained on the ground, one FAC would need to accompany each deployed battalion to ensure each unit received adequate support. However, the Air Force did not have enough FACs to meet that staffing requirement. Another argument was effectiveness. A FAC stationed on the ground with a battalion headquarters may not be able to provide effective support to a company or platoon operating any distance from the headquarters. In contrast, an airborne FAC could fly to each unit whenever needed for support.

Additionally, the larger view of the battlefield gave the airborne FAC an advantage over the limited perspective from the ground. An aerial view of the terrain and the disposition of friendly and enemy forces were critical in order to give proper direction to fighter-bombers. This was especially true after the Air force introduced jet fighters to the theater. The higher operating altitudes and speeds of the jets limited their ability to pick out details on the ground. The FAC provided that service. In the final analysis, the FACs needed airborne mobility and visibility to perform their job effectively and efficiently. Some Army advisors agreed. Red Hat Major Bob Murphy states that he saw Air Force FACs working from the ground struggle to be effective.[29]

September brought a failed coup attempt. The 1st Battalion was tricked into participating in the plot and, for a period of time, helped secure part of the capital.

---

28 Airborne Newsletter, 10 April 1965, p. 5.

29 Colonel Robert Murphy, USA (Ret), questionnaire, 24 January 2011, this was on an earlier tour with the 101st Airborne.

CHAPTER 6 - 1964 - LT COL JAMES MARTIN & LT COL CARLETON CASTEEL

A few tense moments before the jump. Captain Suddath and Lt. Colonel Casteel concentrate. Casteel Collection from the MACV Observer.

Last minute briefing on free fall techniques. Sergeant Lewis briefs jumpers Lindsay and Throckmorton. Casteel Collection from the MACV Observer.

Once informed of the true situation, they withdrew to the Battalion compound, and left the conspirators to their own devices. Several other battalions of the Airborne deployed at Tan Son Nhut as a show of force in support of the ruling junta. By the following morning, the coup attempt collapsed with no bloodshed.[30] Following this abortive coup, the Brigade remained close to Saigon during October.

While the Brigade was inactive during October, many of the advisors went through the free fall training program developed by Lindsay and Paradis. Those who completed the program earned Vietnamese Master Jump Wings. Many of their Vietnamese counterparts also took part in the training. A pictorial report in MACV's official newspaper "The Observer" featured photographs of Lindsay, Casteel and others undergoing the HALO training at Quang Trung Training Center under the watchful eye of Master Sergeant Harold R. Lewis, one of three qualified jumpmaster instructors in Vietnam.[31] The Vietnamese HALO team would later go to at least one international competition.[32]

Michelin Rubber Plantation, Phuoc Long Province, III Corps

In November, Casteel participated in an operation near the Michelin Rubber Plantation in III Corps around Thanksgiving Day. The plantation provided a good staging area for VC operations. The trees provided good overhead cover and there was relatively little undergrowth to impede movement. The Airborne anticipated a sweep of the region might be successful and mounted a huge operation involving four battalions and the Brigade Headquarters. However, the operation had limited results. Casteel was surprised to learn that the French-run plantation was still operating. The operators informed him that, like the villagers in the countryside, they paid taxes to both the Viet Cong and the South Vietnamese government to ensure their continued existence. When Casteel questioned them,

---

30 Airborne Newsletter, 10 April 1965, p. 6.
31 "The Observer," MACV newspaper, 7 Nov. 1964, pp. 4-5.

32 Diary of Brig. General Peter L. Drahn, USAFR (Ret), 13 August 1968, "At 0930 the Halo team (VN jump team to go to Spain parachute jumps) started jumping near Thu Duc south of the water plant."

Michelin Rubber Plantation, Phuoc Long Province, III Corps. Gene McCutchan collection.

they responded matter-of-factly that they could not predict which side would ultimately prevail. Therefore, they needed to stay in good graces with both. In effect, the Americans subsidized those tax payments by compensating Michelin for any rubber trees destroyed by U.S. bombing. Gene McCutchan received the same information on a visit to the plantation later in the war. The operators, dressed in white shorts and white shoes, seemed to be coping with the war quite well.[33]

November also marked the 8th anniversary of the Brigade that the Airborne celebrated in customary high style. This included the usual parachute drops onto a platform in the Saigon River (see Gene McCutchan's stories of being a "wind dummy"), with its attendant miscues. Some jumpers landed in the river, on the roofs of apartments, in the park by the Cathedral, on the roof of the Rex Hotel or in the traffic circle in front of the Rex.[34] Lt. Colonel Casteel jumped from an altitude of 8,000 feet aiming for a target that was a small patch of grass close to the Saigon Zoo. As he descended at what seemed an improbably small drop zone, he spotted a man in a small boat in the Saigon River waving his arms. Casteel made a quick decision and aimed for the river near the boat. He released his parachute harness about three feet above the water. The boatman retrieved Casteel and his waterlogged chute, which was no mean trick, and carried him to shore. Carleton paid him with all the wet money he had in his pocket. About a fourth of the jumpers who parachuted that day were injured from treetop and rooftop landings.[35]

---

33 Interview, 20-21 Jun 2011.
34 Airborne Newsletter, 10 April 1965, p. 7.
35 Colonel Carleton N. Casteel, USAF (Ret), audio notes March 2011.

Binh Gia, Phuoc Tuy Province, III Corps

Late on New Years Eve, the Brigade mobilized a task force to relieve some embattled Marines and Rangers near Binh Gia by 0600 the next morning. Those forces had been attempting for several days to take the village of Binh Gia, which had been seized by a VC unit. A Task Force of the 1st, 3rd and 7th Battalions opened the road and secured the perimeter so that trucks could retrieve the dead. The Task Force then went on a nine-day sweep through the region with no contact. The Viet Cong who had confronted the Marines and Rangers had left the area.[36]

Casteel accompanied the Task Force on this operation and recalls that the Airborne had little sympathy for the Marine and Rangers who had lost comrades in the ambush. As the Rangers' trucks rolled by, some of the paratroopers made universally understood wing-flapping motions with their elbows, accompanied by chicken clucking sounds. Casteel also understands that the Brigade made it clear in coming to the rescue that the other services could recover their own dead, and that the Brigade would only guard their flanks. Casteel deemed such demonstrations a new and vicious low in inter-service rivalry.

---
36 Airborne Newsletter, 10 April 1965, p. 8.

Ap Boc Plain of Reeds. Cebe-Habersky Collection.

Cebe-Habersky and Red Hat Bernie Loeffke in Ca Mau Province. Cebe-Habersky Collection.

SECTION III - THE BUILD UP

- 1965 - Lt Col Carleton Casteel, Major Gene McCutchan
- 1966 - Lt Col Gene McCutchan
- 1967 - Lt Col Gene McCutchan, Lt Col Pete Almquist
- 1968 - Lt Col Pete Almquist, Lt Col Don Glenn

1965–68 AIRBORNE OPERATIONS

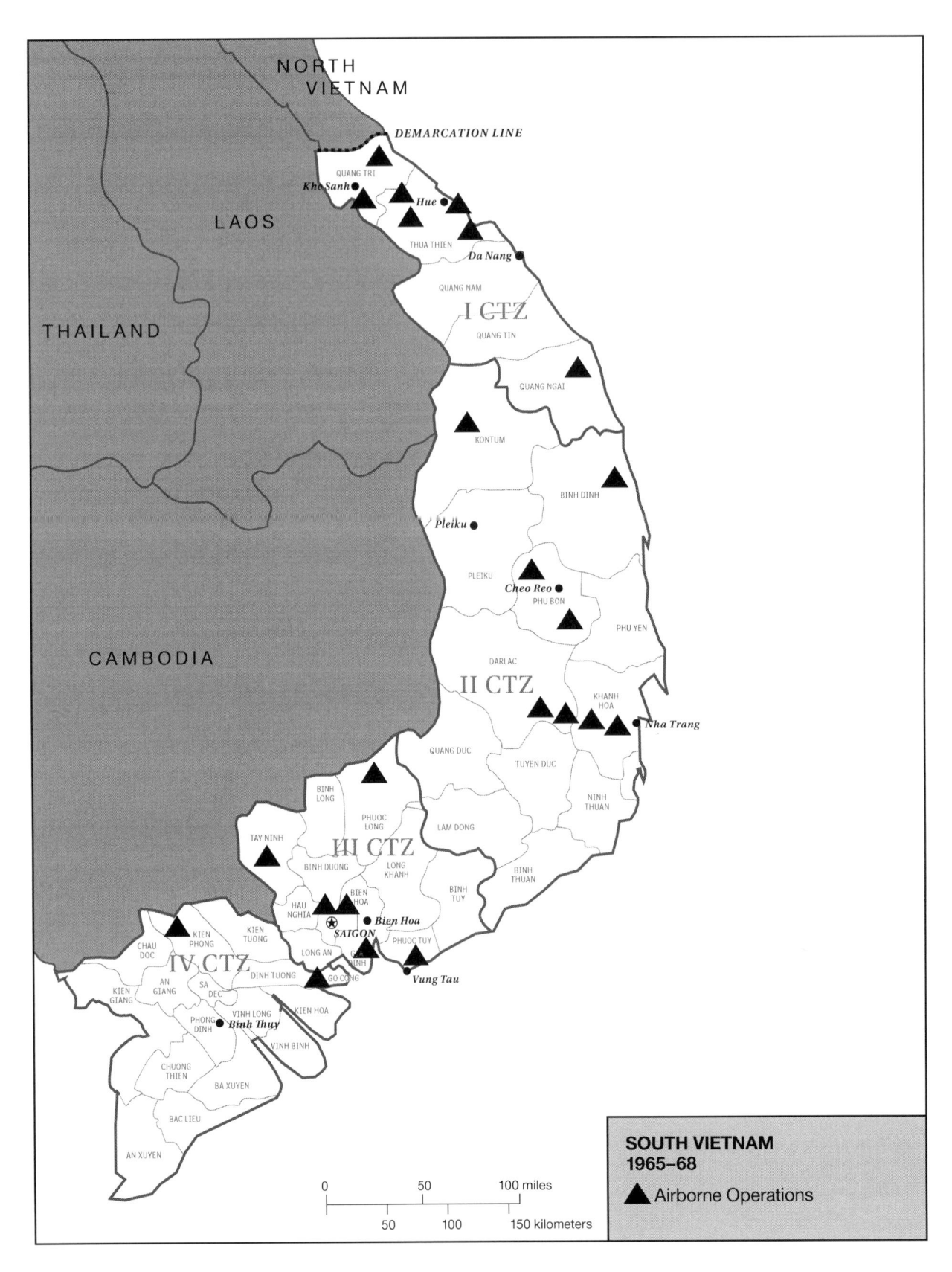

CHAPTER 7

1965 - LT COL CARLETON CASTEEL
MAJOR GENE McCUTCHAN

During 1965, the Red Markers became a full-fledged combat unit having permanently assigned FACs, aircraft, ROMADs and crew chiefs. Operations intensified during the year as the Airborne became increasingly aggressive. Near the end of the year, The Brigade raised and added two additional battalions to its manpower. The unit designation was upgraded to Division, recognizing its increased strength. The Red Marker unit expanded significantly, reflecting the increased American commitment to the conflict. The total American manpower in Vietnam grew from 18,000 at the beginning of 1964 to 240,000 by the end of 1965.[1]

The year, nonetheless, began slowly. Captain Bob Paradis' tour was extended by four weeks as the Air Force looked for a suitable replacement. As a temporary solution 1st Lieutenant Alan L. (Buck) Rennick, a young, cocky A-1E pilot assigned to the 1st Air Commando Squadron at Bien Hoa replaced Paradis. Buck had attended both jump school and the Air-Ground Operations School and was thus well qualified for the Red Marker slot. When approached by his commander with the idea of working as a ground FAC on a temporary assignment, the TDY pay of $16 per diem tax-free decided the matter for Rennick.[2] This pay amounted to $1,440 for 90 days, more than 40% of base pay on an after-tax basis. Buck came to work for Lt. Colonel Casteel and was in the thick of things in short order.

Red Markers 1965

Lt Col Carleton Casteel 01
Captain Bob Paradis 02

Major Gene McCutchan 01
1 Lt Buck Rennick (TDY)
Captain Paul Windle 02
1 Lt Bob Carn 03
Captain Joe Granducci 02
Captain Richard McGill 05
Captain Don Hawley 06
Captain Del Fleener 07
A1C/Sgt Cotton
A2C Jim Henneberry (TDY)
Airman Robinson
Airman Smith

Sgt Tran Dinh Luong
Private Phuong

---

1 Airborne Newsletter, 5 April 1966, p 13.

2 Lt. Colonel Alan L. Rennick, USAFR (Ret), interview 10 January 2011.

A-1Es. 1st Lieutenant Alan L. (Buck) Rennick flew these before and after his Red Marker tour. Casteel Collection

Binh Ghia, Phuoc Tuy Province, III Corps

When a Task Force of two battalions deployed in February, Rennick was the ground FAC for the operation.[3] The 6th Battalion and the 5th Battalion air assaulted by helicopter into an area called Cu Bi in Phouc Tuy Province, south of Saigon and northwest of the village of Binh Ghia. The operation developed into a huge battle. The 58th Viet Cong Regiment attacked the two battalions repeatedly from 1800 hours on the evening of 9 February to 0600 the next morning. The Airborne also received numerous mortar attacks and other indirect fire through the night. Captain Robert Losik, advisor to the 6th Battalion, recalled the difficult defensive position and the action that night as follows:

"Our perimeter was about 30 yards deep and about 80 to 100 yards wide, so it wasn't like Buck had a good deal. He directed strikes all night from a pinned down position. Buck controlled all the air assets supporting us, including flare ships, A-1Es and armed helicopters. He personally directed all the strikes and saved our asses. I thought he deserved the Silver Star; he got a Bronze Star with V."

For the helicopter assault, the Task Force used two landing zones separated by about 1,000 meters of thick woods. It was a large helicopter assault for that point in the war. There were four lifts. The 6th Battalion used LZ One (the first landing zone used in the operation) and were inserted unopposed in two lifts beginning in the morning. Each lift involved 30 slicks[4] flanked on either side by a platoon of gunships. Outside the line of gunships on each side, flights of A-1E Skyraiders bombed and strafed the tree line.

LZ Two had been scouted from the air during the previous few days. This may have tipped off the VC to the planned operation. If the aerial scouting had not

---

3 Lt. Colonel Robert C. Losik, USA (Ret), emails November 2010.

4 Unarmed UH-1 "Huey" helicopters.

tipped them off, the clattering insertion of the 6th Battalion a klick[5] away was surely a wake up call. Intelligence for the mission had pinpointed enemy concentrations in the area, and it was spot on. A VC base camp was located in the tree line just south of LZ Two. When the first wave of the 5th Battalion arrived about 1100 hours, all hell broke loose as the troopers unassed[6] the choppers. About seven choppers were hit, several disabled. The 5th Battalion was pinned down on the LZ, receiving heavy fire from VC emplacements on the south side.

Skyraiders had prepped the south perimeter with napalm before the insertion. However, the napalm had not penetrated the trees and left bunkers below unharmed. Battalion Commander Major Ngo Quang Truong directed his troopers to fix bayonets, prepare grenades and attack directly into the dug-in enemy. The 5th Battalion suffered a lot of casualties, but there would have been many more had Troung not ordered the frontal assault. Troung rapidly rose to become a four-star general and commander of I Corps. He was generally regarded as one of the most brilliant and courageous officers in the Vietnamese Army.

At the same time the 5th battalion was attacking the southern end of LZ Two, the 6th Battalion was moving on a dead run from LZ One to reinforce them. The 5th overran the VC positions just as the 6th arrived. The Task Force command immediately moved two companies from the 6th Battalion to the 5th Battalion in order to replace its casualties.

The afternoon was spent with simultaneous MedEvac, resupply and hoisting the downed choppers out of LZ Two, which was a massive landing zone. With all that activity on LZ Two, the other half of the 5th Battalion, with Red Hat 1st Lieutenant Mick Bartelme, was inserted unopposed into LZ One. These reinforcements ran through the woods and joined the remainder of the force on LZ Two. Bartelme was the only uninjured advisor to the 5th Battalion. Captain Tom Throckmorton and Sergeant Lewis Rowe, who had come in with the first wave, were both wounded assaulting the VC in the initial battle at LZ Two.

Captain Bob Losik and Sergeant First Class Erich Dippel were with the 6th Battalion. The battalion had no Lieutenant advisor, as he had been wounded in the An Lao Valley in January. Major Wesley B. Schull was the Task Force Senior Advisor. Lieutenant Buck Rennick, who landed with the 6th Battalion, represented the Red Markers. As night fell, there were, therefore, five Americans on the ground with about 900 Vietnamese Paratroopers.

At around 1800, the Viet Cong counterattacked. A CH-37 Mohave heavy lift helicopter was in the process of hoisting out the last damaged Huey as the attack began. The Mohave had to release the load to withdraw safely, dropping the Huey from about 50 feet. Buck called for immediate air support, and a flight of four Skyraiders answered. Unfortunately, they were "dry," having dumped all their ordnance on an earlier target. Buck asked flight lead to bring the Skyraiders in a tight four-ship formation, with wheels lowered, at treetop level from north to south in an attempt to scare the attackers. It worked. The VC took cover in the face of the oncoming fighters, giving the Airborne a chance to reorganize and get ready for the fight of their lives.

---

5 A kilometer, approximately 0.6 of a mile.
6 Army talk for "jumped from."

At 1830 hours, the U.S. position was as follows:

- The 5th Battalion with its four depleted companies and reinforced by two companies from the 6th Battalion, was on the south side of LZ Two;

- The two remaining companies of the 6th Battalion were on the north side of the LZ; and

- One badly damaged Huey remained in the middle of the LZ.

Not knowing what was going to happen next, the Airborne decided to blow up the Huey at around 2100 hours. At about 2130, the Task Force Commander, Major Truong Quang An, consolidated his forces.[7] He ordered the 6th Battalion to hurry across the LZ and join the 5th, creating a tighter and more defensible perimeter.

Buck had a pit dug during daylight that was 3 feet square and 3 feet deep. He lined the bottom with bricks of C4 explosives. When darkness fell, he lit the C4, which cast an eerie bluish-green glow that was visible only from the air. That glowing spot became the reference point for the nighttime air support. Every pilot could look down and see it. Buck used terminology familiar to every pilot who had ever made a Ground Controlled Approach to an airfield. He gave them headings to fly from the glowing reference point, and directed them on downwind, crosswind and final approach legs to attack the VC positions. During the long night, Buck controlled flareships, armed Hueys and A-1Es. During attack after attack, Buck directed ordnance onto the VC, helping to break the back of each assault. After beating back an attack at 0600 on the 10th, six of the eight Airborne companies were out of ammunition. Two flank companies had been lightly engaged, and their ammo was rapidly redistributed. If the VC had launched one more frontal assault, the Airborne would have met it mostly with rifle butts and bayonets. Instead, beaten badly, the VC retreated to lick its wounds and the Airborne breathed a sigh of relief.

An Aussie Caribou stood alert all night at Vung Tau with a load of ammunition it was instructed to "free drop" if the Task Force ran out during the night. Having to resort to such a tactic could have ended in disaster. According to Bob Losik, only Buck Rennick's skillful employment of airstrikes allowed the battalions to conserve enough ammunition that they did not need that desperate nighttime Caribou run.[8]

The medal count for this particular fight included a Distinguished Service Cross to Captain Throckmorton, Silver Star to Master Sergeant Rowe, and a Bronze Star with V to Major Schull, Captain Losik, Lieutenants Bartelme and Rennick, and Sergeant First Class Dippel. The Vietnamese also awarded each American with a Cross of Gallantry. The Advisory Detachment Commander, Colonel John Hayes, received the National Order, 5th Class.

After several months on temporary duty as a Red Marker, Lieutenant Rennick went back to flying A-1Es. Major Robert Webb, advisor to the 1st Battalion, recalls that one day a flight of four A-1Es came in so low over Webb's field camp that their prop wash blew down tents and sent papers flying. As the Skyraiders climbed out, Webb's radio crackled. Sure enough,

---

7 Three years later, An was a brigadier general commanding the 23rd Division. He was the first general officer killed in Vietnam. A helicopter carrying him and his wife was shot down 8 Sep 1968 enroute to Duc Lap to celebrate a late August victory by his troops at that location.

8 Losik, email 16 Jan 2012.

it was Buck Rennick, who just wanted to say "hi" and to let Webb know he was leading the flight. The brash lieutenant also made it clear he had a couple of captains and a major on his wing—and, most importantly, that he was flight lead because he was the best damned pilot of the bunch![9] Buck later went on to fly with Continental Air Lines, in part apparently, because the regimentation of military life did not agree with him.[10]

Buck Rennick remembers the February 9th engagement vividly.[11] He recalls his radio operator dug a hole for him, a really shallow depression. Buck lay on his belly but thought his butt was too high in the air. He tried on his back but felt even more exposed. In a quandary, Buck confessed to Major Schull,

"I'm scared shitless. Are you scared, Maj?"

The reply was, "Lieutenant, I am a West Point grad and a trained combat trooper. I'm not afraid of anything! ... Well, maybe a little."

Losik swears, *"We were all scared shitless, so Buck had no corner on that market. As I said before, he was both magnificent and heroic; he saved all of our asses. He was magnificently cool under crushing pressure to perform."*

Buck also claims he does not remember buzzing Major Webb after returning to the A-1Es, but admits, "It sure sounds like me!" He describes Casteel as one of the best bosses he ever had. Casteel wrote a letter stating that Lieutenant Rennick was his representative and that any request from Rennick should be considered a request directly from the colonel. Consequently, Buck was able to borrow aircraft from the VNAF wherever he went on deployments during his several months with the unit.

Buck also notes that Casteel liked to jump, whether from C-119s, helicopters or whatever. Despite Rennick's parachute rating, he did not particularly like jumping; he would rather have been flying.

Lt. Colonel Casteel had to cut his tour short due to a family crisis and left for the states in early April.[12] The Vietnamese Airborne awarded a Corps Level Cross of Gallantry with Gold Star to both Casteel and Bob Paradis for their service to the unit.[13] Lt. Colonel Casteel also received an Air Medal for Meritorious Achievement and an Air Force Commendation Medal. He returned in the states to the same job at his prior duty station, as deputy director of operations for the 12th Air Force. He even moved back into the same office at the same desk. However, his early departure left the Airborne without an ALO.

While working at the TACC early in 1965, Gene McCutchan heard about the vacancy at his old ALO assignment. Gene's boss asked if he would fill the vacancy, and Gene jumped at the chance to leave the rear echelon and return to combat. When McCutchan returned to the Airborne, he met the first flying Red Marker FACs who had permanently assigned aircraft. Captain Paul R. (Windy) Windle, Red Marker 02, had arrived in March. Lieutenant Robert M. Carn, Jr., Red Marker 03, had followed shortly thereafter.[14] Thanks to two

---

[9] Colonel Robert H. Webb, USA (Ret), interview 9 December 2010.

[10] Lt. Colonel Alan L. Rennick, USAFR (Ret), lives in Colorado after a career with Continental and after flying 17 years for the Air National Guard.

[11] Lt. Colonel Alan L. Rennick, USAFR (Ret), interview 10 January 2011.

[12] Per Colonel Casteel questionnaire, his DEROS was 3 April 1965.

[13] Commander in Chief, Republic of Vietnam Armed Forces, postal message to Airborne Brigade, 13 March 1965.

[14] Lt. Colonel Robert C. Losik, U.S. Army (Ret), emails November 2010.

assigned O-1E aircraft, the unit no longer FACed from the ground or depended on Vietnamese FACs for airborne control of airstrikes. A senior pilot, Windle had already served two Vietnam tours in B-26s and was returning for a third tour in A-1Es when he moved into the FAC role.[15]

B-26 Douglas Invader. Courtesy of Wikipedia.

Lt Carn being awarded a Cross of Gallantry. Gene McCutchan Collection.

Carn was a 1962 USAF Academy graduate on just his second assignment after pilot training. They were polar opposites in terms of experience. Neither would live through his tour.

Early in the year, Airborne field operations mimicked those of the past. Battalions deployed singly, or two or more as a Task Force. Sometimes those units operated in conjunction with elements of a local division or the Vietnamese Marines or Rangers. For the first time, the Airborne staged joint operations with American units as they began to arrive in-country. One Airborne Task Force was maintained in II Corps throughout the year. Each battalion joined the Task Force for varying lengths of time. During the year, Red Markers accompanied the Airborne on operations in II Corps at Kontum, An Khe, Duc Co near the Cambodian border (more than once), and Cheo Reo in Phu Bon province.

During the last half of 1965, the Airborne carried out some operations at division strength, posing a new challenge for the command and its Red Hat advisors. The increased size of the Airborne and the number and duration of its deployments dramatically increased the numbers of VC killed and captured. Enemy casualties reached new highs during the year, with 893 KIA, 204 POWs and 313 weapons captured on the field of battle.[16] This heightened activity was not without cost. The Airborne suffered increased losses as well, and the Red Hats and Red Markers were among this sad tally.

Cheo Reo, Phu Bon Province, II Corps

On 30 June 1965, Task Force 1 (1st and 5th Battalions, reinforced by an ARVN Marine mortar platoon) had a significant engagement in the Central Highlands

---
15 Eugene Rossel, Air Commando site, http://home.earthlink.net/~aircommando1/windle2.html

16 Airborne Newsletter, 5 Apr 1966, p. 16.

near Cheo Reo in Phu Bon Province.[17] It became the first fatal operation for a Red Marker. A radio operator and a FAC were both killed. The Task Force's mission was to search out Viet Cong main force units reportedly located south of Pleiku and west of Tuy Hoa. The 5th Battalion led the way. The 1st Battalion followed escorting a convoy of trucks loaded with artillery ammo destined for a firebase in the area. The convoy also included an ARVN infantry unit and a dozen U.S. soldiers, who were apparently headed for the firebase. The force moved out before dawn pausing later for breakfast. The Viet Cong let the 5th Battalion pass unmolested but ambushed the remaining convoy, completely surrounding the trailing units. The 5th Battalion, about five miles in advance, spent most of the day backtracking to link up with the surrounded convoy.[18]

Red Markers were in the air and on the ground during this battle. Captain Paul Windle, Red Marker 02, was flying cover for the operation. Airman 2nd Class James C. Henneberry, a ROMAD on TDY assignment to the Red Markers from the 33rd Air Base Squadron, was on the ground with the Task Force advisor.[19] Henneberry reported to Major William N. Ciccolo, Task Force advisor the day before, stating that he was to accompany the Airborne. This was news to Bill, but he made sure that Henneberry was fed that night by the Airborne and given a spot in the convoy.[20] Henneberry had with him a heavy-weight Single-Sideband radio. Henneberry would be able to contact the DASC if the convoy ran into trouble. However, he could not contact fighter aircraft, helicopters or the FAC.

When the VC fired the first shots as the Airborne ate breakfast, the experienced soldiers took cover and assumed defensive positions. It was the last time Bill saw Henneberry alive. After the first few shots, the VC employed automatic weapons followed by mortars aimed at the exposed convoy. Vehicles rapidly caught fire, and the artillery cargo began to explode. The Airman was killed by small arms or mortar fire near the parked convoy. Presumably, he was trying to get back to his jeep to retrieve his radio. He was the first Red Marker to die in combat.

Henneberry had written to a stateside friend in a letter dated June 23, 1965, that he would be leaving shortly on an operation and was beginning to count the days till he got home. He would have had 100 days left in his tour as of July 24th. He also wrote that,

"...for the first time I am beginning to feel quite nervous about an operation. This will be my second one. The first one I just set up my radio in the rear, but on this one I will be walking through a wooded area. It probably won't be bad once I get started, but I will be glad when it is finished—This will probably be my last operation. In a way I hope it is."[21]

Don Findlay served in the same unit as Jim Henneberry. Don specifically remembers receiving no training with firearms.[22] He recalls only firing a couple of magazines of M-16 ammo at Clark AB in the Philippines. He had not even seen the weapon prior to that time on the range. There was no instruction on care and maintenance of the weapon and no training in defensive tactics. When Don arrived at a forward location assigned TDY to a Special Forces unit, however, he learned

---

17 Current name Gia Lai Province.
18 Colonel Robert H. Webb, USA (Ret), letter 29 Nov 2010, interview 9 Dec 2010. Webb had been the 1st Battalion advisor.
19 Report of Casualty, DD Form 1300, 3 August 1965.
20 Colonel William N. Ciccolo, USA (Ret), interview 30 Nov 2010.

21 http://springfield50.org/pittsfield_henne-berry_letters.htm
22 Donald T. Findlay, former USAF Tech Sergeant, Interview 4 Jan 2011.

A2C James Henneberry (at right), breakfast shortly before the ambush at Cheo Reo. Bill Ciccolo Collection.

some survival skills. The Special Forces knew that Findley might have to help defend their compound at some point. They took him to the range where he fired a case of ammo with each of his weapons (he had two personal side arms in addition to the M-16). The Special Forces also ensured Findley became qualified in firing an M-79 grenade launcher. Don wonders whether Henneberry ever received any such instruction.

Don also speculated about the radio equipment on this mission. Don believes the Single-Sideband radio was probably a PRC-47 and was not really portable. However, it had a power cable to attach it to a vehicle battery. Don suspects that Henneberry connected the radio to the jeep's power supply and left it connected when the convoy dismounted for breakfast. When the attack started, his first move likely was to retrieve the radio so he would be of some help during the fight. Whatever the actual events, the sad fact remains that Henneberry was killed. Don also confirms the reasoning of the task force advisor who wondered about the value of having this HF/SSB radio set. The HF could communicate with the DASC but not with any of the aircraft that would be coming to their assistance—including the FAC.

As the attack began, Windle called in air support in order to blunt the enemy advance and to give the ground forces time to establish positions.[23] He put in several airstrikes in the jungle around the Airborne.[24] Windle carried a passenger during this mission. Army Major Joseph E. Parker, the newly assigned Province advisor, had asked to observe the operation from the air and rode in the backseat.

Major Robert H. Webb, 1st Battalion Senior Advisor, recalls Windy trying to get a better fix on the hostile positions after a couple of airstrikes.[25] The FAC had a flight of F-100s on station while he made several low passes, attempting to get a view under the tree line.[26] Webb remembers telling him on the FM not to get so low. The area was hot, and the FAC was drawing fire. The VC gunners hit Windle's Bird Dog during its third pass. The plane crashed about thirty yards from Red Hat Sergeant First Class Ralph R. Conklin, one of Webb's assistants.[27] Conklin led three attacks of the 11th Company trying to get to the downed craft. The Airborne company commander and several troop-

---

23 Windle probably had been airborne since first light to cover the convoy.
24 Virtual Wall, authored by Major Joseph S. Granducci II, USAF (Ret), online, http://www.virtualwall.org/dw/WindlePR01a.htm
25 Colonel Robert H. Webb, USA (Ret).
26 Rossel.
27 Captain Ralph R. Conklin, USA (Ret).

ers were killed in the futile attempt.[28] Both Windle and Parker were killed. The Bird Dog caught fire during the fight, and their charred remains were recovered after the battle.

Ciccolo remembers the day featured one horror after another. First, the ambush. Then, he lost track of the airman and would not learn till the end of the day that the young man had been killed. Finally, the radio call from the forward locations, "Red Marker is down. Red Marker is down."

Windle had flown just over 100 FAC missions when he was killed. After his death, the small airport at Greensburg, Kansas, where he learned to fly before entering the Air Force, was renamed in his honor.[29] McCutchan wrote to Windle's parents that he had been well liked and respected by both the Vietnamese and the Americans working with the Brigade. When Windy had been flying in support of a battalion and rotated back to Saigon, the unit invariably asked how soon he would be returning, and stated how much they needed him.[30]

The Republic of Vietnam honored the Americans posthumously. Windle and Parker were awarded the National Order, Fifth Class and the Cross of Gallantry with Palm, while Henneberry was awarded the Military Merit Medal and Cross of Gallantry with Palm for their sacrifice.[31]

Webb remembers the battle as a very close thing from the beginning. Among the mortar and automatic weapons fire the VC also used hand grenades, an indication they were nose to nose with the Airborne. After the death of Red Marker 02, an A-1E Skyraider pilot, call sign "Elgin 89," asked Webb if he would like him to stay on scene and control air strikes until a replacement FAC arrived.[32] Webb welcomed the assistance and began calling for closer and closer strikes as the Airborne perimeter shrank. At the height of the battle, the VC were about to split the Airborne forces in two. Webb called for a strike right on top of his lines. Elgin 89 advised it was too close, but Webb told him to do it anyway. The Airborne took some casualties from that strike, including a very good company commander. However, the line held and the VC finally broke contact. The battalion commander personally consoled Webb about the friendly casualties saying, "You had to do it. You had no choice." Webb says that Elgin 89 was the Air Force hero of the day and truly, "Saved our collective ass." He later heard that Elgin 89 ran out of gas just after he landed at his base.

The communication between Elgin 89 and Webb was an anomaly. The A-1E Skyraiders had an FM radio, the only USAF fighter so equipped. Without that piece of equipment on board, Elgin 89 would have been no help, and the Airborne would have gotten no support from the air. After this incident, Red Hats began carrying URC-4 survival radios in the field. These small hand-held units received and transmitted on the emergency Guard Channel on VHF and UHF frequencies (121.5 and 243.0 MHz). Every aircraft, fixed wing or

---

28 Bob Losik remembers Bob Webb and Ralph Conklin as two of the "most courageous sons-of-bitches I have ever known."
29 Granducci, Virtual Wall.
30 Rossel.
31 14 Sep 1965 decree of the Central Executive Committee and Minister of Defense.

32 Webb states that he has tried to locate the pilot with this call sign without success. On-line references indicate that the Elgin call sign was used in 1966-67 by two F-4 Squadrons and an F-105 Squadron. The author has not located a reference to its possible earlier use by an A-1E unit.

helicopter, monitored one or both of these emergency frequencies whenever in the air. Thus, if the Red Hats ever lost a FAC again, they could be in instant communication with someone in the air.[33]

Late in the day, the 5th Battalion arrived, and Webb directed them toward the retreating VC. He took the lead elements of the 5th Battalion right through the destroyed convoy, which continued to cook off ammo. Meanwhile, the main force of the 5th fought along the flanks of the convoy. Webb then returned to his own unit. Moving around during the battle, Webb advised the 12-man U.S. Army team, which was under fire for the first time, to stay put until he gave them directions. After the battle, he learned they had ignored him and tried to return to Cheo Reo. The VC captured and executed the entire team.

The official report states that the battle, which included 84 air sorties, ended with 122 Viet Cong killed and 40 weapons captured.[34] Webb explains that the 84 sorties included USAF, Marine and Navy aircraft employed during the fight, most of which Elgin 89 directed. Further, Webb notes that the tally of enemy KIA was an educated guess. When the battle ended, MACV in Saigon began asking for results. Webb thought it would be folly to start trooping off into the jungle to count bodies and conspired with others on site to provide a reasonable number, which he believes is low. The Airborne had been battling a VC regiment, three battalions against one. Webb is certain the VC sustained a lot of damage. Ultimately, the Airborne and VC each collected their own dead. Ciccolo recalls about 30 Airborne killed. Webb adds

Joe (Duke) Granducci. Gene McCutchan Collection.

that Pulitzer Prize winning photographer Eddie Adams accompanied the Airborne on this operation. That night, Adams and Webb alternately stood watch manning the radio in their defensive position so they each could get some sleep.[35]

Duc Co "I", Phu Bon Province, II Corps

In July, Captain Joseph S. (Duke) Granducci II joined the unit as Red Marker 02, replacing Captain Windle. A ten-year Air Force veteran, Duke also had a senior parachutist rating. He became an excellent FAC and assistant ALO. Before he was even introduced to the rest of the group or issued a red beret, McCutchan sent him to support Task Force 2 (3rd and 8th Battalions) near Duc Co. The Task Force had previously moved to the Duc Co Special Forces Camp at the end of Highway 19 near the Cambodian border to counter an increasing Viet Cong threat. During this particular operation, Granducci flew from Pleiku because the small strip at Duc Co was unsecure and under nearly constant mortar attack.

---

33 Colonel Robert C. Losik, USA (Ret), email 19 Jan 2011. USAF pilots carried the same type radio in their survival vests for communication with search and rescue aircraft in the event of being shot down.

34 Airborne Newsletter, 5 Apr 1966, p 2.

35 Lt. Colonel Robert H. Webb, letter March 12, 2000.

Sweeping the area around the camp, both Airborne battalions engaged well-entrenched Viet Cong forces. They fought until darkness with heavy casualties on both sides, after which the Airborne withdrew to defensive positions near the camp. For a week, the VC surrounded and isolated the camp. The compound took a heavy pounding from mortar attacks. Resupply was only feasible by airdrops. Airstrikes against the bunkered Viet Cong required a direct hit to have much effect.

One of the finest examples of aerial heroism occurred during the week the camp was isolated. A C-123 landed outside the compound on the dirt airstrip, actually just a wide spot in the road. It offloaded ammo and took on wounded troopers. Damaged by mortar fire while on the ground, the C-123 managed to get off the ground and limp into Saigon where the wounded received medical attention.[36]

The 5th Battalion airlifted into Duc Co to reinforce the Task Force. Meanwhile, an additional relief force of Vietnamese Marines, Rangers and armor moved overland from Pleiku, some forty miles away. Granducci and a Province FAC alternated flying cover for this ground relief force. Flying low and parallel to the relief convoy in the early afternoon, Duke discovered a major ambush of NVA troops. He warned the ground forces to take cover and called in immediate airstrikes with several sets of fighters armed with bombs and 20mm cannon. The airstrikes were credited with many NVA casualties. As Duke began to run low on fuel, a Province FAC arrived on scene to relieve him and took control of the last of the airstrikes. The combined ground forces cleared the area almost to the Cambodian border. In the process, they captured 107 weapons and accounted for 486 KIA.

Coordination with Province FACs was the norm during Red Marker operations. Because Red Markers deployed a single aircraft and FAC, they relied on assistance from local FACs to help cover the Airborne's area of operations. The Province FACs shared intelligence gathered from their experience patrolling the same region over a long period of time. The Red Markers lacked such regional expertise because they frequently moved around the country with the Airborne. On the day of this particular battle, the Province FAC covered the relief force headed to Duc Co during the morning, and Duke relieved him at noon. As the time came for them to change shifts in the late afternoon, the Province FAC was aware of the ongoing battle and was right on time to contribute to the action.[37] It was an example of coordination that worked perfectly.

Ban Me Thuot, Darlac Province, II Corps

In August, an Airborne brigade of several battalions airlifted to Nha Trang and moved overland to secure Highway 21 toward Ban Me Thuot.[38] For two and a half weeks, they patrolled the road to allow supply convoys to pass and made sweeps searching for main force Viet Cong units reportedly in the area. However, the Brigade made no significant enemy contacts during this operation.[39]

Granducci initially covered this operation until McCutchan sent Lieutenant Robert Carn to relieve Duke. On 29 August 1965, Carn collided with a Province FAC doing visual reconnaissance in the area.[40] The other FAC made an emergency landing at

---

36 Airborne Newsletter, 5 Apr 1966, p. 3.

37 See Joe Granducci's description of the action at Duc Co in *Cleared Hot, Forward Air Controller Stories from the Vietnam War*, published by the Forward Air Controllers Association, Inc., 2008, p. 98.

38 Now designated Highway 26.

39 Airborne Newsletter, 5 Apr 1966, p. 3.

40 O-1F 56-2530 was destroyed in the crash.

the temporary airstrip near Brigade headquarters. Carn's aircraft crashed, and he was killed.[41]

Other FACs joined the unit during the year to replace Red Marker losses and add manpower to support the expanded number of Airborne battalions. The new FACs included Captain Richard V. McGill (Red Marker 05), Captain Don R. Hawley (Red Marker 06) and Captain Delbert W. Fleener (Red Marker 07). With this expanded staff Gene McCutchan revamped his support of the Airborne. Instead of personally deploying on operations involving only one or two battalions, Gene sent a FAC, an aircraft, a crew chief and a radio operator on these operations. He limited his own deployments to larger formations. This allowed him to maintain closer contact with the division commander and the Red Hat senior advisor, and to deploy only when they did.

In September, the Airborne made a combat jump in Bien Long Province. This was the first time they had deployed in III Corps in quite some time. It was a joint operation with the U.S. 173rd Airborne Brigade, the first U.S. Army combat unit deployed in country. The Americans and four battalions of the Vietnamese Airborne swept from Ben Cat to Quan Loi and back to Ben Cat. The operation resulted in little enemy contact, but the allies destroyed 15 tons of rice and 4 tons of equipment, fuel and explosives.[42]

Later in the year, the 2nd Task Force (5th and 8th Battalions) deployed to Tuy Hoa. The Task Force made little hostile contact. However, the Airborne did capture an enemy courier who possessed a _complete plan_ of the Task Force's deployment. The plan included each friendly unit's identity, its departure point and maneuver plans. These details had been decided only days before at Task Force headquarters. It was obvious that the VC had infiltrated the Airborne.[43] Perhaps this explains why so many Airborne operations resulted in little, if any, contact with the enemy.

Duc Co "II" And Ia Drang, Phu Bon Province, II Corps

In mid-November, the Airborne returned to Duc Co and the Ia Drang Valley to support the U.S. 1st Cavalry Division's attack against major Viet Cong and NVA forces. The battle plan called for the Airborne to block the VC and NVA escape route into Cambodia. The 2nd Task Force (5th and 8th Battalions), located near Tuy Hoa AB, airlifted to Duc Co. The 1st Task Force (3rd and 6th Battalions) followed immediately from Saigon. Staging from Duc Co, the 5th, 8th and 6th Battalions air assaulted to a position astride the Drang River at the Cambodian border. The 3rd Battalion and Task Force headquarters joined them the next day. Meanwhile, the 7th Battalion left Saigon to reinforce the Task Force. All units fought heavily the following week with the 3rd, 5th and 6th Battalions bearing the heaviest burden. The Task Force accounted for 265 KIA, 10 POW and 60 weapons captured.

Red Marker 02, Duke Granducci, flew air cover for the operation. His article in _Cleared Hot_ about the battle reports that he attempted to share information with the 1st Cav regarding the Airborne's earlier engagement with some of the same enemy units at Duc Co. He hoped to coordinate air support with the Cav, but they rebuffed him bluntly. The Americans told Duke things would be just fine if the Viet-

---

41 Virtual Wall, Granducci.
42 Airborne Newsletter, 5 Apr 1966, p. 4.

43 _Id._ at p. 5.

namese stayed "on their side of the road" and out of the way of the Cav. Duke believed the lack of coordination resulted in less than optimal use of the combined firepower of the allied forces and, ultimately, cost some American lives. Red Hat Major Norman Schwarzkopf served as task force advisor to the Airborne during the Duc Co actions. He witnessed firsthand the unorganized fire control and liaison among artillery, airstrikes and helicopter gunships. In Duke's view, Schwarzkopf took the lessons of coordinated action to heart and demanded coordinated fire support from the forces under his command 30 years later in Desert Storm.[44]

Gene McCutchan's view of Granducci is best illustrated by the story of one mission when the Airborne came under attack on a rainy night. Gene called the DASC from the TOC for some immediate air support and went to the flight line to get an O-1 in the air.

Duke intercepted him as Gene was about to get in the Bird Dog, "Major, I'll take this mission."

Gene said, "But Duke, it's night, it's raining, I've done this before."

Duke replied, "Major, you can't do my job for me. Let me do my job, and you go back to the TOC and do yours!" He jumped in the O-1E and took off, putting in airstrikes under the worst possible conditions with no flares and broke the back of the attack on the Airborne.

When Granducci landed later that night and walked into the briefing room at the TOC to give his report of the mission, the Red Hats and Vietnamese gave him a standing ovation. Gene says this is the only time he ever witnessed such a display of appreciation.[45]

---
44 *Cleared Hot*, p. 100.
45 Lt. Colonel Eugene R. McCutchan, USAF (Ret), interview 21-22 June 2011.

Enlisted Support

By the last half of 1965, the Red Marker enlisted roster expanded to include more crew chiefs and permanently assigned ROMADs. Prior to that time, the lack of personnel often meant FACs deployed to remote Forward Operating Locations without a crew chief. The FACs refueled and rearmed the Bird Dogs after each mission. When periodic maintenance was required, the FACs took the planes to Bien Hoa, picked up another plane and returned to the FOL.

Furthermore, all radio operators previously belonged to a central organization. When units deployed to the field for an operation, the central organization assigned a ROMAD to accompany them. The Airborne regularly deployed on operations, requiring a nearly constant stream of these temporary duty radio operators. As the war effort expanded, FAC units supporting American forces placed increased demands on the central communications organization. The increased demand proved the existing structure unwieldy and unworkable. Ultimately, the USAF revised the organization and assigned communications personnel and crew chiefs directly to the various FAC units.

As the first step in decentralizing its organization, 7th Air Force issued a special order dated 6 May 1965 creating four additional Tactical Air Support Squadrons to join the 19th TASS already in existence. One squadron would be responsible for aircraft, equipment and personnel administration for FAC operations within one of the four Corps areas. The fifth squadron had the same responsibility for operations in SEA outside Vietnam. These squadrons assigned crew chiefs directly to the scattered FAC units.

The order creating the Support Squadrons directed that each report to the 505th Tactical Air Control Group. Also reporting to the 505th was the unit containing all the radio communications and maintenance personnel. That unit continued to dispatch ROMADs on a TDY basis as it had done in the past. The 505th also had responsibility for installation and operation of communications, navigation and electrical equipment throughout SEA. A later directive from 7th Air Force created the 504th Tactical Air Support Group as the new parent organization for the five TASSs. That order left the 505th with the major equipment installation function, but moved the FAC radio operators and repair personnel to the 504th. This resulted in direct assignment of radio personnel to each TASS and to the FAC units. During this period, the Red Markers officially became part of the 19th TASS. However, Major Gene McCutchan continued to report directly to the Director of the TACC, who wrote Gene's OERs.[46] Red Markers in a later period had OERs endorsed by the TASS and then by the DASC.

The earliest enlisted personnel assigned permanently to the Red Markers included Sergeant Cotton, Airman Robinson and Airman Smith. Gene especially appreciated Sergeant Cotton's devotion to the mission. On one deployment, the aircraft remained overnight at a remote, unsecure airstrip. Each morning, Sergeant Cotton drove a pilot to the plane, accompanied by an armed guard of several troopers. He completed a security inspection to ensure the Bird Dog had not been sabotaged. Viet Cong reportedly booby-trapped FAC aircraft by placing a hand grenade in the fuel tank. A rubber band held the grenade safety handle in place. Eventually, the gasoline degraded the rubber, which released the handle and exploded the grenade. Cotton checked for grenades by rocking the wings of the parked aircraft and listened for the sound of one rolling around in the tank. When satisfied the aircraft was safe, Cotton launched the FAC on the first sortie of the day. The escort returned to the main base, and Cotton awaited the FAC's return to refuel and rearm the plane for the next mission. Upon learning about this routine, Gene asked if Cotton didn't want to return to the main base with the escort and drive back to the strip when it was time to recover the plane. Cotton responded that he knew everyone was shorthanded. He preferred to stand guard alone all day long rather than eat up an escort's time. Consequently, he spent each day alone on the strip with his M-16 for company.

Airman Robinson, a radio operator, begged McCutchan to go on a ground operation, despite the fact that Red Markers now controlled airstrikes exclusively from the O-1s. Robinson wanted to accompany the Red Hat advisors to the field rather than manning the radios from the TACP back at the field headquarters. Gene finally relented and let him go. On the third day, Robbie sprained his ankle so badly he could no longer walk and had to be evacuated. Rather sheepish, he never again asked to go in the field.[47]

Troops In Contact

The most important FAC mission was controlling airstrikes for Troops-in-Contact (TIC) with the enemy. Mission success depended on both the FAC's direction and the fighters' accuracy. Most FACs had an opinion about the best fighter pilots and aircraft, about which could be trusted to be accurate and aggressive enough to get the ordnance on target without endanger-

---

46 Officer Efficiency Reports.

47 I've found no other information on Airmen Robinson and Smith except for Red Marker memories that they served with the unit.

ing the friendly forces. Duke Granducci expressed his opinion in a personal vignette addressed to the FAC Association for publication in about 2001. That article, with minor editing, follows in its entirety:

"B-57s – Just had a few in the summer of '65. I think they later stood them down for a while after the sappers[48] destroyed some on the Bien Hoa ramp and before the beefed up ones arrived—in the summer of '65, northwest of Bien Hoa, southern edge of the Iron Triangle, working at night under flares. They were laying 250 pound frags by the bushel on the outside of the northwest wall on one of the old French triangular forts.

"A-1Es – Then the A-1s arrived and the poor guys in the fort called for us to take out the western building inside the wall. You know, you can tell by the pitch and frequency of the voice and the speech patterns how serious the guys on the ground are. And the A-1s did the trick. And the good guys held for the night, and were reinforced the next day. Who says air can't hold ground?

"Navy A-4s – The ones I had could drop a 1,000-pounder down a smoke stack. Fall of '65, an ARVN Airborne Battalion was ordered to open the coast road to the DMZ. In I Corps, the local troops had been run south several months earlier by the Cong. Our guys, with a company of engineers, had repaired the road cuts and got to within 15-20 klicks of the DMZ when they came upon a hardened bunker next to the road. The guys in the bunker were blowing heavy firepower across a shallow river draw. Our guy's mortars just seemed to bounce off. Ho, hum. The ARVN Airborne Division troops, not being ones to throw bodies against 50 cal. or 12.7 mm machine gun bullets, called for air. We didn't have any air on station, and I had a hard time getting an immediate airstrike approved. I had to get real insistent. "Forces in contact, Americans forces in contact." (Well, damn it, the U.S. Army Advisor and his NCO were Americans and everyone knew that Red Marker FACs never lied.) Finally, the apologetic controller said he did have a flight of two Navy A-4s that had been diverted out of North Vietnam.

"I said, 'Great! I'll take 'em.'

"He said, 'but they only have one bomb and one can of napalm between them.'

"I said, in an even louder voice, 'I'LL TAKE 'EM!' Seems like the exchange went on for a couple of more rounds, or maybe it was just my frustration. The afternoon was wasting away, and our objective was well on the other side of the river, and the troops needed to get past the bunker so they could hunker down early enough to 'cook rice.' They had already been out two full days, and this would be their 3rd night on the move.

"Anyhow, the A-4s found me in a jiffy by homing on my radio hold-down under the 3,000 foot overcast. The flight leader called, 'Minimum fuel, target quick please.' I immediately rolled in and popped off one of those corkscrewing 3.5-inch WP rocket heads. I guess all the Covey guys got the straight arrow 2.75-inch rocket heads. On a low angle pass you could accidentally shoot down another airplane with one of those 3.5s, right? I could only guarantee I would hit the ground with mine. Fortunately, the bunker was fairly new, my rocket only hit in the vicinity of the bunker and the A-4 guy said, 'The round light spot next to the road?'

"I said, 'Roger.'

"He said, 'One's rollin' in. Clear two in and were headed for home.'

---
[48] VC sapper units carrying satchel charges were occasionally successful at sneaking onto major bases to plant explosives.

"I said, 'Two's cleared in hot.' Or, some sort of neat FAC flyers talk like that. Those A-4 guys preferred high angle stuff and they were going to be lucky if they made it to a 20 degree dive angle under the overcast. But, number one flashed by and WOW! The 1,000 pounder hit. There is no trouble seeing a 1,000 pounder. I waited a split second or two, and POOF! There was a big hole in the ground where the light spot used to be! Seconds later, number two plopped his napalm can in the hole and really sterilized the whole area. The best Air Force cool jargon that my stunned mind could bring forth was something like, 'Thank you gentlemen, have a good trip home.'

"So our guys walked across the draw, past the sterilized hole, found a nice campsite, cooked their next three days rations of rice, and hunkered down for the night.[49] *I don't remember any more of the operation, so I must suppose that the little A-4s had made their point and the rest of the Cong scattered to find another, later, high ground position.*

"Maybe everyone has their own rating, but in my book the B-57s, A-1Es, and A-4s were all great." [50]

Duke's views were probably typical of the FACs of the era. As the weapons systems changed in theater, FACs controlled different types of fighter-bombers. For example, B-57s left the theater except for the Australian contingent. The USAF introduced F-100s, F-4s and A-37s. Consequently, FACs' opinions of the best aircraft for also TICs evolved:

A-1Es – Throughout the conflict, FACs universally respected the accuracy, bomb load and loitering capability of the A-1E Skyraider.

F-100s – The Super Sabres lacked the endurance and payload of the A-1Es but were dependable fighters. Their pilots usually pressed the target and were very accurate.

F-4Es – Phantoms were renowned for an extraordinary bomb load but not for accuracy. Some FACs claimed the F-4s needed gravity to ensure their payload hit the earth. Many would not allow F-4s to drop in a TIC situation. The Phantoms typically released their bombs from a higher altitude than other fighters, which undoubtedly affected their accuracy. FACs orbiting a target area at 1,500 feet often saw other fighters releasing ordnance at or below the FAC's altitude. F-4s regularly release far above the FAC's level.

A-37s – The Dragonfly or "Super Tweet" was slower and smaller than the other jet fighters but usually exhibited pinpoint accuracy. Even with a relatively small payload, they were great in a TIC.

VNAF Fighters – FACs also generally liked the skill of the VNAF A-1 and A-37 pilots, although some experienced communication difficulties. After the American build up in 1965, VNAF flights usually did not include an American advisor. Occasionally, American FACs and Vietnamese fighter pilots did not understand each other.

The most experienced Vietnamese pilots flew F-5 Freedom Fighters. These aircraft were not designed as a close air support weapon. However, in the hands of men who had been flying and fighting for more than a decade, the F-5 was extremely accurate.

---

49 Vietnamese soldiers were issued quantities of rice before each deployment. They cooked three days of the ration, the "shelf" life of the cooked rice, and carried the reminder uncooked. Every three days, they needed to stop long enough to cook another three days' ration.

50 Major Joseph S. Granducci, II, USAF (Ret), unpublished submission to the FAC Association, from his computer files courtesy of his widow.

Due to communication difficulties, VNAF fighter pilots might not adjust the bombing target in accordance with the FAC's instructions. During most missions, a FAC marked the target with a smoke rocket and instructed fighter lead to "Hit my smoke." The FAC then adjusted the subsequent bombing runs to better cover the target. For example, he might instruct Number two in the flight to aim 25 meters long of Number one's strike and Number three to aim 25 meters right of Number two. Because of the language barrier, it was common for all the VNAF bombs to fall on the original smoke mark unless the FAC could get the flight to hold long enough to fire a second smoke rocket indicating a new target.

Song Be, Phuoc Long Province, III Corps

In December, the 2nd Task Force (1st and 5th Battalions) began a sweep of the Michelin Rubber Plantation near Song Be in III Corps, where a provincial force had been partially overrun. While covering this operation on 17 December 1965, Captain Donald R. Hawley, Red Marker 06, was shot down. His Bird Dog crashed between friendly forces and the Viet Cong.[51] While controlling an airstrike at 0730, Hawley directed the fighters to hold high and dry as he made a low pass to look at something suspicious. Shortly thereafter, the fighters realized the Bird Dog had disappeared from sight. No one answered the flight leader's radio calls to Red Marker 06.

About 20 miles north of Hawley's location, Captain Delbert W. Fleener, Red Marker 07, was flying a reconnaissance mission with an Army intelligence officer in the back seat. Del had been monitoring the strike frequency and immediately knew something was wrong. He rushed to the area at full throttle, which took about 10 minutes. Del found the enemy camouflaging the downed aircraft sitting in a clearing with one wing broken off.

Fleener made four passes, dispersing the enemy each time by firing a single WP rocket. He requested additional airstrikes and a flight of F-100s arrived quickly. Several Army helicopters also came to assist. Each chopper tried to get low enough to find and extract Hawley. However, the ground fire was too intense. The VC killed one helicopter pilot and wounded three crewmen during the various attempts. Fleener's Bird Dog also sustained some damage. By 1030, Del had depleted his supply of smoke rockets and needed to refuel. A Province FAC arrived on the scene to continue the airstrikes. Meanwhile, Fleener landed his damaged craft at a nearby strip. Del dropped his passenger, got a different plane and flew back to the crash site.

The ground fire was even heavier during his second sortie. Fleener flew low enough to see that the crashed Bird Dog was empty. A Vietnamese wearing Hawley's flight suit crawled slowly toward a tree line evidently trying to lure Fleener into a trap. On one low pass, heavy machine gun fire blew the door off the Bird Dog and wounded Del in the right leg. He was thrown against the side of the cabin and knocked unconscious. His plane stalled and pancaked to earth in the tall elephant grass. When Del regained consciousness a few minutes later, the Bird Dog was still running, creeping forward through the grass. Del jammed the throttle forward and took off. Because his damaged plane could not immediately climb high enough to get above the surrounding trees, Fleener repeatedly circled the field, the plane gradually climbed, taking

---
51 Aircraft O-1F 57-2873.

Gene McCutchan, Del Fleener and Sgt Luong. Gene McCutchan Collection.

ground fire with each circuit. As soon as he was high enough to escape enemy fire, Fleener began directing an Air Force helicopter that had arrived on scene. After thirty minutes, the wounded Fleener left the area and made it to a friendly strip with his crippled Bird Dog.

The Air Force HH-43 helicopter crew spotted Hawley's body about ten yards from his crashed plane. Despite heavy ground fire, the crew landed and retrieved Captain Hawley's body. Don apparently lived through the crash but could not get far enough away from the plane before the VC found him and stabbed him to death.[52] Fleener received the Air Force Cross for his actions. Through his extraordinary heroism, superb airmanship and aggressiveness in the face of hostile forces, Captain Fleener reflected the highest credit upon himself and the United States Air Force.[53]

Congressional Hearing

The end of the year brought an interesting assignment for Buck Rennick, the hot shot A-1E pilot turned temporary Red Marker. Now a Captain, Buck appeared as one of fifteen witnesses before a special subcommittee of the House of Representatives' Committee on Armed Services.[54] The Congressional hearing focused on the adequacy of close air support and expectations for the future. Rennick testified that close air support required having a forward air controller airborne over the battlefield.

The subcommittee criticized the Air Force for being unprepared to support the Army in Vietnam. The investigation revealed the Army and Air Force communication difficulties. The official report noted that the two services did not even use the same radio frequencies (primarily FM for the Army and UHF or VHF for the Air Force). As a result, ground troops needing support could not talk directly to the fighter-bombers coming to their assistance.

The report further blasted the Air Force for not having developed aircraft to accomplish the mission. The O-1 Bird Dog came from the Army. The best close air support fighter, the A-1E Skyraider, came from the Navy. Furthermore, the Air Force was not developing a follow-on close air support weapon. The subcommittee contrasted these failures with the Marine Corps. The report praised the Corps for its approach to the mission in terms of doctrine, tactics and weapons development. The Ma-

---

52 "Pacific Stars & Stripes," Wednesday, May 18, 1966, page 2, A2C Bob Cutts.

53 From the Citation to Accompany the Award of the Air Force Cross.

54 "Report of Special Subcommittee on Tactical Air Support of the Committee on Armed Services," House of Representatives Eighty-Ninth Congress, Second Session, No. 44, February 1, 1966, page 4859.

rines effectively integrated air power with other fire support for their troops on the ground. As to other Air Force missions, the subcommittee documented the development of weapons systems and doctrine for the Strategic Air Command, Military Airlift Command and for Air Defense Command. The subcommittee concluded that the Air Force placed a higher priority on these other missions than on close air support of ground forces.

Several Congressmen on the subcommittee were Marine veterans. They orchestrated the order of testimony to emphasize Air Force shortcomings and Marine Corps strengths.[55] Regardless, the investigation correctly criticized Air Force brass on several issues, such as the incompatible radios. Years earlier, the Strategic Air Command had adopted the HF radio as its standard. This emphasis on long-range communications blinded the service to the need for short-range radios to work in the field with the Army. As a result, the only portable radios available to the Air Force at the outset of the conflict were HF sets. Later, FACs had access to portable FM, VHF and UHF radios.

As to the men in the field trying to accomplish the mission, the subcommittee concluded,

"...with planes which were not designed for the job, the job is being done to some extent. They are delivering massive attacks on the enemy, and the enemy is being hurt by them. The attacks are increasing in numbers, in intensity, and in effectiveness. The pilots who are flying them deserve a nation's respect and praise."[56]

This certainly was the case with the Red Markers who pressed the attack on the enemy and paid dearly for it.

---

[55] Douglas Norman Campbell, B.A., M.A., *Plane in the Middle: A History of the U.S. Air Force's Dedicated Close Air Support Plane*, Texas Tech University, May 1999, page 113.

[56] Special Subcommittee Report on Tactical Air Support, page 4870.

Gene McCutchan and Big Minh. Gene McCutchan Collection.

CHAPTER 8

1966 - LT COL GENE McCUTCHAN

The Airborne activity increased in 1966. During the first three months, the Division tallied enemy casualties equivalent to the entire prior year: 901 enemy KIA, 203 POW, and 205 weapons captured.[1] The U.S. build up that started in 1965 gathered steam. For FAC units, this meant more pilots, more planes and more enlisted men.

By the fourth quarter, a C-124 Globemaster was landing at Bien Hoa every four days carrying a shipment of seven crated Bird Dogs. Maintenance personnel at the 19th TASS assembled and test flew these craft. When deemed airworthy, the TASS assigned the Bird Dogs to newly formed and expanding FAC units throughout the country. The TASS completed the assembly and flight test program in November 1966, bringing the total USAF in country Bird Dog fleet to 109 aircraft.[2]

Red Markers 1966

Major Gene McCutchan
Captain Joe Granducci 02
Captain Richard McGill 05
Major Del Fleener 07
A1C/Sgt Cotton
Airman Robinson
Airman Smith

Lt Col Gene McCutchan 01
Major Bud Fisher 02
Captain Wayne Kanouse 03
Captain Gene Parker 04
1Lt Mike Morea 04
Captain Bill Stewart 05
Tech Sgt Helmut Knaup
Staff Sgt Balasco
Sgt Art Skillman
A1C Humphries
A1C Ken Karnes

Sgt Tran Dinh Luong
Private Phuong

Bird Dog Modifications

Because the Bird Dog carried no armor at the time, FACs were vulnerable to small arms fire. In one incident, an enemy round struck a FAC from below and stopped just short of his heart.[3] This and other experiences with the Bird Dog in combat conditions provided the impetus for a series of modifications. Captain Rodney Macauley served as chief of maintenance at the 19th TASS through October 1967 and test flew many of the reassembled birds. He knew that developing and getting approval for a permanent solution to

---

1 Airborne Newsletter, 5 Apr 1966, p. 16.
2 19th TASS History, Oct-Dec 1966, p. 7.
3 *Id* at 4.

CHAPTER 8 - 1966 - LT COL GENE McCUTCHEN

Maintenance Ramp at Bien Hoa, newly assembled O-1s ready for assignment. Ken Hinks Collection.

the lack of armor would take months using official channels. As a stopgap, he procured a supply of ¾-inch steel plate. Macauley instructed his technicians to weld a piece to the bottom of the pilot's seat on every plane in the fleet.[4] Two years later, the Air Force finally installed permanent armor in the O-1. This fiberglass-Kevlar shield bolted to the bottom and the back of the pilot's seat with a hinged panel on each side. FACs generally welcomed the added protection, however many found the side panels inhibited their movement and flew without them.

Macauley also specialized in O-1 reclamations. He actively sought Air Force, Army, Marine or VNAF Bird Dogs that had been written off due to battle damage too severe to be repaired in the field. His crews salvaged these craft, transported them to Bien Hoa by truck or helicopter and rebuilt them. During his tenure, Macauley rebuilt and put into service fifteen such craft. He painted fictitious serial numbers on their tails before sending them out to FAC units.[5] A2C Bob Green, a crew chief under Macauley, recalls flying in the back seat several times a week on test flights. Bob always carried a few tools with him. On several flights, Macauley landed in unsecured areas (aka, "Indian country" or "No Mans Land") and instructed Green to adjust the stationary trim tab on the aileron.[6] Additionally, Macauley taught the crew chief to fly the aircraft, but thankfully Bob never had to find out if he could make a landing from the backseat.[7]

Another modification to the plane involved the fuel priming system. The fleet had experienced several instances of engine failure during landing. In landing

---

4 *Cleared Hot*, p. 112. This sounds very similar to the self-help armoring of Humvees in Iraq some 40 years later.

5 *Cleared Hot*, p. 112. Two of these phantom O-1s were subsequently lost in combat, for a net addition to the fleet of thirteen aircraft.

6 The aileron trim tab could be bent upwards or downwards to offset a tendency of the aircraft to roll right or left.

7 E-mail from Robert B. Green, former USAF Sergeant, 9 Jul 2010.

configuration, the pilot set the mixture at full rich and turned on the boost pump. Weak springs on the seal to the primer system allowed pressure from the boost pump to push excess fuel past the seal and into the carburetor. The excess fuel could flood the engine causing it to stall, especially if a pilot opened the throttle suddenly. This might occur, for example, in a go around from a missed landing approach. Over the disagreement of higher headquarters, the TASS capped the primer systems fleet-wide, making them inoperative. The TASS reasoned that pilots rarely needed to prime the engine to start it in the high temperature Vietnam environment. On the other hand, FACs frequently missed approaches at remote fields. Several factors contributed to the likelihood of a go around at a remote field. First, the fields were short and narrow. Second, most were uncontrolled, and civilian traffic, vehicles or animals might appear unexpectedly in the pilots' path. Third, many younger, less experienced pilots operated from these locations. The TASS action made the young FACs' task a little safer.[8]

One safety modification created additional problems. The O-1 did not originally have self-sealing fuel tanks, making the plane vulnerable to catching fire if a bullet hit the wing. Contractors installed self-sealing tanks to correct this problem. However, several planes that had been retrofit with the new tanks suffered engine failure due to fuel starvation. Accident investigators found particles of paper clogging the carburetor and fuel inlet screens. The paper came from installation instructions that had been left inside the new fuel tanks. A fleet-wide inspection revealed three other O-1s with sets of instructions in the tanks.[9]

TASS maintenance personnel made other modifications in response to shortcomings noted by FACs and the fighter pilots who worked with them. The fast jet fighters flying at altitude reported difficulty rendezvousing with the FACs flying low above a target location. In response, the TASS painted the upper surfaces of the O-1's wings and horizontal stabilizers white. The white paint contrasted with the green countryside below the FAC aircraft. The TASS also installed a rotating beacon on the top of the fuselage to aid in night rendezvouses. To prevent making the FAC an easier target from the ground, maintenance personnel fabricated a flared metal shield for the new beacon to direct its light upward. These modifications overturned a 7th Air Force directive to camouflage all allied aircraft in green and brown paint. The command feared enemy MiGs might fly missions into South Vietnam and thought the camouflage would provide protection.[10] After numerous instances of fighters failing to rendezvous with the camouflaged FACs, the command reversed itself and went back to a grey color scheme adding white upper surfaces.

Two other modifications involved armament on the Bird Dogs. The FACs complained they did not have enough smoke rockets for an extended mission. The TASS doubled the rocket capacity by installing four rocket tubes under each wing.[11] Also, the Bird Dogs had no rocket sight or aiming device. The crew chiefs solved the problem by creating a set of "crosshairs." They improvised a vertical crosshair by attaching an 18-inch long piece of welding rod to the engine cowling just behind the propeller. Each pilot provided his own

---

8 19th TASS History, Oct-Dec 1966, p. 5.
9 *Id.* at 4.

10 Major Leo F. Kimminau, USAF (Ret), who as a Captain in 1966 served in 19th TASS and 23rd TASS as a Cricket, Gombey and Nail FAC, emails Sep 2011.
11 This installation included wiring a new arming panel of protected toggle switches on the cockpit ceiling.

horizontal crosshair with a grease pencil.[12] At the start of every mission, the FAC climbed to 1,500 feet, trimmed the aircraft at cruise speed and drew a grease pencil line on the front windscreen along the horizon. That horizontal crosshair automatically adjusted for the height and body position of each pilot.

This makeshift aiming device was remarkably accurate. A Bird Dog FAC executed a rocket pass by first raising the nose in a power-off, climbing wingover, turning to the left or right. He flipped one of the eight overhead toggle switches to arm a rocket tube, continuing a rolling dive to lower the nose below the target. He put the vertical crosshair on the target and raised the nose to align the horizontal crosshair. On a good rocket pass, just as the target came to the intersection of the crosshairs, the diving aircraft had attained cruise speed and was in perfect trim.[13] On more than one occasion, FACs hit relatively small targets dead on. More than one FAC reported hitting enemy personnel.

One of the remarkable aspects of the Vietnam War was the ingenuity of the maintenance personnel in devising ways to address recurring problems and installing solutions in relatively primitive working conditions. They provided these modifications while understaffed and performing regular maintenance and periodic inspections.[14] As a result, the maintenance shop did not enjoy a lot of days off. Crew chiefs were among the unsung heroes of the war.

Major Gene McCutchan's Red Markers began the year with a staff that included two veteran FACs, Captains Joe Granducci and Richard McGill. The losses of Windle, Carn and Hawley during 1965 and the injuries suffered by Fleener in his attempts to rescue Hawley had depleted the unit. Captains Wayne Kanouse and Alfred E. (Gene) Parker soon joined them. Fleener returned to the unit after recuperating in the hospital at Clark AB. Now a Major, he was around long enough to give orientation rides to Captain Bill Stewart, who joined the unit in the spring as Red Marker 05.[15] Shortly thereafter, Del moved to an assignment flying C-118s from Bien Hoa. In May, he transferred to Hickham AFB in Hawaii.

During the year, McCutchan attained the rank of Lt. Colonel, and he extended for an additional tour into 1967. This would bring his cumulative service as Red Marker 01 to more than thirty-six months. The unit began the year with a handful of crew chiefs and radio operators. Additions to the enlisted staff throughout the year provided the Red Markers greater ability to perform at remote locations.

Plain of Reeds, Kien Phong Province, IV Corps

In January, the Airborne's 2nd Task Force left the Michelin Plantation. It joined the U.S. 173rd Airborne Brigade in an assault in the Plain of Reeds in Kien Phong

---

12 Every FAC carried a grease pencil. They regularly wrote mission information on the side windows of the Bird Dog while in the air and transcribed that data after landing.

13 Pilots used trim controls to cause the Bird Dog to fly straight and level, hands-off, at cruise speed. This meant that at cruise speed the aircraft had no tendency to climb or dive, roll right or left, or yaw to either side. The FAC left those trim control settings in place throughout the mission. When the O-1 achieved cruise speed during its dive at the target on a rocket pass, it was therefore back in trim. This meant the rocket was launched at the target without being influenced by inadvertent yaw, pitch or roll of the airplane.

14 19th TASS History, Oct-Dec 1966, p. 7, The 19th TASS aircraft maintenance personnel strength was 231, undermanned by 55, resulting in an average workweek of 60 hours per person.

15 Lt. Colonel William P. Stewart, USAF (Ret), email 7 July 2011.

Province on the Cambodian border below the Parrot's Beak. The 1st and 5th Battalions landed in a hot LZ and assaulted the enemy while Red Markers put heavy airstrikes into the tree line. The 8th Battalion diverted in the air from a scheduled LZ and landed in a position to block any escaping Viet Cong. The 8th became heavily engaged as the VC retreated in its direction. Despite the best efforts of the three battalions and heavy airstrikes, some VC slipped through the net into Cambodia. They left behind, however, 125 KIA, 45 POW and 40 weapons captured.[16]

Bong Son, Binh Dinh Province, II Corps

In late January, the Airborne joined the U.S. 1st Cavalry Division in a major envelopment operation ranging north of Bong Son to the I Corps border. From the Newsletter description of the operation:

"On D-day, while the 2nd Task Force (1 & 5 Bns) attacked north from Bong Son, the 1st Task Force (3 & 6 Bns) conducted a helicopter assault into the northern hills and moved south. The 8th Battalion was reserve. Simultaneously, the 1st Cavalry Division lifted three Infantry and one Artillery Battalions to the area immediately to the west." [17]

The five Airborne battalions and the American forces together made up a major operation. The Red Markers sent a large contingent in support. McCutchan headed a team of two FACs, plus ROMADs and crew chiefs. They lived together in a ten-man tent with a separate six-man tent next to the radio jeep serving as a control center. In addition to the air support for the operation, the Cavalry's artillery unit was equipped with

MRC-108 Jeep on deployment. Gene McCutchan Collection.

new 155 mm howitzers. These weapons were touted as a panacea for indirect fire support. These so-called "Penny-Nickel-Nickel" guns packed a larger punch and had almost twice the range of the smaller "Dime-Nickel" 105 mm howitzers.[18]

The 2nd Task Force landed in the late afternoon and began moving north at first light the next morning. The operations plan gave priority of fire to the Cav's artillery to support this effort. When the Airborne could not move for a day and a half, however, Airborne commander General Dong asked Gene McCutchan if he could help get them unstuck with airstrikes.

Gene responded, "Certainly, but you must give the airstrikes priority so we can turn off the artillery." Shutting off the artillery meant that FACs and fighters would not have to fly through the artillery fire. After the guns shut down, twelve sorties of airstrikes caused the enemy to retreat, and the Airborne moved out.

The next day, a general from the Cav came over to the Airborne demanding to know who shut off his artillery. McCutchan informed him that General Dong had given

---
16 Airborne Newsletter, 5 Apr 1966, p. 7.
17 *Id.* at p. 7.

18 Approximately 22,400 meters versus 11,500 meters.

CHAPTER 8 - 1966 - LT COL GENE McCUTCHEN

priority to the airstrikes and had shut off the artillery. The Cav brass wanted to know why he had done that, to which McCutchan replied, "General Dong did it at my request so we could put in airstrikes since your artillery was not getting the job done!" The Cav general stalked off fairly tight-jawed.

The Newsletter reports that Viet Cong heavily engaged the 2nd Task Force during the first two days as it moved north, including night attacks. However, airstrikes turned the enemy back with heavy losses. McCutchan, Joe Granducci and Captain Alfred E. (Gene) Parker, who had just joined the Red Markers before the operation, each directed some of those strikes.[19]

Meanwhile, the 1st Task Force moved slowly south in open terrain against deeply entrenched forces. Some enemy tunnels were twelve feet deep and ran four hundred meters long beneath the village of Gia An. Red Markers put in numerous airstrikes, but even direct hits with 500 lb. bombs had little effect on some emplacements.[20] The reserve 8th Battalion teamed up with a squadron of APCs and two companies from the Air Cav to form the 3rd Task Force and joined the battle. After nearly three weeks, the Viet Cong suffered 393 KIA, 107 POW and 53 weapons captured. The American advisors also suffered casualties. Red Hat Sergeant First Class John E. Milender, 5th Battalion advisor, was killed. Six others were wounded, four seriously. Additionally, two advisors with the APC company were wounded. Gene McCutchan and Gene Parker each received a Cross of Gallantry with Gold Star and Joe Granducci received a Cross of Gallantry with Silver Star for their contributions to this operation. The citation for McCutchan noted that he conducted airstrikes in inclement weather on 27 Jan 1966. The citations for Parker and Granducci mention the accurate airstrikes they controlled in the face of withering ground fire on 25 Jan 1966.[21]

For several days prior to this operation, the Red Marker team did reconnaissance near Bong Son. After the FACs finished their recon flights for the day, they generally made one last stop before returning to Bong Son. They landed at a larger base such as Qui Nhon to buy a couple of cases of Cokes or beer and hauled these refreshments in the back seat of the O-1 to the thirsty advisors and the rest of the team. As a result, the Red Hats appreciated the Air Force contribution even before the operation kicked off.

In those evenings before the operation began, Gene took his troops into Bong Son for dinner. Exhibiting his independence from the Army, he continued that practice even after the Army declared the town off limits due to a crime committed by an American soldier. McCutchan theorized that the Army orders restricted its personnel, but such restrictions did not apply to the Air Force.[22]

In late February, the 8th Battalion was dispatched to Quang Tri to serve as a reserve for the Vietnamese 1st Division. The battalion fought three major battles

---

19 Airborne Newsletter, 5 Apr 1966, p. 12, according to the Newsletter, the FAC roster at the end of March 1966 included only Major McCutchan, Captain Granducci and Captain Gene Parker, who joined them just before Bong Son. We can infer that Richard McGill left between January and March, and that Kanouse, Morea, and Stewart had not yet arrived.

20 Id. at 8.

21 Republic of Vietnam, Joint General Staff, Official Order No. 171/TTM/CL, awarding Corps Level awards to McCutchan and Parker, and Division Level awards to Granducci and to Captain Kenneth L. Kerr, call sign "Herb," the Sector FACs in Binh Dinh Province who supported the 22nd ARVN Division.

22 McCutchan Interview, 1 Sep 2011.

with an NVA battalion recently arrived from the north, inflicting serious damage. There were 185 enemy KIA, including an enemy commanding officer.[23]

Quang Ngai, Quang Nai Province, II Corps

In early March, the 1st Battalion deployed to Quang Ngai to join a U.S. Marine battalion in a helicopter assault on the 21st North Vietnamese Regiment. Reinforcements, including the 5th Battalion, arrived to encircle the enemy during two days and nights of attack. Out of total enemy killed of 583, the 1st Battalion claimed 236 KIA, plus five POW and 60 weapons captured.

Additional Personnel

In May, Captain Michael J. Morea joined the Red Markers by a circuitous route. A young but seasoned transport pilot, Mike had flown numerous times into Tan Son Nhut a couple of years earlier. In 1966, he drew a Vietnam tour as an O-1 FAC, initially attached to the 25th ARVN Division in III Corps at Duc Hoa west of Bien Hoa AB. After serving there a few months, Mike transferred to another regiment of the 25th Division at Tan An to take the place of a FAC who had been wounded during a mission. In May, the 19th TASS selected him to become an instructor pilot at Bien Hoa. He would be teaching some VNAF students to fly the O-1 and others to become FACs, one of the original missions of the 19th TASS.

Preferring to stay in the field, Mike asked the commander of the TASS for permission to find someone willing to trade assignments with him. After a few hours on the radios talking to other units, Captain Morea found a Red Marker willing to take

Mike Morea at Hue Citadel Strip. Morea Collection of the Texas Tech Vietnam Archive.

the instructor slot and switched jobs with him. Mike became Red Marker 04 and served in that role until the end of his tour the following February.

Mike flew to Tay Ninh in late May 1966 and met Joe Granducci and Staff Sergeant John Balasco for the first time.[24] They met in the rather dimly lit mess hall in the provincial headquarters, a French colonial structure. Two camouflage-clad, swarthy characters with large mustaches welcomed him to the Red Marker team. Mike felt he had stepped into a spaghetti western. He met Lt. Colonel McCutchan later in the day.[25] Gene was not immediately available because he was flying a crippled Bird Dog with a cracked cylinder, to Bien Hoa.

Other FACs assigned during the year included Major Oliver Paul "Bud" Fisher, who replaced Granducci upon completion of Duke's tour; Major Wayne E. Kanouse,

---
23 Airborne Newsletter, 5 Apr 1966, p. 8.

24 *Cleared Hot*, p. 126.
25 Apparently, Gene had been recently promoted from Major, since the Newsletter shows him at the lower rank as of March 1966.

CHAPTER 8 - 1966 - LT COL GENE McCUTCHEN

Bud Fisher, Red Marker 02. Morea Collection of the Texas Tech Vietnam Archive.

FAC Villa on Yen Do Street. Morea Collection of the Texas Tech Vietnam Archive.

Red Marker 03 and Captain William P. Stewart, Red Marker 05.

Enlisted personnel who joined the unit in 1966 included Staff Sergeant Helmut Knaup, who was soon promoted to Technical Sergeant, A1C Humphries and A1C Kenneth W. Karnes. Sergeant Knaup was a German national who became a naturalized American citizen. Gene named him NCOIC, and Knaup provided direction and training for the younger enlisted men.

McCutchan used the call sign "Red Marker" without a numerical suffix, as he had since 1962. As the second ranking officer in the unit, Bud served as assistant ALO and took the call sign Red Marker 01. That came to an end during a summertime deployment in II Corps when the DASC commander in that region got upset about the "unnumbered" Red Marker. McCutchan took his argument to the TACC director and lost. Gene was ordered to use the "01" designation and Bud Fisher became Red Marker 02.

Living Conditions

The Red Marker officers established a long term living arrangement in a French villa at 134A Yen Do Street, Saigon. The enlisted men stayed in quarters in the Cholon District.[26] The officers' villa was plush by Vietnamese standards. It was two stories with thick walls, high ceilings, large windows, tile floors and ceiling fans, making it comfortable even in Saigon's heat. A Vietnamese family cared for the place, cleaning the house and cooking provisions bought by the FACs from the local market or the commissary. The normal routine was for a FAC to reside at the Saigon villa before going out on assignment. The FAC remained in the field until relieved or until the Airborne unit being supported returned to Saigon. Each officer and enlisted Red Marker carried an off-duty pass, which allowed him to be in Saigon during curfew hours.[27] This pass allowed Red Markers to get to Tan Son Nhut in case of an emergency. The off base living tradition established by Gene McCutchan when denied room in the MACV quarters lasted until late 1970.

---

26 Cholon is the Chinese district of Saigon on the west bank of the Saigon River. It contained many large markets and a military commissary.

27 U.S. military imposed a curfew in Saigon between the hours of midnight and 6:00 am.

Captain Wayne Kanouse. Bill Stewart Collection.

Gene McCutchan and Bill Stewart (RM 01 and 05). Bill Stewart Collection.

Phu Bai, Thua Thien Province, I Corps

A deployment to Phu Bai in I Corps during the first half of 1966 brought to a head the old argument whether it was more effective to have FACs in the air or on the ground. After a few beers one evening, the Red Hat Senior Advisor to the 1st Task Force, then Lt. Colonel (and later Major General) Guy S. Meloy invited Captain Mike Morea, Red Marker 04, to accompany him on the ground in an armored personnel carrier during the upcoming operation. The Army argued, as always, that the FAC should be on the ground side-by-side with the people he supported. The Air Force countered that this created two blind mice rather than just one. The theory was that an airborne FAC would have the best view of the battle and could provide better control of the airstrikes. The discussion of the two positions grew heated, and Meloy "ordered" Morea to stay on the ground. Mike refused. He reasoned that the Army had no authority to order a FAC to do anything. Furthermore, Lt. Colonel McCutchan had already issued his FACs standing orders to the contrary. This refusal led Meloy to accuse Mike of being a coward, which led Mike to invite him outside for a knife fight! Cooler heads prevailed and nothing was ever said about this incident.[28]

After the operation began, Captain Morea began flying extended hours covering the Airborne. Sometimes he logged twelve hours a day. In time, worn ragged by the grueling schedule, Mike radioed Saigon for relief. McCutchan sent Captain Wayne Kanouse, new Red Marker 03, to assist him. The next day, Morea put Kanouse in the front seat for an orientation mission while Mike rode in the back seat. During the mission, the Airborne got into a running firefight with an NVA unit northwest of Hue. With the NVA in the open, retreating along dry creek beds, Wayne directed fighters and helicopters with good results. On one attack, however, Red Marker 03 showed his inexperience. He rolled in to mark a concentration of NVA in a line of banana trees and hit within feet of the target. He knew it was a good shot and pulled up rolling on one wing to admire his handiwork instead of breaking sharp-

---

[28] Information on Colonel Michael J. Morea, USAF (Ret), is from personal interviews, his personal biography essay, his story in *Cleared Hot* and from his interviews under the *Oral History Project, The Vietnam Archive at Texas Tech University*, conducted by Steve Maxner, various dates Dec 2000, Jan and Feb 2001.

CHAPTER 8 - 1966 - LT COL GENE McCUTCHEN

Ken Karnes. Morea Collection of the Texas Tech Vietnam Archive.

Lt Vuong Dinh Thuyet. Bill Stewart Collection.

ly away from the target. At that point, the enemy soldiers stepped out of the tree line and opened fire. Their aim was bad that day. Luckily, the enemy missed, and Wayne learned an important lesson about combat tactics.

Dong Ha, Quang Tri Province, I Corps

During October, the Airborne deployed to I Corps near the North Vietnam border. Captain Mike Morea, Red Marker 04, and Captain Bill Stewart, Red Marker 05, flew support from the American Marine base at Dong Ha. On October 3rd, the 2nd Task Force of the 2nd and 8th Battalions assaulted by helicopter into LZs two kilometers south of the DMZ. Stewart flew cover for the landings and controlled a number of airstrikes for LZ prep. Accompanying Stewart in the backseat was 1st Lieutenant Vuong Dinh Thuyet, an Airborne trooper.[29] The trooper served as a flying communications relay from the field troops back to their command post using the FM radio. This lieutenant would eventually rise to the rank of Lt. Colonel commanding the Airborne Engineering Battalion.[30]

At dawn a few days later, the NVA unleashed a massive mortar attack followed by waves of infantry against the Task Force perimeter. Stewart and Vuong immediately took off from Dong Ha to assist the Task Force, which was in danger of being overrun. Stewart directed Air Force, VNAF and Marine TACAIR onto the enemy positions along with AC-47 gunships and artillery. This near continuous stream of firepower broke the enemy attack and resulted in an estimated 300-500 hostile casualties. In the afternoon, Stewart and Vuong returned. They used air strikes to silence enemy artillery positions just north of the Ben Hai River. While conducting attacks throughout the day, they were exposed to almost constant ground fire. One helicopter lifting out wounded troopers was hit during the operation, but nonetheless managed to limp out of the area. Both Stewart and Vuong received the VNAF's Air Gallantry Medal with Silver Wings for the action and

---
29 Lt. Colonel William P. Stewart, USAF (Ret), email, Nov 2011.
30 Major Truc Van Tran, email 15 Nov 2011.

the Air Force awarded the Distinguished Flying Cross to Stewart.[31]

Late in the day on October 15th, Mike Morea was flying cover for the operation when a battalion of Airborne ran headlong into an NVA unit. Both sides were surprised. During the ensuing confused firefight, the Airborne had difficulty identifying the enemy concentrations. Flying repeatedly over the battlefield, Mike could clearly differentiate friendly and enemy forces because the area was relatively free of vegetation. He relayed the NVA locations to the Red Hats using various techniques. He fired smoke rockets and dropped smoke grenades into the largest enemy dispositions. He instructed one advisor to lie on the ground and rotate his body until it pointed like an arrow to one of the main formations. The Red Hats then advised the Airborne where to concentrate its mortar fire and bolster its defenses against possible attack. Mike called his radio operator, A1C Kenneth W. Karnes, requesting air support. Fighter-bombers were on the way when ground fire hit Mike's aircraft. Mike had inadvertently descended as he circled the area concentrating on the battle. His Bird Dog was at about 600 feet when a soldier stepped out of the trees and fired a burst from his AK-47. The enemy fire hit the generator and ripped through the cabin, shattering the left rudder pedal and both side windows.

Mike keyed the radio, "I'm hit!" Karnes immediately called for a rescue helicopter and told Marker 04 it was on the way. Morea cancelled the rescue because the plane was still flyable. Remarkably, he was not wounded. Mike ran low on fuel and had to leave the area before the fighters arrived on station. However, the Red Markers had coordinated with the local Province FACs to provide extended coverage for the Airborne. Dan Riley, Trail 65, arrived on the scene in time to direct the airstrike.

Morea briefed Dan and headed to Dong Ha. He made one of his less sterling landings: tail-dragging, propeller driven aircraft are difficult to fly with no left rudder control. By the time Mike borrowed an airplane from the Trail FACs and returned to the area, Dan Riley had inflicted severe damage on the NVA. The enemy retreated to a sanctuary across the border. Mike helped the Airborne secure its position for the night. He ensured a flare ship and fighters were available if the NVA regrouped and attacked, which they did not. Captain Morea received the Distinguished Flying Cross for his actions during this engagement.

FACs who worked for McCutchan unanimously believed he was a good boss. When asked about this, Gene described his approach to dealing with his subordinates. He told each privately that they were professional pilots and officers. He expected them to act that way and to get the job done. If they complied, there would not be any Mickey Mouse from him.[32] On the other hand, if someone did something foolish, Gene preferred to handle it and not involve outsiders. For example, one of his pilots performed an aileron roll in his Bird Dog above an FOL. Someone on the ground reported him, and the TASS wanted to court martial the FAC. Gene adamantly argued to impose his own discipline. After an extended period of discussion, Gene won and the TASS dropped the idea of a court martial. While serving with the Division as G-3 Air, Major Truc

---

31 Citations to accompany Air Gallantry Medal and DFC, Stewart email Nov 2011.

32 McCutchan Interview, 21-22 June 2011. At the same time, Gene says that he was an "Iron Ass," but the author believes he chose his spots to exercise that aspect of his character.

CHAPTER 8 - 1966 - LT COL GENE McCUTCHEN

Van Tran remembers seeing a hangman's noose in Gene's office as a reminder to any other FAC about such aerobatics. No one repeated that foolishness.

In another instance, McCutchan was riding in the back seat with a new FAC flying his first airstrike control mission. The FAC instructed fighter lead to rendezvous by flying a specific heading from Black Virgin Mountain. This mountain, Nui Ba Den, was the highest peak in Vietnam and the most prominent landmark in Tay Ninh Province. Lead asked instead that the Red Marker provide the coordinates of the rendezvous point, and he would find his own way there. The new FAC did not know that information off hand and got flustered. Gene intervened on the radio and reiterated the instructions to fly a certain heading departing Nui Ba Den. After some amount of griping, Lead finally followed the directions, located the Bird Dog and the rest of the mission went without a hitch.

After the Red Markers landed, Gene received a call from the fighter lead, who happened to be the squadron commander. He berated the FAC, saying it was the worst controlled strike he'd ever encountered. Gene let him say his piece and then calmly explained that the FAC was on his first mission and there were certainly some things to be improved. Then Gene unloaded, telling him that it was the most screwed up rendezvous Gene had ever seen, especially for a pilot as experienced as the squadron commander. He was flabbergasted that flight lead could not follow the simple directions to find the FAC in the most efficient manner. His refusal to follow the FAC's instructions wasted fuel and time on target. The squadron commander shut his mouth. The new FAC became highly qualified in short order.

McCutchan remained fiercely independent of the Army command structure, which endeared him to his Air Force brothers and most of the Army as well. Upon returning from a deployment, Team 162 advisors usually hosted a celebratory dinner. At those dinners the participants traditionally broke their empty glasses on the floor after a toast honoring any friendly casualties. A new and rather prim Red Hat senior advisor prohibited this behavior. Some Red Hats who disagreed with that order asked if Gene would be willing to disobey it. He agreed without hesitation. That night McCutchan flung his glass to the floor after the ritual toast to the cheers of most of those around him.

Instrument Flying in the Bird Dog

Red Marker FAC missions were primarily conducted under daytime VFR (Visual Flight Rules) conditions. Positive control of bombing and strafing required that FACs and fighter pilots have visual contact with each other, with the target and with friendly forces on the ground. As a consequence, most airstrikes were conducted during daylight hours and in reasonably good weather. Exceptions to this general rule occurred from time to time in extraordinary circumstances. For example, FACs and fighters worked in darkness and bad weather if a friendly position was in danger of being overrun. After controlling an airstrike in those adverse conditions, however, merely flying from the target area to a safe landing at a forward operating location in the Bird Dog was a challenge.

Both environments required reliance on the Bird Dog's inadequate instruments. A somewhat questionable vacuum pump system powered the plane's gyroscopic instruments ... the artificial horizon, gyrocompass and turn and slip indicator. Failure of system components meant inaccurate readings from the instruments. Additionally, the little plane was not a stable platform for instrument flying. Wind and turbulence affected the Bird Dog far more than they would a larger and heavier aircraft.

Gene McCutchan and other highly experienced pilots met the challenge of night flying easily. If required to land at night on an unlighted field, Gene merely called on a couple of jeeps to light each end of the runway and landed between them. Younger pilots found it more difficult but succeeded.

Flying in weather presented different problems. The first problem was navigation. The Bird Dog's navigation system was an outdated ADF (Automatic Direction Finder) fixed-card system. As the name implies, the circular face of the instrument was stationary. The face was marked clockwise in degrees with zero degrees at the top and 180 degrees at the bottom. The needle on the instrument pointed toward the radio station tuned by the pilot. Therefore, the needle indicated the direction and the number of degrees a pilot should turn to fly directly to the station. Keeping the needle at the top of the face, i.e., zero degrees, guided the aircraft directly to the station. However, the pilot had to reference the gyrocompass and magnetic compass to determine the aircraft's heading. More modern systems incorporated a moveable instrument face. Those systems automatically rotated the ADF face to display the aircraft's magnetic heading at the top.

The Air Force's 505th Tactical Control Group and its predecessor organizations installed and maintained navigation beacons and radar throughout the country and at major airports. Most of those Navaids were TACAN rather than ADF.[33] The unit also provided air traffic control and flight following services for aircraft transiting South Vietnam airspace and staffed the radar control for Ground Controlled Approaches (GCA) at the major airports operated by the USAF. The U.S. Army's 125th Air Traffic Control Company (later Battalion) had similar responsibilities at airfields controlled by the Army. The frequency range of the ADF receiver in the Bird Dog extended from the low frequencies of the non-directional beacon broadcast by the ADF stations up through the normal band for AM radio stations. FACs could therefore listen to rock-and-roll music on the Armed Forces Radio Network while flying missions.

Even though ADF stations dotted the landscape, Red Markers did not frequently use these stations because most of their flights were local. When flying from a forward location to a target area or area of operation only minutes away and returning to the same FOL, Red Markers usually did not need instrument navigation. Further, the ROMAD at the deployed TACP served as the FAC's flight following service. FACs checked in usually every fifteen minutes to confirm their location. If the FAC did not radio in, the ROMAD called to check on him. In the local area, the term IFR (Instrument Flight Rules) usually meant "I Follow Roads." If there was an overcast, the Red Markers flew under it to the AO or climbed through it and tried to find a hole in the clouds

---

33 CHECO Report, "Tactical Control Squadron Operations in SEASIA (U)," 15 Oct 1969, HQ PACAF, Mr. Melvin Porter at p. 6, during the last six months of 1964, the Tactical Control Group installed five TACAN stations, four control towers and six radar facilities as compared with two radio beacons and two UHF/VHF DF stations.

CHAPTER 8 - 1966 - LT COL GENE McCUTCHEN

at the destination. However, when flying long distances to or from a remote deployment, Red Markers planned their trip using the ADF stations and the radio frequencies of the flight following service along the route. If they encountered weather along the way, the ADF helped them fly to the destination.

However, the second problem with instrument flying was landing after arriving at the destination. If flying to a large airfield with approach control radar, the Bird Dog FAC could make a precision approach under the direction of the radar controller. This presented a challenge for the GCA controller because the O-1 presented such a small return on his screen. Furthermore, the controller had to sequence the slow flying Bird Dog into a traffic pattern that included fast moving jets and large transports. Regardless of the difficulty, if caught in the bad weather, the radar approach was the FAC's only option for a precision approach.

A precision approach provides runway alignment and glide slope information. In contrast, a non-precision approach provides only alignment data. This was the case with ADF approaches. A typical non-precision approach followed a teardrop shaped ground track designed to align the plane with the active runway. The pilot flew a defined heading outbound from the radio beacon for a certain amount of time while descending to a designated altitude. At the proper time, he turned inbound to the station on a bearing that approximated the runway heading and descended to a minimum altitude. He continued inbound holding that minimum altitude until sighting the runway and landing. Following this procedure guaranteed terrain and obstruction clearance. Furthermore, the airfield's controller cleared the airspace of other aircraft.

The official ADF approach "plate" for each field diagramed the ground track for the approach showing the heading to fly, the minimum altitudes to be observed, the runway headings and layout, and the approach control frequencies to use to contact the controllers. However, Red Markers rarely if ever had access to the published approaches. Without the official approach plate, a Bird Dog FAC flying in the weather to a field without radar control could use the ADF to navigate to the field, but could not be assured a safe descent.

When Gene McCutchan flew in weather conditions, he planned his route to approach the destination at a point away from the airfield where he knew the ground elevation and was reasonably certain there would be little air traffic. He then descended under the overcast weather and proceeded visually to the destination airfield. With all the possibilities for mishap, Red Markers avoided flying in bad weather needlessly.

In *Cleared Hot*, Captain Bill Stewart relates an unintentional instrument flight from Saigon to Dong Ha with an improvised instrument approach. On a trip to deliver a fresh aircraft to a Red Marker deployment in I Corps, Bill departed from Tan Son Nhut with a crew chief in the back seat.[34] The 420-mile trip was a long hop in the Bird Dog, which has a range of only 530 miles cruising at 104 mph at 5,000 feet. The weather was forecast to be VFR for the entire trip, but Bill was not surprised to see an undercast forming as he went north. Weather conditions changed rapidly in Vietnam. As he arrived in I Corps flying at 5,500 feet, the cloud layer beneath him became solid.

Bill dialed in the Army beacon at Dong

---
34 *Cleared Hot*, p 132.

Ha on his ADF set to navigate to the field. Not having a published approach plate for Dong Ha, Stewart planned a makeshift teardrop instrument approach that he hoped would keep him clear of traffic. Dong Ha was near the coast and very close to the DMZ. If Bill missed the station and overflew it, he would quickly be in North Vietnam. Therefore, his plan was to turn immediately due east at station passage. He planned to descend to 3,000 feet outbound from the station over the ocean, then turn back inbound and descend to 1,000 feet, hoping he would be under the cloud layer by that time. All went as planned, almost.

Bill noted station passage as the ADF instrument needle swapped ends. He turned east and put the ADF needle on the tail of the aircraft while descending. At 3,000 feet he turned back inbound and kept descending. At 1,000 feet he was still in the clouds, so he descended further. At 700 feet, he broke out of the clouds. At that point, however, he could not see the coastline. Bill chugged along for several minutes with the clouds above and the water below, beginning to worry that he had enough fuel to make it to land. Finally, the coast came into sight, and he found his way to the Dong Ha field uneventfully. The crew chief in the back never suspected the pucker factor level in the front seat.

McCutchan and Tech Sergeant Helmut Knaup at Dalat. Morea Collection of the Texas Tech Vietnam Archive.

Lt. Colonel Gene McCutchan being awarded the National Order of Vietnam Knight by President Thieu. Gene McCutchan Collection.

91

CHAPTER 8 - 1966 - LT COL GENE McCUTCHEN

Corporal Phuong. Morea Collection of the Texas Tech Vietnam Archive.

Red Marker Over III Corps. Bill Stewart Collection.

Airborne Patch on a Red Marker O-1. Bill Stewart Collection.

ROMADS A1C Humphries and Staff Sergeant John Balasco operating radios. Pleiku, South Vietnam. Bill Stewart Collection.

CHAPTER 9

1967 - LT COL GENE McCUTCHAN
LT COL PETE ALMQUIST

In late 1967, Lt. Colonel Gene McCutchan completed his final tour as ALO for the Vietnamese Airborne. Lt. Colonel Peter W. Almquist replaced him. McCutchan and A1C Kenneth W. Karnes were each awarded a Bronze Star prior to departure.[1] Gene added the 17th through 21st Oak Leaf Clusters to his Air Medal for the period from 19 October 1965 through 25 July 1967.[2] He was also the first American to be awarded the Vietnamese nation's highest award, the National Order of Vietnam Knight.

Gene's next assignment was another overseas tour, this time in Europe. He had several jobs, one of which was to install a Tactical Air Control System for the German Air Force, complete with a TACC, DASCs and TACPs that were functional in time for a NATO exercise. While performing that task, he ran into former Red Marker Colonel Carleton Casteel, commander of the 601st DASC at Frankfort, Germany. Remarkably, neither learned of the other's history with the Red Markers until they provided information for this book.[3]

The Vietnamese Airborne Brigade expanded to a Division in 1965, and the Red Marker organization expanded with it. Eight new FACs joined the unit during 1967. When the unit was shorthanded near the end of the year, the TASS temporarily assigned three FACs who normally covered the US 101st Airborne Division. A number of enlisted men also came into the unit.

Red Markers 1967

Lt Col Gene McCutchan 01
Major Bud Fisher 02
Captain Wayne Kanouse 03
Captain Mike Morea 04
Captain Bill Stewart 05
Tech Sgt Helmut Knaup
Staff Sgt John Balasco
Sgt Art Skillman
A1C Humphries
A1C Ken Karnes

Sgt Tran Dinh Luong
Private Phuong

Growing Pains

Unit expansion brought some problems. According to the "End of Tour Report" from Captain Bill Stewart in March 1967,

---

1 See 19 TASS History, Jul – Sep 1967, for listing of awards.
2 McCutchan Interview and files, 21-22 June 2011.
3 Per emails dated 17 Jan 2011.

the 19th TASS treated the Red Markers as if they still supported a brigade size unit. In his report, Bill noted that the Airborne Division:

"...requires the ALO to furnish three mobile TACPs (Tactical Air Control Parties) ... and one Division TACP at the division headquarters. The mobile TACPs operate in all Corps of Vietnam and in many cases these TACPs are set up in locations where no living facilities exist and no means of transportation exists." [4]

He pointed out that regulations required that Red Marker TACPs must be equipped to operate in field conditions with tents, cots and other field supplies. Captain Stewart noted that the Red Markers did not have all the required equipment. He also observed regulations authorized two M-series jeeps for a division TACP and one jeep for each regimental or brigade TACP. Instead of having the five "slick" jeeps authorized, the Red Markers had only one, which would have been appropriate if they were still supporting a single brigade. Further, the unit had been informed they would only get a second jeep in the near future.

Stewart documented the disparate treatment between the Red Markers and the ALO/FAC units supporting the Vietnamese 1st and 22nd Divisions in I and II Corps, respectively. Both of those units had more equipment, notwithstanding that each operated in a relatively static environment from established FOLs rather than in the field.

Stewart had flown from locations in each of the four Corps areas during his tour. He reported that no two situations were identical. Instead, each ALO and each FAC on remote assignment dealt with unique problems. He challenged the 19th TASS and the 504th TASG to learn each of these situations and provide appropriate support. Stewart finished his report with praise for the Red Markers' relationships with both the Airborne and the Red Hats. He stated,

"The Airborne Division Advisory Detachment enjoys the best U.S. Air Force – U.S. Army relationship I have observed in Vietnam." [5]

Capital Military District, III Corps

Captain Mike Morea was scheduled to rotate home near the end of January. As his DEROS (Date of Estimated Return from Overseas Station) approached, McCutchan scheduled him for missions generally out of harm's way. However, on 20 January 1970, Mike flew one of the

---

New Red Markers 1967
Lt Col Pete Almquist 01
Major John Giles 02
Major Laurie Kivisto 02
Major Jack Taylor
Captain Jim Frail (TALO)
Captain Duane Andrews
Captain Pete Drahn 06
Captain Bill Jenkins 09
Captain Rip Blaisdell (Two Mos)
Captain Gary Blake (TDY 101st)
Captain Art Greiner (TDY 101st)
Captain George Varner (TDY 101st)
SSgt Raymond Moore
Sgt Walt Stepaniak
Chico Hernandez
Sgt Pat Lind
Sgt Doug Hedensten
Sgt Garza
Sgt Funk
Sgt Valliant
Sgt Reguera

---

4 Captain William P. Stewart, Air Liaison Office, ARVN Airborne Division, End of Tour Report, for the period 23 Apr 1966 – 15 Mar 1967, to Commander 504th Tactical Air Support Group.

5 Id.

most demanding missions of his tour. He was shuttling an O-1 due for a periodic inspection on a short hop from Tan Son Nhut to Bien Hoa to swap airplanes. An Airborne lieutenant rode in the back seat. Per the usual procedure, he tuned the FM radio to the tactical frequency of the local Airborne unit. Enroute to Bien Hoa, the lieutenant, who had been listening to the troops on FM, tapped Mike on the shoulder and told him that a unit northwest of Tan Son Nhut was in trouble. It had run headlong into a VC unit in a village and was heavily engaged. Mike flew to their aid in minutes. He called in artillery, controlled helicopter gunships from Bien Hoa and Tan Son Nhut, and controlled a flight of F-100s scrambled for the TIC. Because of the open terrain, Mike easily spotted the enemy forces and directed strikes where they could do the most damage. In his words:

"At one point I think I was talking to the U.S. Advisor on the ground, the lieutenant in the back seat, the gunship commanders, several fighter flight leaders, the artillery fire control center, Red Marker Control at Tan Son Nhut – all on different frequencies, and more or less all at once." [6]

Only a seasoned FAC could have accomplished this mission. As a result of the availability of air assets and the skill of Captain Morea, enemy casualties topped 100 KIA in less than an hour. The Red Hats awarded him a well-deserved Army Air Medal with V. A few days later, Mike headed back to the states, leaving a big gap in the Red Marker ranks.

Quang Ngai, Quang Ngai Province, I Corps

In February, the 1st Task Force went to Dong Ha for another operation in I Corps. Bill Stewart, Red Marker 05, led the Air Force contingent on this operation. As he tells the story in *Cleared Hot*, he was highly experienced by this time. He planned the air operation to complement the Airborne's ground operation. He coordinated the plan with I DASC and the local sector FACs.[7] However, a day and half after the Task Force arrived at the Marine base at Dong Ha, Airborne headquarters ordered a redeployment to a new operation near Quang Ngai—175 miles to the south. With no airlift available, the Task Force and the TACP jeep convoyed down Highway 1 with Stewart flying cover for the three day trek.

After the convoy reached Quang Ngai without incident, Bill repeated all the planning steps for the new operation. He coordinated extended coverage of the Airborne with the Jake FACs who supported the 2nd Vietnamese Division in the region. As the operation began, Stewart directed the LZ prep and flew cover for the Airborne's helicopter assault into the new AO.

The Airborne contacted the enemy on the afternoon of the first day. The Red Hats called for air support, and Stewart requested an immediate airstrike from the DASC. Bill had spotted a tree line where the enemy was most likely concentrated, but the DASC failed to scramble a flight. He then went directly to the Vietnamese side of the DASC, repeated the request and received a flight of four A-1Hs in short order. They precisely laid a series of 500-pound bombs on the enemy tree line with great effect.

Red Hat Sergeant Charles A. McDonald reported on this same operation in *Angels in Red Hats*.[8] He makes it clear that the Airborne 7th Battalion was used as bait.

---

6 *Cleared Hot* at p. 130.

7 This story is published in *Cleared Hot*, pp. 133-135.

8 Martin at pp. 103-111.

The target was the 21st NVA Regiment, which the allies hoped would attack the smaller Airborne battalion. The Vietnamese Marines and Korean troops making up the rest of the Task Force planned to encircle and trap the enemy. The 7th Battalion air assaulted into a defensive position, with a semicircular perimeter backed up to a river on their south side. To the east and west were relatively open areas, and to the north was the area of most danger—a wooded area where the enemy could concentrate.

The engagement began in the morning. Heavy fog prevented immediate air support. The Airborne suffered significant casualties while fighting off wave after wave of khaki-clad NVA infantry assaults. As the fog began to lift, McDonald radioed Stewart, who was overhead looking for break in the clouds. The FAC found a hole and descended beneath the overcast at extremely low altitude, exposing himself to enemy ground fire. Stewart told McDonald to pop smoke to mark his position. A flight of A-1s had followed Red Marker 05 under the cloud layer and was ready to bomb the tree line. In addition to the tree line, McDonald requested that the A-1s napalm the cane field just outside his east perimeter. Many NVA perished in the ensuing conflagration.

Stewart then directed a flight of B-57s under the cloud layer. The flight streaked so low and close to McDonald that he was afraid they would hit his lines. Bill assured him he would not be hurt. These Aussie B-57s were already dry, having expended their bombs on another target. They were just making a low pass with bomb-bay doors open to scare the NVA. McDonald is confident that it worked on the enemy, because he was certainly scared.

Following the A-1 strike, the Americans at I DASC came on Stewart's radio frequency demanding to know why Bill had communicated directly with the Vietnamese counterparts at the DASC. Red Marker 05 replied:

"Because I had troops in contact, and I wasn't getting any action from you!"

During the remainder of the operation in I Corps, the Airborne had no further problem getting the air support it needed.

Stewart had arranged that the local Jake FACs would fly the first mission the next day covering the Airborne operation. The Airborne position came under attack, and Red Hats asked for an immediate air strike from the Jake flying "dawn patrol." A series of strikes were in progress when Stewart arrived on scene to relieve the Jake. The Province FAC didn't want to leave. It was the first time he had seen South Vietnamese troops slug it out with the enemy. In Bill's words,

"I reminded him that these guys were Airborne troopers – the Red Hats – they stayed and fought." [9]

The Jake FAC reluctantly relinquished control and Stewart took over for the next three hours, putting in strikes from A-1Es, F-4s, VNAF A-1Hs and USMC fighters. Ordnance included napalm, CBU anti-personnel bomblets, rockets, and 500-pound high-drag Snake Eyes. When the Jake FAC returned on station for the next shift, Bill headed back to Quang Ngai to refuel and rearm. On Stewart's last mission of the day he directed a flight of F-4s down a line of massed NVA. The Phantoms unleashed CBU with devastating effect. The attack broke up, and the NVA withdrew.

---

9 *Cleared Hot*, p 134.

Stewart's ROMAD passed the word to him that additional relief was on the way. Red Marker 02, Major Bud Fisher, would fly up on the following day. By the time Fisher arrived, the Task Force had orders to pull back to Quang Ngai, so Fisher stayed with them and Stewart returned to Saigon.

Major Fisher attended the victory parade held at Quang Ngai and accepted on Captain Stewart's behalf a Cross of Gallantry with Palm awarded by the Airborne. The US Army awarded Bill an Army Commendation Medal on the recommendation of the Task Force Senior Advisor, a unique honor for an Air Force officer. The citation to accompany the award reads, in part:

"During the cited period Captain Stewart controlled a continual stream of high performance aircraft and systematically destroyed the attacking enemy. He directed them so effectively that the NVA troops broke contact and withdrew, carrying an estimated 100 dead with them. The body count on the ground was over 340 dead left on the battlefield, and 150 enemy weapons were captured. Captain Stewart's actions on this day saved the lives of numerous friendly troops, and seriously crippled the enemy forces. The professional competence, aerial skill, and devotion to duty displayed by Captain Stewart reflect great credit upon himself and the United States Air Force." [10]

Bill Stewart completed his time with the Red Markers shortly after this engagement. He returned to SEA for another tour in 1971-72. He initially served with the 555 Tactical Fighter Squadron at Udorn Royal Thai AB, where two of his squadron mates were aces. He served the last four months of that tour as a member of the briefing team for the Seventh Air Force.

10 *Cleared Hot*, p. 135.

Bud Fisher Wearing Bill Stewart's Cross of Gallantry. Stewart Collection.

Quang Dien, Thua Thien Province, I Corps

In March, the 2nd Battalion, with an attached platoon of M113 APCs, swept an area near Quang Dien, eleven miles northwest of Hue Citadel. About 1700 hours, the troops approached the village, their last objective. Lieutenant Truc Van Tran, the Airborne Division G-3 Air, was in the backseat with a Red Marker flying cover for the operation. Truc reported to the Battalion Commander that there were camouflaged foxholes and trenches in front of the village. Ten minutes later the troops made contact, the APCs firing and moving forward with Airborne troops following behind. Truc called the Vietnamese 1st Infantry Division TOC requesting air and artillery fire support and Dust Off.[11] Over the target, the Red Marker adjusted artillery fire as he and Truc watched the Airborne troops in hole-to-hole combat. About 30 minutes later, helicopter gunships and fighter-bombers arrived. Red Marker worked the air support on target where it was most needed. The FAC and Truc covered the battle until dark. Before leaving the AO, they chased the retreating NVA, firing smoke rockets and directing artillery.

The next morning, a helicopter brought a group of media and members of the 1st Infantry Division staff to see the battlefield. They found more than 60 NVA dead and wounded along with weapons and ammunition. In this battle, Major Tang, 2nd Battalion S-3, was seriously wounded. Truc and Tang served together later on the G-3 staff of the Airborne Division.[12]

Ben Hai River, Thua Thien Province, I Corps

In June, the 2nd Brigade conducted "Operation Protect" to install an electric sensor fence along the Ben Hai River on the south side of the 17th Parallel (the DMZ). The NVA shelled the south side of the river each night, firing hundreds of rounds of mortar, rocket and artillery shells from north of the river. During one such shelling, a Red Marker FAC flew blacked out along the river to locate the position of the NVA firebase. He then requested counterfire from the 7th Fleet and an immediate air strike. The Navy answered with 8-inch guns and a flight of F-4s. A few days later, the morning briefing at the TOC by the G-2 Air included a photo of two NVA 130 mm artillery pieces destroyed by the Navy guns and F-4s. On another day, a Red Marker directed a flight of Navy F-4s that knocked down an NVA flagpole on the north side of the Ben Hai River Bridge.[13]

West Of Hue, Thua Thien Province, I Corps

Throughout most of 1967, the Airborne deployed a Task Force of from two to four battalions in I Corps. Usually the Task Force operated under direction of the 1st Vietnamese Infantry Division. During May, three Airborne battalions operated in Quang Tri Province, while the 9th Battalion helped provide security for Hue in Thua Thien Province. On May 27, the 9th and a troop of APCs conducted a sweep to engage a reported battalion of VC west of Hue. A battalion of the 1st Division went into a blocking position, while the 9th Airborne and the APCs crossed the Song Bo River. The 9th split into two teams with the battalion senior advisor, Red Hat Captain Marshall B. Johnson, accompanying Team 1 and the battalion assistant advisor and NCO advisor with Team 2.

Moving parallel to each other, the teams proceeded through the first two of four objectives with little contact except snipers. Nearing the third objective, both units came under intense fire from well-prepared positions. A Red Marker FAC overhead brought immediate airstrikes to the battle. The battalion fought hard for several hours. Red Marker directed napalm strikes within 100 meters of the Airborne lines. The senior advisor made the following comments about the air support:

"The air support...was some of the best I have experienced. The FAC remained airborne for the entire contact (with the exception of refueling stops) and as a result was able to very effectively direct aircraft into the target area. This allowed us to drop ordnance much closer to friendly troops

---

11 "Dust Off" was the call sign for MedEvac helicopters.
12 Major Truc Van Tran, email Nov 2011.
13 *Id.*

Hue Citadel. Morea Collection of the Texas Tech Vietnam Archive.

than would normally be advisable." [14]

As darkness approached, the battalion withdrew under flares from a flare ship toward their previous objective to establish a night position. The next day they moved through the next two objectives and linked up with the blocking force. The Airborne suffered 60 casualties while killing 156 VC during this operation.

Hue Citadel, Thua Thien Province, I Corps

The Red Markers received short-term as-

sistance during the middle of the year from Captain Michael P. "Rip" Blaisdell. Rip was a 1962 Air Force Academy graduate and a career fighter pilot. He flew F-100s at Lakenheath AB prior to his assignment to Vietnam. On arriving in country, he flew Huns with the 3rd Tactical Fighter Wing at Bien Hoa from January through May 1967. Rip had attended Air-Ground Operations School at Ramstein AB in 1964 and worked in numerous training operations in Germany as a ground FAC. With the American force buildup creating a shortage of FACs in Vietnam, headquarters chose Rip to "upgrade" from the F-100 Super Sabre to the O-1 Bird Dog. He served with the Red Markers during June and July 1967 before moving to the

---
[14] Captain Marshall B. Johnson, Battalion Senior Advisor, "Operations of the 9th Battalion, Airborne Division (ARVN) in a Search and Destroy Operation 27-28 May, 1967 in Thua Thien Province, Republic of Vietnam," United States Army Infantry School, Ft. Benning. GA, 2 April 1968, p. 17.

173rd Airborne Brigade for the remainder of his tour.

Captain Blaisdell spent most of his time as a Red Marker flying from Hue Citadel or Dak To. Most of the duty was uneventful, although the VC scored a kill on the radio jeep at Hue. They shoved a satchel charge under the jeep one night and blew it to smithereens. Thankfully, no one was injured.

Rip remembers the Airborne as relatively inactive during his time with them, giving him the impression they were more interested in being a palace guard. However, he recalls one particular battle near Hue. The Airborne, reinforced by APCs, chased the enemy through a rubber plantation. The Airborne advanced so rapidly they would not permit Rip to call in any air strikes in support. In frustration, he fired a smoke rocket at the retreating VC, hitting one.

The Red Markers added more FACs during the year at the same time that the FAC unit supporting the U.S. 173rd Airborne Brigade was shorthanded. Rip had flown some missions in the Dak To region, the new area of operations for the 173rd. He was also fighter-qualified, making him a "Class A" FAC. Under agreement with the Army, the USAF would support Army units with FACs having prior fighter experience. Consequently, Rip transferred to work for the 173rd as a Tonto FAC in August 1967. One of the most memorable battles for that unit was the fight for Hill 875 over Thanksgiving 1967. The 173rd attacked an entrenched NVA force in a bloody slugfest. Rip was recognized for his contribution by the Commanding General's award of a Bronze Star with V. However, the Air Force did not recognize it.

In December, about six weeks before Rip's scheduled rotation home, he flew a Bird Dog to Pleiku from Dak To for a 50-hour check. He arrived late in the afternoon. Some local FACs invited him to join them for dinner downtown. Rip told them not to wait for him. He would shower and catch the next bus. As the bus let him off downtown, Rip heard an explosion. The VC tossed a satchel charge over the wall of the restaurant where the FACs were eating, severely injuring a couple of them. Blaisdell reflected that had he been earlier, he might have died.

After that incident, he decided to remain on base for the rest of his tour. He felt safer on base despite frequent random mortar attacks. At Dak To, his tent sat atop a deep bunker. One day, the attack sirens sounded as he was walking back to the tent after a shower. Rip dove into the shelter just as a mortar hit the tent. He was unhurt, but a can of chocolate milk and a can of tuna on his desk in the tent mixed with the odor of burning canvas to create an awful smell. He destroyed what was left of the tent.

Enlisted Help

Sergeant Walter Stepaniak was among the enlisted men newly assigned to the unit during the year. He had been in the Army from 1963 to 1966 and left at the end of his enlistment.[15] When Walter was called back to duty in late 1966, he joined the Air Force rather than re-enlist in the Army. Orders sent him almost immediately to Vietnam as a radio operator assigned to the 20th TASS at Tam Khe in I Corps.[16] At that time, Stepaniak's brother was serving in Vietnam with the U.S. 1st Infantry Division in III Corps. The two de-

---
15 Walter Stepaniak, telephone interview 13 Oct 2010.
16 Blanket TDY orders dated January 1967 authorized up to 29 days duty in the field.

Sergeant Walter Stepaniak. Stepaniak Collection.

cided that Walter would try to transfer to a post further south, closer to the 1st Division's AO. The 504th Tactical Air Support Group personnel office reviewed his qualifications, noting that he was infantry trained and jump qualified. They agreed to his transfer request and assigned him to the ALO supporting the Vietnamese Airborne. Walter recalls, "This was fine with me. The Airborne had a reputation for hard fighting. My family is Ukrainian so we like to fight Communists." He made training jumps with the Airborne and wore the Airborne badge of both nations. When Colonel Almquist learned that Stepaniak had a brother nearby, he helped facilitate visits between the two during Walter's off-duty time.

Walter extended his first tour for six months. After returning to the states, he volunteered to go back to the Red Markers for another eighteen months. His two tours, extending from late 1966 to mid 1970, made him the longest serving enlisted Red Marker.

Hue Phu Bai, Thua Thien Province, I Corps

In September, the 7th Airborne Battalion made an operational sweep near Hue Phu Bai, with an attached platoon of M-113 APCs. A Red Marker FAC flew cover for the sweep with Lieutenant Truc, G-3 Air Operations, in the back seat. About noon, the ground force entered a large rice paddy area. It featured a grid of dikes in a chessboard pattern, with many stacks of rice straw. The APCs opened fire as they advanced across this area, and the Airborne troops reported enemy contact. While the FAC requested air from Red Marker Control, Truc reported the contact to the 1st Infantry Division TOC and requested air, artillery and a Dust Off helicopter. Using the FM radio, he reported enemy locations and movements to the battalion commander on the ground. Within thirty minutes, Red Marker controlled helicopter gunships and a flight of fighters onto the enemy positions. An artillery fire mission provided additional support. The battle finished at dark, resulting in more than 60 NVA bodies with weapons and ammunition. The Airborne lost 12 soldiers.[17]

Dak To, Kontum Province, II Corps

During 1967 and 1968, Red Hat Captain Joseph W. Kinzer worked several times on deployments with Major John K. Giles, Red Marker 02.[18] They spent months together near Dak To in Kontum Province during the fall of 1967. Joe remembers John as one of the best FACs he knew. Kinzer provided this statement about Giles:

"I first met John at the village of Tan Kanh in the II Corps Tactical Zone of South Vietnam in mid November 1967. He provided FAC coverage for the 3d Brigade of the RVN Airborne Division, which had deployed from Saigon via C-130s. It was just before Thanksgiving of 1967. He flew out

---

17 Major Truc Van Tran, emails Nov 2011.
18 Lt. General Joseph W. Kinzer, USA (Ret), interview 4 Jan 2011.

101

Red Hat Joe Kinzer, his RO, Sgts Moore and Stepaniak, Cpl Phuong. Stepaniak Collection.

of the airstrip at Dak To, which was the Tactical Headquarters for the U.S. 4th Infantry Division at the time.

"Our operation was part of a major combined offensive to drive the NVA from the Central Highlands and restore security along the Cambodian border. It wasn't long after commencing operations that we engaged the 64th NVA Regiment about six to eight kilometers north-northwest of Dak To. We were in contact for more than seven consecutive days. Red Marker 02 was on station from sun up to sundown throughout the entire battle.

"I recall that on one occasion he brought in some 32 sorties of close air support in one day. I don't know if that's meaningful to the Air Force, but it sure made a hell of a lot of difference to those of us on the ground. I remember very vividly this response from John when one of the U.S. advisors on the ground made a call for air support. John's reply was, "Roger, just hang on for a few minutes Red Hat, I have wall-to-wall napalm on the way." That's a most reassuring feeling when you are up to your ass in bad guys bent on killing you. Bottom-line in all of this was we knew that we could always count on Red Marker 02. We owe him more than he knows for what he did."

Joe specifically recalls one day with miserable weather when he needed air cover badly. John Giles "strapped on his O-1, took off at dawn from Dak To, climbed through the overcast layer" and gave Joe a call saying, "I'm on my way!" Giles flew multiple missions till after dark...Joe thinks he must have refueled four or five times.[19] On one particular mission when John was flying out of Dak To, he supported an Airborne operation in relief of the Special Forces camp at Dak Seang. John's Bird Dog was hit by ground fire that day while putting in an airstrike, but he safely returned to land at Dak To.[20]

Giles remembers flying multiple missions, sometimes so pressed for time that he didn't get out of the aircraft while the crew chief refueled and rearmed it. He just shut down the engine and sat in the cockpit while the chief pumped gas and filled the rocket tubes. Through the cockpit window the chief or radio operator might hand him a C-ration can they'd heated by sitting it on one of the radios... and maybe a cold beer, if Giles asked for one.[21]

New Red Markers

In late November, Lieutenant Peter L. Drahn, a 1964 West Point graduate, arrived in country following jungle survival school in the Philippines. He signed in with the 504th TASG and headed to the Theater Indoctrination School at Binh Thuy AB. The school, which lasted about three days, included refresher courses on the O-1 systems and instruction regarding in country procedures related to the FAC mission. During several orienta-

---

19 Lt. General Joseph W. Kinzer, USA (Ret), email 3 March 2011.
20 Colonel John M. Lenti, USA (Ret), email 13 May 2012.
21 Colonel John K. Giles, USAF (Ret), Interview 2 Mar 2011.

tion flights, Pete fired smoke rockets and dropped smoke cans, practiced ADF procedures and made numerous landings on dirt, gravel, PSP and concrete runways.[22] After completing the orientation school, he returned to Bien Hoa, where he learned he had been promoted to Captain. Captain Drahn began in-processing at the 19th TASS, expecting an assignment in III Corps. Instead, the 19th directed him to the Vietnamese Airborne at Tan Son Nhut. At the time, the Airborne had troops deployed in I Corps and II Corps.

Pete hitched a ride to Tan Son Nhut in the backseat of a test flight by 19th TASS maintenance. Major Giles met him at the airfield and escorted him to headquarters and to the villa downtown, where Pete shared a room with Major Lawrence E. "Laurie" Kivisto. At the time, the Red Markers flew O-1F aircraft with variable pitch propellers. Three were stationed at Tan Son Nhut while others were deployed.

Pete soon learned that one of the advisors to the Airborne was Captain Ernie Westphalen, who had been in the same company with Pete at West Point. Ernie graduated a year after Pete, but made Captain sooner. The Army at the time promoted officers from 2nd Lieutenant to 1st Lieutenant in one year and to Captain after another year. In contrast, the Air Force promotion schedule took three and half years from graduation to Captain's rank.

After a week at Tan Son Nhut, Pete and John Giles flew to Dak To. During a week and a half at that location, they supported an Airborne battalion that convoyed to Kontum and swept the area without much enemy contact. Giles flew with Drahn to familiarize him with the area. Then they

Captain Pete Drahn. Drahn Collection.

shared duties, alternating flying cover for the battalion. Pete controlled his first airstrikes during this deployment.[23]

During the fall of 1967, two brigades of the 101st Airborne Division deployed to Vietnam to reinforce one brigade already in country. For some time, the Air Force had staffed some stateside Army units with complete FAC organizations. The Air Force assigned about 25 FACs and 50 ROMADs to work with the six battalions of the 2nd and 3rd Brigades of the 101st. When those brigades deployed to Vietnam, the attached USAF personnel deployed with them. The number of FACs and ROMADs far exceeded the staffing for other formations already in combat. Consequently, the 504th TASG reassigned a number of them, some permanently and others temporarily.[24] The Red Markers benefited from the assignment of three FACs from the 101st. Captains Art Greiner, Gary Blake and George Varner served with the Red Markers for a time in late 1967 and early 1968 before returning to support the 101st Airborne.

During 1965, Major Donald T. Glenn had been ALO of the stateside FAC organization attached to the 101st. ROMAD

---

22 PSP is Perforated Steel Planking used to make runways, taxiways and ramp areas at some FOLs.

23 Brig. General Peter L. Drahn, USAF (Ret), from his Diary kept during his Vietnam tour.

24 Timothy Painschab, ROMAD with the 101st Airborne, emails February 2012.

Sergeant Jerry Marsh had served under Major Glenn at Fort Campbell. Jerry deployed to Vietnam with the unit in late 1967. In early 1968, Marsh ran into Glenn, by then a Lt. Colonel, at the 19th TASS. Glenn had been recently assigned to the Red Markers. He convinced Marsh to ask for a transfer to the Vietnamese Airborne, which the TASS approved. As a result, Sergeant Marsh joined the ranks of the Red Markers.

Tan Son Nhut AB, III Corps

Pete Drahn returned from the Dak To deployment in late December and met veteran Red Markers Major John Taylor and Captain Bill Jenkins, due to rotate home soon. Pete inherited from Bill the duty of Awards and Decorations officer. On two occasions before the end of the year, Pete flew to Baria near Vung Tau to shuttle Red Marker Captain Duane Andrews to Saigon. Duane and another Red Marker FAC were covering for an Airborne unit operating from Baria. When Duane needed to return to Tan Son Nhut, he left the aircraft at Baria for the use of the other FAC.

The year ended with Christmas and New Year's Eve parties. Red Marker officers hosted a party for the enlisted men. The day after Christmas, John Taylor and new TDY Red Marker Art Greiner flew to Pleiku to catch the Bob Hope Show in person.

CHAPTER 10

1968 - LT COL PETE ALMQUIST
LT COL DON GLENN

The year 1968 marked a transition for the Red Markers and the American war effort. In late January, the Viet Cong began the TET Offensive, a bloody and costly affair especially for the enemy. After initial limited success in achieving its objectives, the VC met overwhelming allied response. Many enemy main force units were decimated. The absence of any popular uprising in the south was particularly important to the failure of the offensive. Northern strategists had expected local sympathizers to help the insurgents.

However, the lasting impact of the offensive was political rather than military. In the eyes of the American public, the TET Offensive made it painfully clear that the war was far from over—and, indeed, might not be winnable at an acceptable cost. Primarily because of the unpopular war, President Johnson announced he would not run for re-election. Richard Nixon ran on a pledge to end the conflict by bringing about peace with honor. After Nixon's election, U.S. forces began turning the war over to the South Vietnamese under a program of "Vietnamization." Under that plan, the Americans and other allies would begin extracting their troops.

However, prior to implementation of the Vietnamization program, the Americans continued their force buildup, and the war increased in violence and destruction. In 1968, thirteen new FACs and eleven en-

---

Red Markers 1968

Lt Col Pete Almquist 01
Major John Giles 02
Major Laurie Kivisto 02
Major Jack Taylor
Captain Jim Frail
Captain Duane Andrews
Captain Pete Drahn 06
Captain Bill Jenkins 09
Captain Gary Blake (TDY 101st)
Captain Art Greiner (TDY 101st)
Captain George Varner (TDY 101st)
SSgt Raymond Moore
Sgt Walt Stepaniak
Chico Hernandez
Sgt Pat Lind
Sgt Doug Hedensten
Sgt Garza
Sgt Funk
Sgt Valliant
Sgt Reguera
Sgt Tran Dinh Luong
Cpl Phuong

listed men joined the Red Markers. Lt. Colonel Donald T. Glenn served for several months with the unit before taking over as ALO from Lt. Colonel Almquist.

Dak To, Kontum Province, II Corps

January began without fanfare. On New Year's day, two Red Marker O-1s headed in formation from Tan Son Nhut to Dak To. John Taylor and George Varner flew in one bird and Pete Drahn and Gary Blake in the other. Radio failure interrupted the trip. Both landed at Nha Trang for fuel and to repair the radio in Drahn's plane. Drahn and Blake spent the night awaiting repair, while Taylor and Varner completed the trip. After waiting for bad weather to lift the next day, Drahn and Blake flew under a solid overcast to Pleiku and then to Dak To. The original plan had been for Drahn and Blake to replace John Giles at Dak To for an extended deployment. Instead, the ALO instructed Blake to stay at Dak To with the fresh airplane. Giles would remain to orient Blake to the AO, and Drahn would fly Giles' O-1 back to Saigon.

The following day, Pete flew to Saigon at 9,000 feet after climbing through an overcast. Usually, FACs flew the O-1 at 1,500 feet and rarely above 5,000 feet.

Drahn returned to Dak To the following week to relieve Giles. The two FACs, Pete Drahn and Gary Blake spent an uneventful week in Dak To with ROMAD Sergeants Pat Lind and Fred Palmer and crew chief Chico Hernandez. During the week, the Airborne's sweeps of the area yielded little or no enemy contact. On January 14th, Blake went back to Saigon on a C-130, leaving Drahn at Dak To. On January 19th, the Airborne unveiled plans for another sweep operation. The next afternoon, Drahn flew Red Hat Captain Bill Binlich, Senior Advisor to the 6th Battalion, over the new AO. For the next several days, Drahn flew cover for the operation. On January 21st, the FM radio failed again and Pete flew to Pleiku for repairs with Chico Hernandez in the back. The repaired radio failed once more on the return trip to Dak To. To maintain communications with the ground forces the next day, Pete took Sergeant Pat Lind in the back seat with a portable PRC-25 FM radio. It worked as a stop-gap measure.

On January 23rd, Gary Blake arrived to

New Red Markers 1968

Lt Col Don Glenn 01
Major Bill Fulton 01
Major Jim Leach 02
Captain/Major Ken Kreger
Captain/Major Harold Magnuson
Captain Bill Marlin 04
Captain Roy Moore 09 (TALO)
Captain Bruce Bechtel 03
1Lt Stuart Wheeler 09
Captain Ed Fairchild 06
Major Dale Dickens 07
2Lt/1Lt Don Spooner 07
Captain Jack McKessy 08
Captain Ken Munson 03
SSgt Bill Mackey
SSgt Bob Jones
Sgt Fred Palmer
John Carpenter
Sgt John Kokoski
Sgt Jim Fuller
Sgt Larry Lauber
Sgt Perry Timpson
Sgt Jerry Marsh
Sgt Matt Fischer
Mike Roberts
Sgt Pressley
Sgt Coppage
Sgt Brown

replace Drahn, who caught a C-123 from Pleiku to Tan Son Nhut. In late January, Lt. Colonel Don Glenn and Captain Roy Moore joined the Red Markers. Glenn was slated to replace Almquist as ALO in April. Moore took over Captain Jim Frail's job as the unit's Tactical Airlift Liaison Officer (TALO).[1] That position assisted in planning air movements for both deployments and resupply of the Airborne. These activities were larger and more complex since the Airborne had increased in size to a division.[2] Two days before the end of the month, the 6th Battalion made contact with the enemy near Dak To and inflicted serious damage. As the battle intensified, the Airborne command considered sending another battalion as reinforcement. Lt. Colonel Almquist visited Dak To to determine whether Blake needed assistance providing air support. Both the Airborne and the Red Markers decided not to send reinforcements.

TET Offensive

The enemy's TET Offensive began in the early morning hours of 31 January 1968. Airborne units operating in II Corps at Dak To and in I Corps north of Hue stood in the path of two Viet Cong thrusts. At Dak To, Red Marker Captain Gary Blake helped the 6th Battalion defeat two enemy regiments. During the battle the battalion was reduced to just 200 effective troopers.[3]

Meanwhile, Major Lawrence Kivisto, Captain George Varner and a new FAC, Major Ken Kreger, were supporting the I Corp Task Force. The Red Marker team at Hue included crew chief Sergeant Douglas J. Hedensten and radio operators Sergeants Robert Eyer and Walter Stepaniak. The group had arrived in late January with two aircraft and a radio jeep. Both aircraft were destroyed on the ground by the opening mortar and rocket salvos, leaving the Airborne without FAC support. The weather was so abysmal that the FACs would not have been effective anyway. The 9th Battalion, with Red Hat senior advisor Captain Richard Blair, fought two NVA regiments near Quang Tri without air support. The Airborne unit was badly decimated in the process.

A third FAC team was located at Red Marker headquarters at Tan Son Nhut AB. This team included Lt. Colonel Almquist, Lt. Colonel Glenn, Majors Giles and Taylor, Captains Drahn and Greiner (another TDY FAC from the 101st) and Sergeant Raymond Moore.[4] The TET Offensive started in Saigon about 0230 hours on 31 January. Numerous rocket and mortar attacks from various locations in the city preceded enemy troop movements against many government installations. The Red Markers felt relatively vulnerable at their off base quarters. They could hear the sound of small arms and machine gun fire just down the street. For the first day, they could not leave the villa. When they were able to get to the base, they beefed up their armament in case they should be attacked. Pete Drahn's Diary entry for February 1, 1968, states:

"John Giles, Taylor, Sgt. Moore and myself drove back to the villa and set up 3 M-16s, a .38 & .45 and ammo to burn; also a PRC-25."[5]

Pete also secured a supply of hand grenades from the Red Hats. Luckily, none were needed. However, the battles against main force VC units in and around the

---

1 Drahn Diary, 24 and 25 Jan 1968.
2 Colonel John M. Lenti, USA (Ret), email 13 May 2012.
3 Martin, p. 18, from MACV official account.

4 Brig. General Pete Drahn, USAFR (Ret), Diary entry for 30 Jan 1968, "The two majors [Giles and Taylor] and I drove to TSN O'Club and ate supper, then back to the villa."
5 Id.

Red Marker O-1 before its destruction at Hue. Drahn Collection.

Sergeants Eyer, Stepaniak and Hedensten at Hue. Stepaniak Collection.

city made it clear that Saigon was no longer the relatively safe metropolitan area it had once been.

The Airborne's reserve battalions engaged in many of those battles. The 8th Battalion drove an enemy regiment off Tan Son Nhut AB, then sent two companies to reinforce the battered 6th Battalion at Dak To. The 1st Battalion held off an attack on the Presidential Palace, recaptured the radio station and defeated the enemy forces in Cholon. The 5th Battalion fought north of DaNang and then returned to Saigon while the 3rd Battalion fought north of the capital.[6] Pete Drahn, Red Marker 06, and others put in airstrikes in and around Saigon. Many were within half a mile of the runways at Tan Son Nhut. In support of U.S. troops in contact, Drahn controlled one flight of F-100s that leveled a Saigon city block near Cholon.[7]

The situation in Hue was more serious than in Saigon. The VC captured part of the city and the historic Hue Citadel. After the FACs lost their aircraft, Almquist ordered Kivisto, Kreger and Varner to evacuate to DaNang where he would bring replacement Bird Dogs. The FACs went to Phu Bai by chopper and then to DaNang. Kivisto ordered the Red Marker enlisted men to hang tight and keep the radio jeep going. It was the only backup communication system available to the allies at Hue.

Some of the airmen attached to the sector FACs were isolated in a house outside the secure part of the compound. Upon learning of the situation, Sergeant Doug Hedensten volunteered to guide some U.S. Marines to get the airmen to safety. Doug was seriously wounded in the ensuing fight. He was evacuated to a Cam Ranh Bay hospital and then to Clark AB where he recovered.[8]

Shortly after Hedensten was evacuated, an enemy mortar round destroyed the radio jeep and wounded Bob Eyer, although not severely. With no further responsibility for the radio jeep, Stepaniak began working with the U.S. Marines who were moving to push back the invading NVA. Using a Marine deuce-and-a-half armed with twin fifty caliber machine guns mounted in the back, Stepaniak joined a group of volunteers who pushed across the Perfume River bridge, tossing ammo to the Marines providing covering fire and

---

6 Martin, p. 18, from MACV official account.
7 Drahn email Jan 2012.

8 Drahn Diary, March 6, 1968, "I completed the rough draft on Sgt Hedensten's award, probably Silver Star. He saved a few lives up at Hue and was badly wounded."

Red Markers 1968 - Back Row - Jack McKessy, Bill Marlin, Pete Drahn. Front Row - Jim Leach, Ken Kreger, Hal Magnuson. Drahn Collection.

picking up wounded Marines on the return trip across the bridge.

On 3 February 1968, Kivisto heard his troops had been wounded and ordered Eyer to leave the area.[9] Kivisto arranged for a Trail FAC to give Eyer a ride in the right seat of his O-2 from Phu Bai to DaNang and from there to Saigon. Walter Stepaniak left Hue when the Marines wanted their deuce-and-a-half relocated to the south, and he volunteered to drive it. When news reporters heard that Stepaniak was leaving, Walter Cronkite and others gave him rolls of film to deliver to their offices in Saigon. Some of the first pictures of the battle at Hue were therefore transported courtesy of the Red Markers. Stepaniak received a Bronze Star with V for his actions at Hue.

Lt. Colonel Almquist sent reinforcements to link up with Kivisto, Kreger and Varner at DaNang. Lt. Colonel Don Glenn and Captain Art Greiner caught a ride in an O-2 to Nha Trang, where they picked up replacement Bird Dogs and flew to DaNang. Pete Drahn followed by transport. According to his diary, on 4 February 1968:[10]

"I caught a C-130 to Quin Nhon [Qui Nhon] and then Danang [DaNang]. Art [Greiner] and Col Glenn picked me up at the field and we went to the club for steak. Met Ken Kreger, our new FAC, and Lorry [Laurie Kivisto] & George Varner were there ..."

The group flew several missions from DaNang to Hue without any success due to the weather. On 6 February, Majors Kivisto and Kreger flew one VR mission without ever getting above 300 feet. They

---

9 Lt. Colonel Lawrence E. Kivisto, USAF (Ret), Diary, 3 February 1968, "Eyer wounded. ROs to leave area."

10 Drahn Diary, 4 February 1968.

CHAPTER 10 - 1968 - LT COL PETE ALMQUIST & LT COL DON GLENN

Stepaniak and a Red Hat during TET. Stepaniak Collection.

spotted some enemy troops and were hit with small arms fire. They directed artillery fire on the enemy location; no fighter aircraft could work under the low overcast.

After that flight, Kivisto and Kreger went back to Tan Son Nhut with a stop at Cam Ranh Bay to check on Hedensten. They learned that Doug's wound was an open break to a femur, and that he'd been MedEvac'd to Clark. Further, he was scheduled to return to the states within sixty days.[11] Given the severity of the wound, Doug was medically retired from the service. They did not learn that Doug had suffered an additional wound, a friendly fire M-16 round to the foot. Evidently, his Vietnamese Airborne fatigues stood out from the Marine greens. As he was taking cover beside a road, one of the leathernecks he was leading decided he must be one of the enemy!

On 10 February, Lt. Colonel Almquist informed the DaNang group that Captains Blake, Greiner and Varner had completed their TDY service with the Red Markers and would be returning to the 101st. The news was disappointing. After working together for several months, the FACs felt like part of a team. The next day, Greiner and Varner flew one of the Bird Dogs to Tan Son Nhut and reassignment. The remaining Red Markers left DaNang on 14 February without putting in a single strike. Day after day, the FACs had taken off under 200-300 foot overcasts and had flown up the coast looking for a hole in the cloud cover. The weather was so bad that no fighter aircraft could work beneath the overcast, and the FACs were in danger of being shot down flying under the low ceiling.

Within a week after the departure of Blake, Greiner and Varner, two replacement FACs arrived. On 17 January, Captain Bruce C. Bechtel reported to the office, and a day or so later, Captain Harold R. Magnuson arrived. They were quickly folded into the routine, initially flying orientation rides with an experienced FAC before going on independent missions.

Airborne Battles For Hue, I Corps

Meanwhile, the Airborne sent the 2nd and 7th Battalions to reinforce the battered 9th Battalion in an attempt to take back the Hue Citadel.[12] However, the reinforcements were ambushed enroute, and the 7th Battalion was reduced to a single effective company.[13]

Red Hat advisor Staff Sergeant Michael

---

11 Lt. Colonel Lawrence E. Kivisto, USAF (Ret), interview 17 Jan 2012.

12 Martin at p. 18, MACV official account.

13 *Id.* at p. 113, article by Michael H. Smith, Advisor.

A break the flight line, Hal Magnusen, Don Glenn, Jack McKessy and Bill Marlin. Drahn Collection.

H. Smith, fighting with the 91st Company of the 9th Battalion, recounts the battle in *Angels in Red Hats*. One company, the 94th, lost all but 10-15 troopers. Mike's company was isolated from the rest of the battalion and was reduced to two platoons. Most of the casualties died in their fighting positions, not retreating. He praises the courage, tenacity and esprit of the Airborne. After taking the beating near Quang Tri, the remaining troopers of the 9th were ordered to relieve a battalion of the elite 1st Vietnamese Infantry Division. In Smith's words:

"While changing positions, as we crossed paths enroute to the fighting, our ... paratroopers were 'cat calling' and making chicken sounds, and in general making fun of the retreating leg infantry; not unlike our U.S. 101st Airborne Division when they were relieving a leg unit at Bastogne in WWII." [14]

After fighting for weeks since the beginning of TET, the remnants of Mike's company linked up with the rest of 9th Battalion. Captain Dick Blair, the Battalion Senior Advisor, was the first American Mike had seen since the beginning of the attacks.[15] After two more weeks of battle, a fresh task force relieved the Airborne. The U.S. Marine Infantry retook Hue two months later.[16] Dick Blair, by the way, was the only Red Hat to have a brother who would serve as a Red Marker: Lieutenant David Blair, who served during 1969-70.[17]

New Mission

Saigon's vulnerability to further attack

---

14 *Id.* at p. 112.

15 *Id.* at p. 113.

16 *Id.* at p. 113.

17 Colonel Richard Blair, USA (Ret), emails 2011. Dick Blair once leapt from the third floor balcony during a party at Red Hat Manor in Saigon. He made a great PLF on the forty-foot jump, breaking both ankles but only one wrist.

CHAPTER 10 - 1968 - LT COL PETE ALMQUIST & LT COL DON GLENN

Awards Ceremony after TET. Lt. Colonel Don Glenn trails General Westmoreland. At right, Ken Kreger saluting, Jim Frail, Stuart Wheeler, Pete Drahn. Drahn Collection.

created a new emphasis on protecting the capital. The Snap FACs, which were responsible for the Capital Military District (CMD), began flying "rocket watch" missions throughout the night during TET. The purpose was to locate the launch points of rockets aimed at the city and to respond with airstrikes or artillery. Almquist agreed that the Red Markers would carry part of that workload. Pete Drahn and Art Greiner flew the first such missions.[18]

The Red Markers incorporated this new requirement into their existing daily schedule supporting the Airborne's repeated ground sweeps around Saigon. On nights when no mission was scheduled, a FAC and a radio operator stood alert at the Tan Son Nhut office. They slept on cots until called to launch. Some of the missions carried a backseater who used a starlight scope to spot activity on the ground.

In June 1968, the rocket watch was transferred to FACs flying O-2As. The Skymaster was much better suited for night flying. Initially, four O-2A FACs and four navigators were transferred from Nakhon Phanom Royal Thai AB, Thailand to fill that role. The unit became the "Sleepytime" FACs, with exclusive responsibility for flying the cap over Saigon. Despite the creation of the Sleepytime FACs, the Red Markers continued to stand night alert for the remainder of the year. They launched many times when the VC attacked the Airborne at their night bivouacs in the vicinity.

---
18 Drahn Diary 2 February 1968.

On 25 February, the Airborne kicked off one of its sweeps near the Capital. Ken Kreger flew the early morning mission covering the operation. Pete Drahn took over at 1030. At noon, the Airborne made contact with the enemy. Circling overhead, Pete's aircraft was hit by several AK-47 rounds in the left strut and wing. Thanks to the self-sealing fuel tanks, the round in the wing did not cause a gasoline leak or a fire. Pete directed helicopter gunships onto the enemy position before Bruce Bechtel relieved him on station. Per his diary, when he landed:

"... I was met by the whole crew including a flight surgeon with a beer & combat ration of brandy." [19]

Drahn received a DFC for his actions during this mission.

My Tho, Dinh Tuong Province, IV Corps

Mid March saw continued activity by the Airborne. A two-battalion operation swept an area near My Tho in IV Corps, while other units deployed around Saigon. Newly promoted Major Ken Kreger and Captain Bruce Bechtel covered the IV Corps operation flying from Binh Thuy AB. During a mission on 13 March, Bruce's Bird Dog (tail number 890) received a number of hits as he directed airstrikes during an Airborne battle. He would receive a Silver Star for the mission.

The following day, Pete Drahn flew a replacement aircraft to Binh Thuy while maintenance patched the holes in 890. With that task completed on 15 March, Pete returned to Saigon with Red Hat advisor Sergeant Noll in the back seat. Noll had been wounded in the fighting. Pete dropped him off at Tan Son Nhut and took off to replace Major Laurie Kivisto, Red Marker 02, on station covering an Airborne unit on maneuvers near the capital. Pete put in an airstrike of F-5s in support. Two and a half hours later, the same unit again came under attack. Pete ordered an immediate airstrike. He was running low on fuel by the time the fighters arrived, and Kivisto returned to direct the attack. Pete landed, rearmed, refueled and took off again. This time, he headed for the Rung Sat to control a pre-planned strike of A-37s.

West Of Saigon, III Corps

At the end of March, Captain Jack McKessy came to Vietnam and joined the Red Markers with eight years service under his belt, but as a new pilot. He had been a navigator for many years and completed pilot training in June 1967. With a growing need for FACs, he transferred to O-1s from his initial assignment in C-123s. After Vietnam, Jack flew C-141s and then had an assignment in the long-winged RB-57, flying at 70,000 feet... quite a contrast to the Bird Dog. As Red Marker 08, McKessy flew out of Quang Tri and DaNang during the Airborne's relief of U.S. Marines at Khe Sanh. He also flew on deployments from Tay Ninh and from Saigon. Jack earned a DFC, a Bronze Star, 16 Oak Leaf Clusters to his Air Medal and three Vietnamese Crosses of Gallantry during his tour. The mission he remembers most vividly was a series of flights in support of some besieged Vietnamese Marines.[20]

The Marines were heavily engaged near a small village west of Saigon. The battle had raged all day. Jack got into the fight late in the day, putting in multiple airstrikes. As it began to get dark, he was

---

19 Drahn Diary 25 February 1968. This is the first mention the author has heard of combat ration brandy. References by other contributors indicate the practice continued until late 1969.

20 Colonel John D. McKessy, USAF (Ret), interview 20 February 2011.

running low on gas and smoke rockets. Jack knew it was time to head for the barn and turn the fight over to another FAC coming on scene. However, as Jack was leaving the Marine Senior Advisor came up on frequency and asked if he would refuel, rearm and return. His argument was that Jack knew the tactical situation inside and out, they really needed his help, and he was doing a great job! McKessy answered, "OK." How do you say no to a request like that? McKessy refueled and returned for a second mission, and then a third, and then a fourth. It was a very long night. He flew a total of 10.9 hours that day and night. Jack claims he was just doing his job.

Quang Tri City, Quang Tri Province, I Corps

Red Hat Joe Kinzer worked with Red Marker John Giles for a second time in the spring of 1968 in I Corps. Following the successful repulse of the TET Offensive, the Airborne mission was to help establish a series of combat outposts along the DMZ from the South China Sea to the Laotian Border. During this operation, Joe got to fly with John for a day and experience first hand how he did his job. In Kinzer's words,

"I am not an aviator, but I have to say that he made that Bird Dog perform far beyond its capabilities. He was nothing short of spectacular albeit in one of the most vulnerable flying machines ever built. As long as we stayed above 1,500 feet we were out of small arms range and relatively safe from being shot-down. He made it look easy.

"John was key and essential in building the bond between the Red Hats and the Red Markers during our time together in RVN. Again, when we were in a tight situation we always knew that we could count of Red Marker 02 regardless the time of day or the weather.

"John was a team player, professional, dedicated, competent, loyal, selfless, and enthusiastic in getting the job done. In my professional opinion, John Giles ranks in the top five percent of all the Air Force officers I ever met in the 40 years in America's Army. Many of us owe our lives to him for what he did in support of us. He is a true professional by any measure." [21]

New Red Markers

At the end of March, Captain Roy Moore, Red Marker 09, transferred to the 173rd Airborne Brigade at An Khe as their new TALO. In April, First Lieutenant Stuart K. Wheeler arrived as a new Red Marker FAC. In mid April, Captain William F. Marlin, Red Marker 04, joined the unit. He came from an assignment in C-130s and would return to that aircraft stateside at the end of his tour. In June, Major F. Dale Dickens transferred to the unit after a six-month assignment in a staff position at 7th Air Force. April 1st also marked the beginning of Lt. Colonel Don Glenn's tenure as Red Marker 01 and Major Laurie Kivisto's as Red Marker 02 while the incumbents, Peter Almquist and John Giles prepared to return to the states.

Khe Sanh, Quang Tri Province, I Corps

During early April, Major Ken Kreger and Captain Jack McKessy supported an Airborne task force sent to relieve Khe Sanh Combat Base. The Airborne 3rd, 6th and 8th Battalions were part of Operation Pegasus. One battalion helilifted into the base, and the other two were part of the allied force that reopened Route 9 from Quang Tri to the base. Captain Hal Mag-

---
21 Joseph W. Kinzer, Lt. General US Army (Ret), email 3 March 2011.

nuson joined the Red Marker deployment on 11 April, along with Sergeants Kokoski and Hernandez. The team flew sorties from Quang Tri through the end of the operation on 15 April. At that time, the Airborne moved south into mountains west of Hue.

Hue, Thua Thien Province, I Corps

A week later, Captain Pete Drahn and Lieutenant Stew Wheeler went to I Corps to relieve Jack McKessy and Ken Kreger. Pete and Stew caught a C-130 shuttle to DaNang. McKessy had brought one of the two Bird Dogs there for a periodic inspection. From DaNang, Jack caught a return shuttle flight to Tan Son Nhut. After maintenance completed the inspection, Pete and Stew headed for Hue in the O-1. The last part of their flight into the Citadel was under a 150-foot overcast. Ken Kreger met them at the strip and flew with Stew back to DaNang to catch a flight to Saigon. Stew returned to Hue the next day after some mechanical problems with his aircraft.

Meanwhile, Hal and Pete were covering the Airborne's operation west of Hue as best they could. In Pete's words, "the terrain was bad and the weather was worse."[22] On 23 April, Pete took off for his second sortie of the day with an artillery observer in the back seat. However, the weather was so poor they had to return to base. On the way back, he received a radio call from Bilk 14, Art Greiner, the former Red Marker. At the airstrip, Art told him that a VNAF Bird Dog had landed on top of Art's O-1 as each was attempting to land. The planes collided when about ten feet in the air. Both were totaled. However, none of the four people in the two aircraft was seriously injured. Chico Hernandez removed the propeller from Art's aircraft and gave it to him as a keepsake.

Bad weather plagued the rest of the deployment. Each FAC flew missions in marginal conditions, putting in airstrikes under very low ceilings. Pete Drahn cites one set of Navy A-4s that bombed with remarkable accuracy when the ceiling was less than a 1,000 feet. At other times, missions had to be scrubbed because of weather.

Late in the month, Lt. Colonel Glenn arrived, and Hal Magnuson departed for Saigon along with Chico Hernandez. Glenn, Drahn and Wheeler battled the enemy and the elements for the rest of the month while supporting the Airborne. On 29 April, a mortar attack at 0100 destroyed one of the team's aircraft on the ground. Red Marker 01 and 09 (Glenn and Wheeler) took the other aircraft to DaNang to prevent it from falling victim to another attack. The following day they returned. The FACs' operating plan for the next few weeks was to fly support sorties from Hue during the day and to evacuate the aircraft to DaNang each night to avoid mortar and rocket fire. On 30 April, Lt. Colonel Glenn and Sergeant Perry Timpson rotated back to Saigon. On 1 May, Captain Bill Marlin, new Red Marker 04, flew aircraft #675 to DaNang as a replacement for the lost Bird Dog, then caught the shuttle back to Saigon.

Drahn and Wheeler spent their days flying support when the weather allowed. They spent bad weather days coordinating with Red Hats Joe Kinzer and Wes Taylor in the Airborne TOC at Hue. May 3rd was a particularly clear day. Taking off from DaNang, Drahn flew at 3,500 feet directly to the valley where the Airborne operated and directed several airstrikes on Hill 333. Wheeler relieved him later

---
22 Drahn Diary 23 April 1968.

in the morning and controlled additional strikes.

On 5 May, Captain Bruce Bechtel arrived at DaNang via a shuttle flight to relieve Stew Wheeler. After Pete gave Bruce a three-hour orientation flight, all three FACs recovered at DaNang, with Stew scheduled to catch the shuttle to Saigon the next day. On 6 May, Bruce took off for the Hue AO while Pete waited for Captain Bill Marlin to arrive from Saigon as his replacement. By the time Pete flew into the AO with Bill in the back seat, Bruce had already controlled six airstrikes. Following an orientation ride, the FACs again flew to DaNang where Drahn would catch a shuttle to Saigon the next day.

Rung Sat Special Zone, Gia Dinh Province, III Corps

In late June, Red Markers were relieved of flying the nighttime rocket cap over Saigon. The unit picked up an alternative ongoing assignment, flying two missions per day of visual reconnaissance of the Rung Sat Special Zone. The Rung Sat was a vast area of interlocking waterways on either side of the Long Tau River, connecting the inland port of Saigon with the coast. The river was a vital route for military and commercial supply of the capital region. The Rung Sat was also a known VC haven.

Previously, Red Markers had controlled an occasional preplanned airstrike in the region. The new mission required daily sorties to patrol the area. Pete Drahn and others covered the region with flights from Tan Son Nhut. Pete spent some time coordinating the Rung Sat effort in the TOC in Nui Ba, which was located at the northern edge of the zone. The U.S. Navy participated in that coordination. It staged Swift Boat missions of "The Brown Water Navy" to patrol the waterways.

Another change in the routine occurred as the TASS replaced the Red Marker F-model Bird Dogs with O-1Es and Gs. The E and G models had a fixed pitch propeller rather than the variable pitch, constant speed prop of the F. The F models were more powerful during certain modes of flight. Pete Drahn noted in his diary on 13 May:

"Went to Bien Hoa and picked up [tail number] 663. A pig. We are losing all our F models to TIS." [23]

In these post-TET months, the Airborne remained closer to Saigon than usual. Captain Bill Marlin, Red Marker 04, flew a number of missions from Tan Son Nhut supporting sweeps around the capital. He lived in the relative comfort of the Red Marker villa at 134 Yen Do. Many of the airstrikes controlled during that period were within sight of Tan Son Nhut AB. Marlin was awarded a DFC for one action against targets on a big peninsula at a bend in the Saigon River. He directed F-4 strikes on targets so close to Tan Son Nhut that the attack path of the fighters impinged on the traffic pattern at the air base. Bill had the control tower on the radio during the strikes and made them divert some inbound traffic until he could complete his strikes.

Personnel Moves

On 1 June, the Red Markers lost the services of Captain Jim Frail as he transferred to duty with Combat Control. In the middle of June, Sergeant Pat Lind contracted hepatitis while on duty with the I Corps team. He was treated at Nha

---
23 Drahn Diary 13 May 1968. (TIS is Theater Indoctrination School.)

Trang and then in the hospital at Cam Ranh Bay prior to being MedEvac'd home. Also in June, Second Lieutenant Donald A. Spooner arrived in country as an O-1 FAC on his first permanent assignment after pilot training. He reported to the Allen FACs supporting the ARVN 25th Division flying out of Tay Ninh and Duc Hoa. In late July 1968, the TASS determined the 25th ARVN needed a more senior FAC. Red Marker Major F. Dale Dickens and Don were ordered to swap jobs. As a result of the new orders, Dickens became an Allen FAC in late July and Spooner became Red Marker 07.

At that time, it took eighteen months after commissioning to be promoted from 2nd to 1st Lieutenant. Don Spooner was one of only two FACs to make it to the Red Markers while still wearing a brown bar. He was not the only new officer to go straight from pilot training to a FAC job. However, for all but one other who followed the path from commissioning, pilot training, upgrade training in the O-1, survival school, in-country orientation and assignment to the Red Markers, it took longer than eighteen months.

Don's inexperience may have had something to do with an air mishap that occurred early in his tour. In the aftermath of TET, the Airborne conducted a training exercise in city combat a few miles from Tan Son Nhut. On August 14th, Don was flying cover for that operation. At the request of the Red Hats, he marked a location with a smoke grenade. Distracted while circling the area and talking to the ground forces, Spooner lost track of his altitude and crashed into a two-story building. He blacked out for a moment. He awoke to find himself hanging upside down in his harness. When he released his seatbelt, he fell from the aircraft and landed in a lavatory area. He passed out again and regained consciousness cursing, leaning against a tree. Don suffered severe lacerations to his face, particularly around his right eye, and burns to both arms. He had been flying with sleeves rolled up and gloves rolled down, which he never did again. Red Hat NCO Ed Taglieri got Don into a jeep and took him to the hospital, where Army Major Edwards spent a lot of time sewing him up. Don's bruises and scrapes healed in short order with only minimal scars on his face. He returned to duty, but many of his "friends" accused him of trying to wipe out a VC latrine.[24]

Shortly after Don Spooner joined the Red Markers, Captain Bruce Bechtel transferred to Bear Cat as a FAC for the new Thai Brigade to be based there. On 8 August, Captain Ken Munson joined the unit as Red Marker 03. Ken had flown transport MedEvac from McGuire AFB and completed the Air Force Flight Safety School.

Two days later, Ken flew an orientation ride in the Rung Sat with Pete Drahn in the back seat. During the flight, Pawnee Target (III DASC) informed the Red Markers that a ship in the main river channel had been hit with a B-40 rocket and asked that they direct an airstrike. Ken had not yet seen a live airstrike and was not checked out to direct the mission. However, Pete could not control the strike from the back seat. Radio controls, arming switches and the rocket firing trigger are all in the front cockpit. Pete talked Ken through the process, instructing him where to orbit, when and where to mark the target and how to direct the fire of a set of Huey gunships followed by a flight of F-100s.

---

[24] 19th TASS Unit History, Jul – Sep 1968, "O-1E, 56-2519 crashed near Tan Son Nhut and was substantially damaged by the crash and subsequent fire. Pilot received minor injuries; cause unknown."

Tay Ninh, Tay Ninh Province, III Corps

On 3 September, the Airborne 3rd Brigade deployed to Tay Ninh. Newly promoted Major Hal Magnuson and Captain Ken Munson covered the operation, flying from Tay Ninh City and Tay Ninh West. The dirt strip at Tay Ninh City was particularly poor. It was short and had power lines running perpendicular to the runway near one end. Bill Marlin recalls always landing toward the power lines and taking off in the opposite direction, away from them. One VNAF FAC crashed taking off the wrong way.

On 17 October, Major Dale Dickens was killed, shot down landing at Tay Ninh after a mission. Pete Drahn's Diary entry reads,

"Bad news from Tay Ninh – Dale Dickens crashed on a nite landing and was killed. He was in 7AF for 6 mos., spent a month with us before going to Allen FACs. He was due to rotate soon. A great guy." [25]

This news hit Don Spooner particularly hard. Had he and Dale not traded positions, it very well might have been Don who died at Tay Ninh. As it was, Lieutenant Spooner finished his tour as a Red Marker about June 1969. [26]

Personnel Changes

On 12 October, Major James A. Leach joined the Red Markers. He replaced Laurie Kivisto as the assistant ALO, Red Marker 02, until June 1969. At that time, Jim moved to Xuan Loc as ALO for the 18th Vietnamese Division. Another highly experienced transport pilot, Captain Edward A. Fairchild, joined the group as Red Marker 06 in October. He had flown C-141s in and out of Vietnam from August 1967 until his assignment as a FAC. Following his tour, he returned to C-141s, again flying to and from Vietnam, through December 1971. Ed logged 985 hours and 566 sorties in the Bird Dog and became the Tactics IP for the unit. [27] After nine months with the Red Markers, he moved to Xuan Loc to work for Jim Leach as assistant ALO and lead FAC for the 18th ARVN Division, call sign Kenny 02.

Fairchild's first assignment with the Red Markers was supporting an operation involving the Vietnamese Airborne working with American and Australian infantry units. Major Magnuson and Fairchild spent about two months living in a wooden floored tent in the Australians' compound near a small dirt strip carved out of a rubber plantation.

In November, Captain Pete Drahn completed his tour and returned to the states. During his time in Vietnam, he had put in his papers to resign his regular commission. Later, Pete joined the Air National Guard and rose to the rank of Brigadier General, the only Red Marker to earn a star. Sergeant Jerry Marsh went back to the states at the same time and separated from the service. He completed an engineering degree and pursued a career in the gas pipeline business. Captain Ken Munson also left the Red Markers in November. He transferred to the 504th TASG in the Safety Office. Also in December, Lt. Colonel Don Glenn completed his tour and returned home. Major William H. Fulton, Jr., replaced him as ALO.

In December, First Lieutenant Bruce M. Freeman arrived in Vietnam. Bruce had worked hard for two years to ensure he

---

25 Brig. General Peter L. Drahn, USAFR (Ret), diary.
26 Colonel Donald Spooner, USAF (Ret), 4 Mar 2011 email. Don said that he thinks often of Dale Dickens.
27 Each FAC unit assigned one of its most capable pilots the role of Combat Tactics Instructor Pilot. The Tactics IP checked out new FACs before they performed solo airstrike missions.

got to Vietnam in a combat role. While a cadet at the Air Force Academy, Freeman was slated to pursue a master's degree in international affairs following his June 1967 graduation. However, he turned down the opportunity, believing that the war in SEA might begin winding down. Instead, he opted to go through pilot training as soon as possible. In August 1968, he completed pilot training at Craig AFB in Selma, Alabama. He got an assignment to an O-1, with orders to begin training at Hurlburt Field two months later. Until then, he would remain at Craig as a student squadron duty officer. Freeman believed that building up flying time would be more useful than answering telephones. He got the student squadron commander to agree to release him if he could find a short term flying job. Bruce had already found a National Guard unit in nearby Montgomery, Alabama, that flew Bird Dogs and was happy to have "the blue suiter" join them prior to his going to SEA.

When Freeman reported to Hurlburt, he was already thoroughly checked out in the Army L-19. In his Army Bird Dog, he had checked fence lines, herded cattle and landed on multiple dirt roads to recon some of Alabama's fishing holes. Bruce credits these flying experiences with helping him survive his first combat tour. After completing the course at Hurlburt and in-country orientation at Phan Rang, Freeman was sent to the 19th TASS for assignment. At TASS headquarters in January, he met Major Bill Fulton, the new Red Marker 01. Noting that Freeman wore jump wings, Fulton asked if he had an assignment yet and if he would like to work with the Airborne. Later that day, Freeman was taken to Tan Son Nhut and became Red Marker 08.

Ed Fairchild recognized Bruce's aggressiveness as soon as he joined the unit. Ed recalls that Freeman had a stated goal of amassing 1,000 combat hours. From time to time, Bruce would be missing and so would an airplane. Even when not scheduled to fly, Bruce could be found over the AO doing additional recon and keeping an eye on the troops. As a senior pilot and the Tactics IP, Fairchild felt he had to hold the young pilot in check without stifling his initiative and aggressiveness.

Bruce soon began sleeping with a portable FM radio by his bedside so he could monitor the Airborne troops during the night. Ed remembers having to go toe-to-toe with Freeman at 0400 one morning when Bruce wanted to take off under an 800 foot overcast in drizzling rain because he thought the troops might be in trouble. As later actions would prove, Lieutenant Freeman's aggressiveness was not hampered. He would be awarded the Silver Star, two DFC's and five Vietnamese Crosses of Gallantry, becoming one of the most highly decorated Red Markers.

Fairchild's more cautious approach was undoubtedly influenced by some near misses he experienced with a couple of the unit's Bird Dogs. One was dubbed the Super Pig, but the other was normally a very good plane. Tail number 595 was a great aircraft. It had good power, was responsive and would fly in good trim. One day while Ed flew cover for an Airborne sweep, the Red Hat advisor on the ground was taunting Ed for allegedly flying in the "stratosphere."

"We can't even see you up there you're so high. Hope you've got on your fur-lined boots so you don't get frost bite," came the taunts over the FM.

Goaded enough, Fairchild buzzed the troops as they crossed a rice paddy single file on one of the dikes, trying to keep their feet dry. Ed laughed over the radio as they dove into the water on either side of the dike, "Well, did you see me that time?"

Ed swallowed his glee about twenty seconds later when the engine coughed and sputtered as he was pulling up. The engine lost a valve keeper and digested two pistons, vibrating so much it seemed the engine would rip off its mounts. Declaring an emergency on Guard Channel as he limped back to Tay Ninh West, Fairchild coaxed the Bird Dog the 25 miles toward safety, certain that any minute he would be forced down. However, 595 came through for him. It kept running until, with the runway in sight, he reduced the power just a bit to start a descent. The engine quit altogether at that point, and he made an uneventful glider landing. He vowed his buzzing days were over.

The Super Pig, tail number 622, was another story. On four or five occasions with Fairchild at the controls, 622 would begin missing and losing power with the aircraft descending to just a few hundred feet above the jungle canopy. Then the engine would begin running smoothly, and Ed would recover to a normal altitude and finish the mission. His crew chief, Sergeant Matt Fischer, could not identify the problem. The strangest thing was that it never happened to any other pilot flying the plane. Despite his position as Tactics IP and with several hundred missions under his belt, Fairchild felt that everyone suspected he was making it up. He was greatly relieved when Captain James A. Hill returned from a mission in 622 one day and reported the same problem. Jim said the engine just started running rough and losing power, exactly Ed's experience. Jim was an experienced pilot who joined the Red Markers in December.

He served as the unit's safety officer in addition to his FAC duties.

Later that week while taxiing out for a mission in another aircraft, Ed passed 622 sitting on the flight line with its cowling open ... its normal condition. What was unusual this time was that crew chief Sergeant Matt Fischer had the oil filler cap off, and was holding a file in one hand and a large nail in the other. Matt put enough metal shavings in the engine to set off the chip detector and get Super Pig in line for a new engine. The engine change did the trick. Tail number 622 became one of the best Bird Dogs in the Red Marker fleet, although it caught some abuse at the hands of the author when he hit a runway marker at Quan Loi.[28]

Engine fouling due to continuously running at full rich mixture was a relatively common occurrence in the Bird Dog. Especially early in the war, many FACs without experience in flying reciprocating engines flew this simple plane like they flew a jet, never adjusting the mixture. Better practices and training helped solve some of these problems. Full rich mixture was used for takeoffs and landings and during airstrikes. At all other cruise conditions (such as providing convoy escort or doing visual reconnaissance) FACs learned to lean the mixture. Not only did the practice conserve fuel, extending the Bird Dog's range and time on station, it prevented fouling the spark plugs. The fouled plugs could cause the engine to run rough and lose power. This may have

---

28   Fairchild reports that some time after getting a new engine, 622 sustained damage on the ground in a mortar attack. While being hoisted back to Bien Hoa for repairs it caused a crash of the Chinook carrying it. The author could not verify the accident because the records for 1969 are not available at AFHRA. However, 622 definitely was in service until at least July 1970. Some reports have the plane transferred to the Royal Khmer Air Force. Ed may have confused the tail number with 662, another Bird Dog in theater.

been part of the problem with 622. On the other hand, it may have just been a Super Pig.

Vietnamese Red Marker

In 1966, First Lieutenant Truc Van Tran moved from his position as a FAC at the 112th L-19 Squadron to the staff of the Airborne Division as G-3 Air Operations. He was promoted to Captain in 1968 and to Major in 1970, serving with the Airborne until 1971. He had flown with Gene McCutchan in 1962 while with the 112th, and he continued to fly in the back seat while with the Airborne. Truc amassed more than 800 hours in the Bird Dog during his time with the 112th, and another 600 hours with the Airborne. During his tenure with the Airborne, he was known as a Red Marker with a call sign "DO(Red)" (Director Operations – Red Marker). In recognition of his service, he was awarded the USAF Air Medal in 1968. Lt. Colonel Don Glenn presented the medal at a ceremony at the Airborne Division Headquarters in Tan Son Nhut. Truc also earned his parachute rating while with the Airborne, eventually qualifying as a Master Parachutist.[29]

---

29 Major Truc Van Tran, emails Oct 2011.

Pete Drahn, Ken Kreger, Jim Leach, Jack McKessy, Don Spooner. Drahn Collection.

CHAPTER 10 - 1968 - LT COL PETE ALMQUIST & LT COL DON GLENN

From left, Ken Kreger, Pete Drahn, Roy Moore receiving award, Bruce Bechtel. Drahn Collection.

Sergeant Matt Fischer. Freeman Collection.

Major Laurie Kivisto in the Snoopy Bird Dog. Stepaniak Collection.

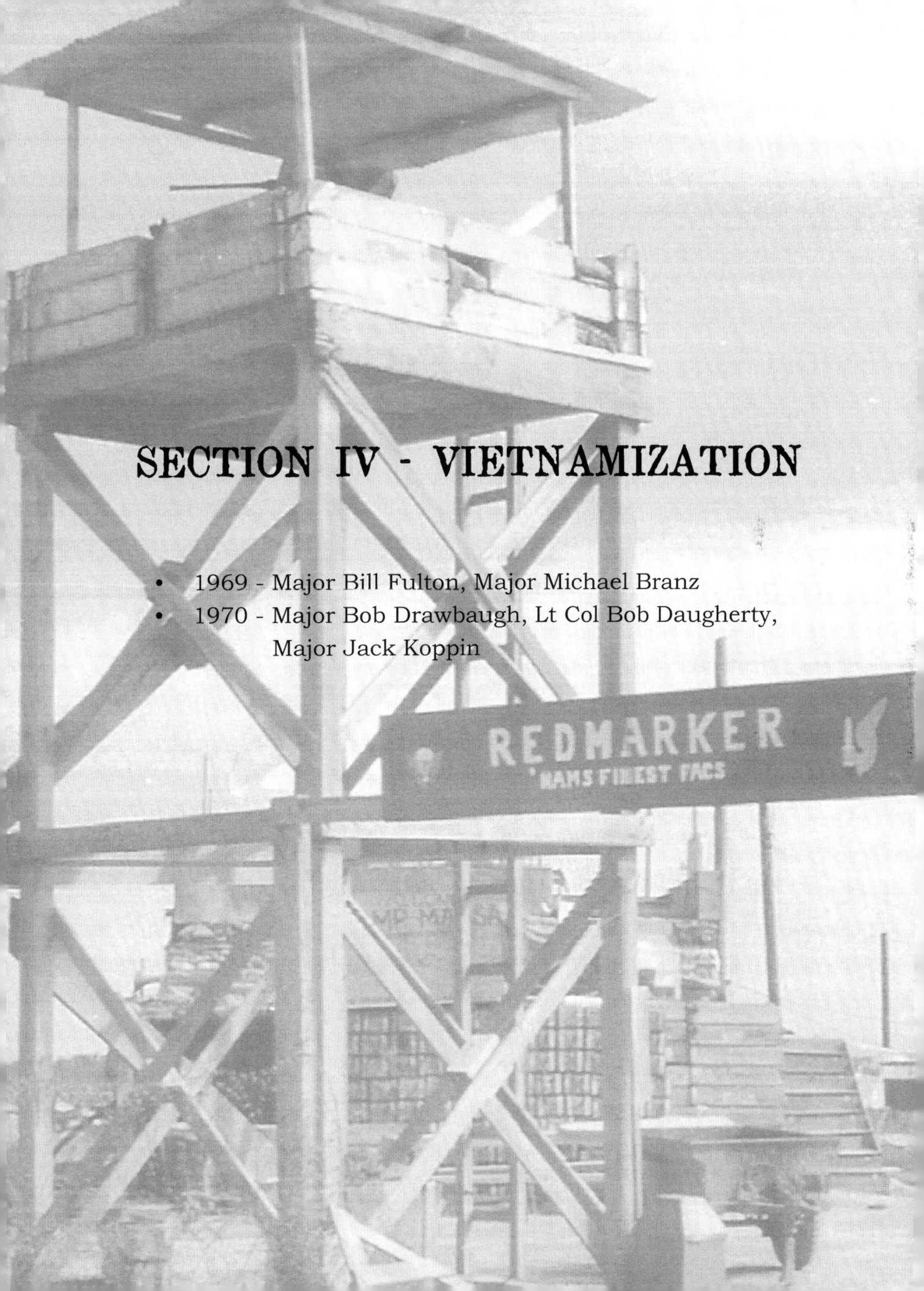

SECTION IV - VIETNAMIZATION

- 1969 - Major Bill Fulton, Major Michael Branz
- 1970 - Major Bob Drawbaugh, Lt Col Bob Daugherty, Major Jack Koppin

1969–70 AIRBORNE OPERATIONS

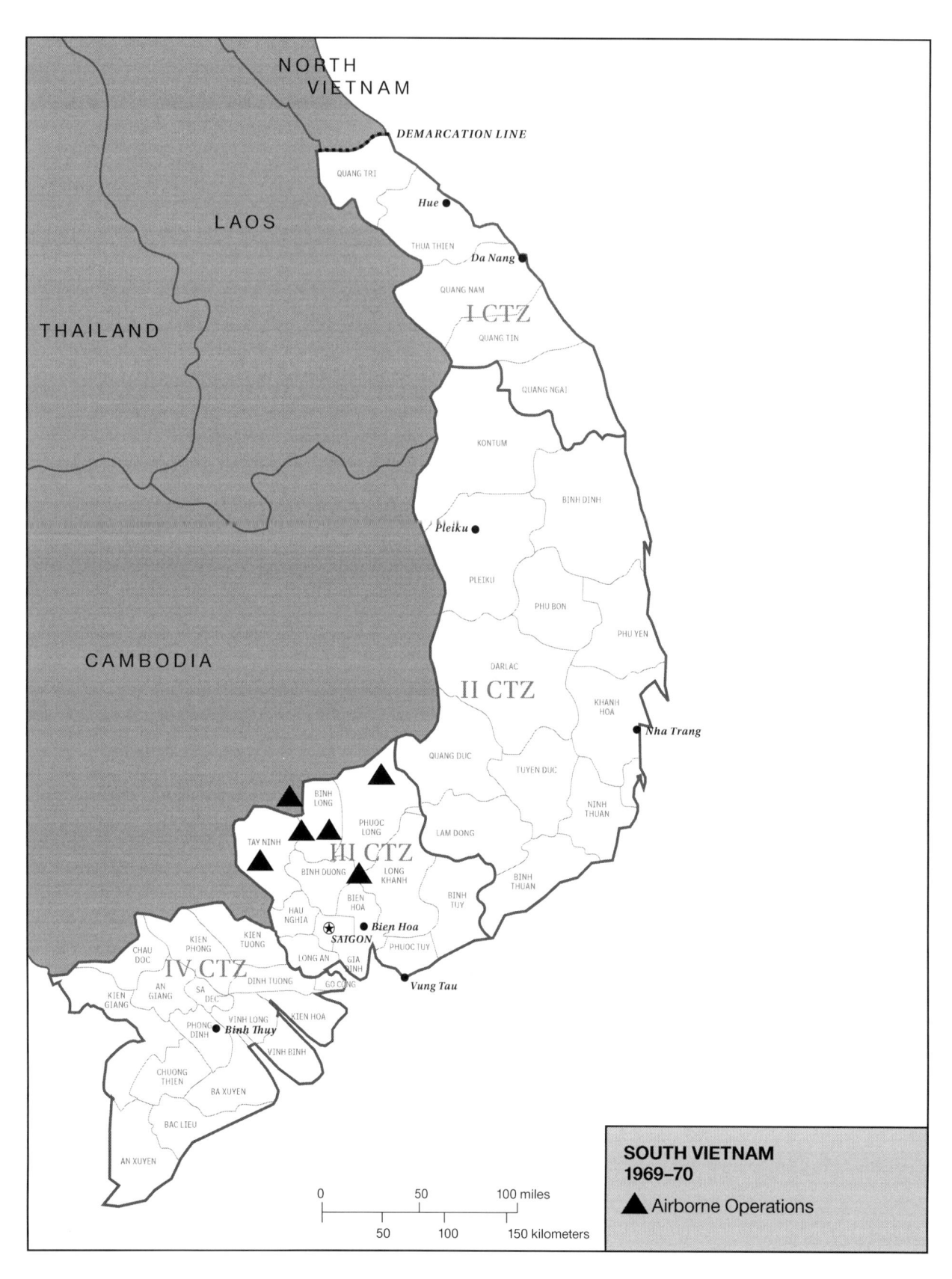

CHAPTER 11

1969 - MAJOR BILL FULTON
MAJOR MICHAEL BRANZ

During 1969, the Red Markers continued to expand in personnel and equipment notwithstanding the Vietnamization program. Many of the detachment's equipment problems were a thing of the past, although staffing remained an issue. Other units supporting ARVN divisions that were spread among several locations would generally field a permanent ALO and several FACs at each location. The Red Markers, on the other hand, had a single ALO and assistant ALO despite operating out of three or more locations at a time. This required a flexible command approach and considerable reliance on individual FACs and senior radio operators to maintain contact with the ALO or assistant responsible for activity at a particular FOL.

Major William H. Fulton, Jr. took over as ALO from Lt. Colonel Glenn near the end of 1968. Major Jim Leach was second in command of the unit. However, Fulton frequently spent time at Bien Hoa. Consequently, Leach ran the Red Markers for extended periods. In May or June, Major Leach transferred to Xuan Loc to fill a vacant ALO position. Shortly thereafter, Major Fulton transferred permanently to Bien Hoa. Major Michael H. Branz replaced Fulton as ALO and served till December. By the end of 1969, Major Robert E. Drawbaugh joined the Red Markers as ALO. Branz moved to a position at the 504th TASG at that time.

The shorter ALO assignments that began in 1969 may have been an unintended result of Vietnamization. It had become clear that the U.S. was going to disengage in Vietnam in the relatively near term. American

---

Old Red Markers 1969

Major Bill Fulton 01
Major Jim Leach 02
Major Harold Manguson
Captain Bill Marlin 04
Captain Stuart Wheeler 09
Captain Ed Fairchild 06
1Lt Don Spooner 07
Staff Sgt Raymond Moore
Staff Sgt Bill Mackey
Staff Sgt Bob Jones
Sgt Walt Stepaniak
Chico Hernandez
John Carpenter
Sgt John Kokoski
Sgt Jim Fuller
Sgt Larry Lauber
Sgt Perry Timpson
Sgt Matt Fischer
Mike Roberts
Sgt Pressley
Sgt Brown

Sgt Tran Dinh Luong
Cpl Phuong

manpower committed to SEA reached a peak during the year and began to decline. Any career officer seeking combat command and combat flying time needed to get on track or be left behind. In any event, the Red Marker ALO position became a six-month assignment rather than a year from 1969 forward. Two officers held the position in 1969, two in 1970, three in 1971 and two in 1972. Previously, the usual tour was a year. The shortest tour had been about nine months, terminated early by an emergency.[1]

There was also a marked increase in junior company grade officers serving as FACs. Earlier in the war, it had been rare to see a lieutenant serving in that role. From 1969 onward, it was common. The personnel pipeline was graduating successive classes of FACs from Hurlburt, despite the upcoming decrease in U.S. involvement in SEA. Most of these graduates were junior officers straight from pilot training. Before the end of the year, the Tactical Air Support Squadrons began reporting surpluses of company grade officers. This overstaffing caused newly arrived FACs to encounter weeks of delay before being assigned to a unit.

One factor in the number of lieutenants arriving for duty with the Red Markers was the military's distinction between FACs with fighter pilot experience versus those without. Under an agreement between the U.S. Air Force and Army, only FACs with prior fighter experience ... so-called "Class A" FACs ... could support American units. The remainder were designated "Class B" FACs, who could work as Sector FACs or to support Vietnamese units such as the Airborne. As the fighter-experienced FACs went to American divisions, more green lieutenants right out of pilot training went to units like the Red Markers.

The vast majority of Class B FACs did a good job and many were clearly outstanding. Most FACs never knew about the distinction that affected their assignment. In practice, the classification may have been a distinction without a difference. With so

> ### New Red Markers 1969
> Major Michael Branz 01
> Major Robert Drawbaugh 01
> Major Gerald Schwalb 02
> Captain Warren Paxton 03
> 1Lt Bruce Freeman 08
> Captain Dave Langas 04/14/24
> Captain Jim Hill 05
> Captain Fred Bishopp 05
> Captain Doug Lobser
> 1Lt Art Intemann 09
> 1Lt Ed Weiss 03
> 1Lt Terry Weaver 07
> 1Lt Dave Blair 16
> 1Lt Larry Shaevitz 24
> Captain Bill Dunne 25
> 1Lt Lloyd Prevett 26
> 1Lt Gary Willis 18
> 1Lt Byron Mayberry 19
> 2Lt Bill Smallman (one month)
> Sgt Greg Lockwood
> Sgt Ron DeVries
> A1C/Sgt Barry Schupp
> Staff Sgt Bill Bradley
> A1C Bob Byrnes
> Sgt Charles Cude
> A1C Roger Egleston
> Terry Elliott
> Richard Guy
> A1C David Janssen
> Staff Sgt Billy Johnson
> A1C Bill Kaeser
> Sgt Orlando Metcalf
> Staff Sgt Ken Poteet
> A1C Henry Presswood
> A1C George Smith
> Sgt James Stokes
> A1C Ron Wessell
> Sgt Pat Williams

---
1 Lt. Colonel Carleton Casteel in 1964-65.

many joint operations involving American and Vietnamese forces, and with American advisors on the ground with the Vietnamese units, Class B FACs invariably directed strikes that supported the U.S. Army.

As a result of the Class A versus B distinction, most of the captains assigned as Red Markers came from transport aircraft rather than fighters. For example, Captains Jim Hill and Ed Fairchild had flown C-141s prior to their FAC assignments. Jim Hill reported that he thoroughly enjoyed his tour as a FAC. After 2,500 hours in the C-141, it was a pleasure to fly an aircraft without an autopilot. He logged 1,000 hours in the O-1, flying almost every day. During seven months as a Red Marker, he flew in support of the Airborne near Tay Ninh. Hill was awarded a DFC, numerous Air Medals, a Vietnamese Cross of Gallantry and an Honor Staff Medal. In August, he transferred to Bien Hoa and served the last five months of his tour as an O-1 check pilot for the 19th TASS.[2]

Captain Ed Fairchild also enjoyed his tour. He joined the Air Force at age nineteen and completed navigator training as an Aviation Cadet. He flew for four years as a navigator before going to pilot training and subsequently flying heavy transports. As a consequence, Ed brought a lot of Air Force experience and common sense to his Red Marker assignment. Upon his arrival, he spent two months near the rubber plantation at Nui Dat with newly promoted Major Harold Magnuson. Following that operation, he flew primarily from Tay Ninh or Tan Son Nhut. Magnuson soon returned to the States, leaving Fairchild as ranking officer after the ALO and assistant ALO. Ed then served as

Captain Ed Fairchild. Jim Hill Collection.

scheduling officer as well as combat Tactics IP.

Fairchild spent nine months with the Red Markers before transferring to Xuan Loc to join Major Jim Leach. Ed counts both the Red Marker and Xuan Loc assignments among the best of his Air Force career. Leach had requested Ed be transferred to help improve the unit. The facilities at Xuan Loc ranked near the bottom of the forward operating locations in III Corps. Red clay dust blew constantly during the dry season. The aircraft parked in a quagmire when it rained. On-base amenities were virtually nonexistent.[3] Naturally, the adverse environment affected the men in the unit. Several young FACs and most of the enlisted men approached their jobs in a lackluster manner. According to Fairchild, many in the outfit drank to excess and did not maintain their quarters or their personal appearance.

---
2 James A Hill, questionnaire, 2010.

3 USAF MOBs contained air conditioned quarters, movie theaters, separate clubs for officers, NCOs and enlisted men, and well stocked BXs. FOLs might have an air conditioned club for officers and a minimal Army PX. Xuan Loc had none of these.

Ed first tackled the aircraft facilities by announcing that the group would rebuild the revetments. The airmen moaned, thinking they would be doing all the work while the officers sat on their hands. Privately, Ed told the young FAC lieutenants they could do as they pleased, but he was going to wield a pick and shovel and work on the revetments with the enlisted troops every day after he finished flying. The young FACs responded and joined the project. In time, the men's personal appearance and mission execution improved along with the aircraft ramp facility.

To compensate the men for the improvement, Leach and Fairchild sent each on a three day in-country R&R to Vung Tau. Ed announced the reward by calling a meeting of the detachment and stating that he had a project in mind and needed two volunteers. After a long hesitation, two crew chiefs said they would volunteer. Ed said, "Great, you are the first two to get some time off in Vung Tau for all your hard work. Everyone else can come up here and sign the list and we will send you in due course."

When Fairchild landed from his last mission prior to going back to the States, his crew chief came to his quarters to inform him he was needed at the airstrip. Ed asked why, and the crew chief responded that it was an emergency. They got in a Jeep and drove to the strip where they were joined by another Jeep with enlisted crewmen, who popped smoke grenades as they drove around the ramp area to the cheers and applause of the rest of the detachment.

Tay Ninh, Tay Ninh Province, III Corps

In March, the 8th and 9th Airborne Battalions began ground sweeps west

Lt Bruce Freeman and O-1 at Tay Ninh. Bruce Freeman Collection.

of Tay Ninh along the southern edge of the Straight Edge Woods. The area was a known concentration point for units of the 7th and 9th NVA Divisions. In a major engagement, which began as the Airborne was about to terminate the operation, Red Markers saved countless lives and prevented the Airborne from being overrun. The aggressive Lieutenant Freeman, Red Marker 08, was awarded the Silver Star for his part in this fighting.

On the afternoon of 9 March, following a series of largely uneventful sweeps, the Airborne units lined up for Huey extraction in a large east-west LZ. The Airborne was spread out in a "pick-up line," a series of evenly spaced groupings of 8-10 troopers. A dense tree line was located approximately two hundred meters north of the troops. Freeman was the FAC on station. Minutes before the Hueys arrived,

Lt Ed Weiss. Jim Hill Collection.

the NVA opened fire from along the entire tree line, instantly inflicting casualties among the troopers. Freeman radioed for an immediate airstrike. Before the fighters arrived, however, an estimated two to three hundred NVA soldiers charged across the field in an attempt to overrun the Airborne positions. Freeman dropped his Bird Dog to treetop height and flew directly over the Airborne positions and north into the oncoming attackers. In the short but critical time that the NVA redirected their fire at the O-1, the Airborne were able to better organize their defensive line, some getting cover in old bomb craters.

Shortly thereafter, Freeman directed a flight of VNAF A-1Es to bomb and strafe the tree line. The next two days were a virtually continuous TIC until the NVA were forced to withdraw and the Airborne were extracted. Freeman and Red Marker 03, Lieutenant Edward D. Weiss, directed fighters, helicopter gunships, Navy OV-10 "Black Ponies," AC-47 "Puffs," and 105s/155s/8-inch artillery into the NVA positions. They maintained an almost constant cap over the Airborne.

In a classic "small world" story, the fighting that first night brought Freeman and one of his former AF Academy instructors together. Visibility had deteriorated to less than a mile in fog and rain as Bruce continued to fly over the battlefield that night. The NVA undoubtedly heard the Bird Dog overhead, but chose to attack. Perhaps the NVA believed that air support was not possible under those conditions. Freeman called for "anything with ordnance on it that can get through the weather." A flight of Navy OV-10s from Vung Tau responded. They were carrying wall-to-wall Zuni rockets.[4] At two in the morning in a driving rain, Freeman could not stand off and mark the target with a smoke rocket. With his top rotating beacon on, he told the Broncos to black out their lights, follow his beacon as he dove toward the target and to open fire as soon as he called that he was breaking left. The Navy pilots followed his instructions, scoring direct hits and buying the friendlies more valuable time.

Later that morning, after a brief nap, Freeman prepared to relieve Weiss on station. His crew chief, Sergeant Ron Devries, walked in and told him the "Black Pony" flight lead was in a nearby hootch and wanted to meet the FAC with whom he'd worked the previous night. Lt. Commander John A. Butterfield greeted Bruce when he came into the hootch. Bruce had last seen John when the naval aviator was an exchange officer teaching one of the Political Science courses at the Academy.

Ironically, after receiving numerous awards for his combat actions, Bruce almost died near the end of his tour in a

---

[4] Zuni 5" air to ground rockets were fired from a cylindrical rocket launcher, the Lau-10 series, with four rockets per launcher. Each Bronco carried four pods/16 rockets, a lot of firepower.

Sergeant Schupp and MRC-108. Barry Schupp Collection.

Schupp's Quarters at Tay Ninh. Barry Schupp Collection.

non-combat aircraft accident. His Bird Dog crashed taking off into the wake turbulence caused by a C-130 in front of him. Just ten days after facial repair work at Saigon's 3rd Field Hospital, Bruce returned to flying status. He flew missions for the three weeks remaining on his tour. Some of those missions were to various FOLs where he lectured on the hazards of wake turbulence, a phenomenon not fully studied or understood at the time.[5] He finished his tour logging 612 sorties and just over 1,000 flying hours.

Freeman returned to the states to fly F-100s, expecting to go back to Tuy Hoa AB as a Misty Fast-FAC. He remained stateside when that program was canceled. He returned to SEA two years later flying F-4s during the Linebacker I & II campaigns over the North. He subsequently served as an IP in the German Air Force's Top Gun program, during which he did get his master's degree ... at night.

---

[5] Tower had cleared Freeman for a midfield takeoff behind the heavyweight C-130, exactly the wrong place to be. Instead, he should have been directed to the takeoff end of the runway where his takeoff climb would have been well above the turbulent vortexes spiraling off the C-130's wingtips.

Sergeant Barry R. Schupp, a Red Marker radio operator, remembers the battles around Tay Ninh. On 10 April 1969, Schupp was supporting the 1st Brigade. The Brigade Tactical Operations Center was located in a building within the province chief's estate in the city of Tay Ninh. Sergeant Schupp's MRC-108 radio jeep and tent were just outside the TOC. The FACs were in the Tay Ninh Base Camp (Tay Ninh West), separated some distance from the TOC.

Army intelligence had alerted base personnel to increased enemy activity and the possibility of an attack. All units were directed to review and improve defenses as necessary. Schupp had previously created a small bunker from an unused concrete water cistern that stood near the MRC-108 by putting metal sheeting and sand bags over the top of the concrete enclosure. He prepared for the expected attack by getting all the portable radios from the jeep ... the PRC-41, PRC-47 and PRC-25. He checked that each had fresh batteries. He tested each by radio checks with Pawnee Target, the DASC at Bien Hoa, as well as random aircraft in flight.

Red Markers 1969, Back Row: Art Intemann, Ron DeVries, Jim Leach, Jim Hill, Warren Paxton. Front Row: Bruce Freeman, John Kokowski, Ed Fairchild, Jim Fuller, Ed Weiss. Bruce Freeman Collection.

Finally, he placed the portables in the cistern. Barry planned to use the portables if the radio jeep was destroyed or if enemy activity precluded his occupying an exposed position at the jeep to communicate with the FACs.

Shortly after midnight, the first rounds came in. Small arms fire was sporadic, but mortar and rocket fire was significant. The TOC came under heavy rocket and mortar attack. Enemy fire detonated two ammunition storage areas several hundred meters away, causing a hail of flying projectiles, shrapnel and other debris in and around the command post. At the same time, two Airborne battalions located southwest of the city received mortar and ground attacks and requested air support. The TOC commander told Schupp that landline communications to Tay Ninh Base Camp had been severed. He could not contact the FACs at Tay Ninh West.

Schupp put out an emergency call on Guard Frequency and asked for any gunship to respond. A C-119 Shadow answered the call. Schupp explained the situation, gave the pilot the battalion Red Hat's call sign and radio frequency and informed the TOC commander. The Shadow's four mini-guns helped beat back the VC attack.

For a short time, Schupp attempted to conduct radio operations from the cistern-bunker. However, the reception on the portable HF radio was too poor to stay in contact with III DASC, which Schupp

131

needed to request additional air support. Therefore, he left the bunker and remained at the MRC-108 throughout the night. As dawn broke, a FAC scheduled for a preplanned airstrike got airborne and diverted the strike to close air support.[6]

All the while, projectiles from the burning ammunition storage areas, incoming rounds of all sizes, and other shrapnel were flying around the TOC and the jeep. Windows and roof tiles from some buildings shattered, sending shards of glass, clay and concrete flying. The windshield of the MRC-108 was damaged by shrapnel, but not destroyed. Glass fragments left numerous minor wounds in Schupp's arms and neck.

A 105mm round from the burning ammunition dump tore a gaping hole in Schupp's tent. The shell destroyed the tent and his aluminum cot, and embedded itself in the ground. Since it was not fused, it did not explode. Sergeant Schupp remained at the MRC-108 for what became nearly twelve hours of flareship and airstrike control. Army crews extinguished the fires at the ammunition dumps, but the battle continued. The VC held part of the city for a few days. Barry recalls a lot of discussion with III DASC the following morning. Some people safely behind the wire at Bien Hoa were upset that a three-striper diverted the Shadow from its pre-planned target. The Airborne, however, was not upset. Sergeant Barry Schupp was awarded the Army Commendation Medal with V for his actions during this engagement.[7]

On 12 March 1969, Captain Jim Hill flew cover for the Airborne during further contact with the enemy. The Airborne took some casualties that needed to be evacuated. While under heavy fire, Hill coordinated the MedEvac at the same time he directed a set of fighters on the enemy position. The helicopters safely extracted the wounded troopers. Jim received a DFC for his actions that day.[8]

Captain Jim Hill. Jim Hill Collection.

The Airborne awarded a Cross of Gallantry to many Red Markers who supported the Tay Ninh operation during the period 30 January to 26 March.[9] The orders issuing awards listed the following recipients:

Major James A. Leach
Captain Warren K. Paxton
Captain Edward A. Fairchild
Captain James A. Hill
1st Lt. Edward A. Weiss
1st Lt. Bruce M. Freeman
1st Lt. Arthur J. Intemann
Staff Sgt. William C. Mackey
Sgt. William F. McAlexander
Sgt. John E. Kokoski
Sgt. Lawrence L. Lauber

---

6 Attempts to identify this FAC have been unsuccessful. It may have been Fairchild, Freeman or Weiss.
7 Lt Colonel Barry R. Schupp, USAR (Ret), Red Marker Questionnaire, 19 Jan 2011.
8 From Citation to Accompany the Award of the Distinguished Flying Cross.
9 General Order NR 073/SDND/TQT/CL dated 17 April 1969.

Captain Dave Langas and O-2A. Dave Langas Collection.

Captains Fred Bishopp and Dave Langas. Dave Langas Collection.

Sgt. James L. Fuller
Sgt. Ronald J. Devries
Sgt. Walter Stepaniak
Sgt. Perry Timpson
Sgt. Barry Schupp

O-2A Skymasters

In mid-1969, the Red Markers received some of the new FAC aircraft, the O-2A Cessna Skymaster. Compared with the O-1, the O-2As were vastly superior in armament, range, speed, max altitude, time on station and weather navigation capabilities. It carried two external pods, each with seven rockets. This was almost twice the armament of the Bird Dog. The O-2's top speed was 206 miles per hour versus 151 for the O-1, and it cruised at 120-130 versus 100. Its range was about 1,400 miles, which was triple the O-1's. Furthermore, the Skymaster had a full array of instruments and NavAids including TACAN with glideslope and DME for instrument approaches. In contrast to the Skymaster's NavAids, the Bird Dog had an Automatic Direction Finder (ADF). The Bird Dog could make weather penetrations and non-precision approaches, except that the FACs did not carry approach plates for the published approaches. The Bird Dog FACs instead used the ADF (which was just an AM receiver with a direction needle) to listen to Armed Forces Radio Saigon. They heard rock and roll music and knew the general direction of Tan Son Nhut AB. The O-1 was, however, superior to the O-2 in two areas: visibility of the ground and rough field landing capability. That last shortcoming of the Skymaster would limit its usefulness in certain areas of operation.

In advance of the Skymaster arrivals, the personnel pipeline began adding O-2 qualified pilots to the unit. The first to arrive, Captains Carl D. "Dave" Langas and Fred T. Bishopp, Jr. preceded the aircraft by almost two months. They landed in Vietnam in late March and processed through the Theater Indoctrination School, which at the time was located at Phan Rang. Upon their return to Bien Hoa, they waited for a couple of weeks before being assigned to the Red Markers. By late April, they were taking area orientation rides in the back seat of O-1s, awaiting the arrival of their planes.

Captain Douglas B. Lobser also arrived

Captain Doug Lobser, Lt. Terry Weaver and local children. Dave Langas Collection.

before the unit got its first O-2. Other Skymaster pilots, Major Gerald P. Schwalb, Captain William E. Dunne, Lieutenants Lawrence H. "Larry" Shaevitz and Lloyd L. Prevett, Jr., each arrived in short order.

Unlike the O-1s, which had been shipped in crates to Bien Hoa to be reassembled and test flown, the O-2s were ferried across the Pacific using extra gas tanks installed in the cabin to extend their range. This 9,100-mile trip was flown in legs landing at Hawaii, Midway, Wake, Guam and Clark AB in the Philippines before arriving in Vietnam. Groups of O-2s followed a lead cargo plane that provided long-range navigation, scouted ahead for good weather and winds and served as a Search and Rescue platform if needed.

Between June and the end of the year, the Red Markers received four Skymasters. The Red Marker Tactics IP was Captain Edward A. Fairchild. He was O-1 qualified, but nonetheless, gave the tactics check rides to the first several O-2 pilots. Captain Fred Bishopp remembers being given his area orientation by O-1 FAC Bruce Freeman. Subsequently, Bishopp became the Red Markers' O-2 Combat Tactics IP. He served in that role until September 1969 when he transferred to 19th TASS Stan/Eval Section as an O-2A instructor pilot. When Bishopp moved to the TASS, Langas assumed the role of Tactics IP.

Dave also had the additional duty of operations officer, tracking the accumulated flight time for the unit's aircraft and scheduling them for periodic maintenance at Bien Hoa. That coordination role with the TASS may have been the reason Dave became the point man on an investigation into an alleged cross-border rocket-firing incident. Someone reported that a smoke rocket had been fired into Cambodia from Tay Ninh Province, where Red Markers were operating. The TASS bureaucrats contacted Langas and came to the field for a day to investigate. He could not answer any of their questions, and eventually they went away. According to Dave, flying at 5,000 feet near the border of the Parrots Beak, one could see some metal roofed buildings in the distance. These were believed to be part of an NVA base camp and were the apparent target of a "spare" rocket.[10]

More Personnel

The personnel pipeline also added several new O-1 pilots to the roster. First Lieutenant Arthur J. Intemann joined the Red Markers early in the year. Lieutenants Terry L. Weaver and David G. Blair were assigned by mid-year. Lieutenants Byron L. Mayberry and Gary N. Willis arrived before year-end. Lieutenant Intemann became the O-1 Tactics IP after Captain Fairchild moved to Xuan Loc with the 18th Division.

With the expanded number of pilots and

---

[10] That camp became an objective of the Vietnamese Marines during the Cambodian Incursion in May 1970. Possibly the TASS was trying to prevent further incidents which might tip off the enemy to U.S. intelligence knowledge of their location.

O-2A Servicing at Tay Ninh. Dave Langas Collection.

the O-2A aircraft in the unit, the Red Marker ALO modified the FACs' numerical call signs. In the past, the calls signs were random except that 01 and 02 were reserved for the ALO and assistant ALO. Now it seemed appropriate to create a distinction between FACs flying the Bird Dog and those in the Skymaster. Such a difference would allow everyone in contact with the pilot to know immediately the aircraft type and capabilities.

Major Branz instituted the first iteration of a new numbering system by assigning numbers beginning with "zero" to the Bird Dog FACs, with the exception of 01 and 02. The Skymaster pilots received numbers beginning with "one," i.e., 10 through 19. Shortly, however, there were not enough numbers to accommodate all the O-1 pilots. Branz revised the system to give the O-1 FACs numbers beginning with "one" and the O-2 FACs numbers beginning with "two." This system made sense and for a while provided enough numbers to account for a growing outfit.

The result of these various schemes was that some FACs had several call signs during their tour. For example, Captain Dave Langas was first Red Marker 04, then 14 and finally 24.

Tay Ninh, Tay Ninh Province, III Corps

During 1969, the Airborne Division's nine maneuver battalions usually operated as three brigades. The Red Markers mirrored this organization with mobile TACPs, generally assigning three or four FACs, two aircraft, two crew chiefs and two radio operators to each. As of mid-year 1969, one TACP was based at the unit headquarters at Tan Son Nhut because the 1st and 3rd Brigades were operating in the vicinity of Saigon. Another TACP was at Tay Ninh supporting the 2nd Brigade.[11] Later in the year, the Airborne began operations at Phouc Vinh and Song Be and would briefly close its Tay Ninh operations, all

---
11 "Seventh Air Force News," story by Sgt Bob Palmer, photos by SSgt Ron Smith, 3 Sep 1969, pp. 10-11, interview of Major Michael H. Branz, ALO.

Tay Ninh Hootch. Willis Collection.

within III Corps. A Red Marker TACP deployed to Phuoc Vinh and the Tay Ninh TACP moved to Song Be.

When Red Markers first moved into Tay Ninh West, they were assigned a screened hootch on prime real estate ... right next to the transient helicopter pad and a seven-hole latrine. The Army really knew how to take care of their Air Force compatriots. The Red Markers made the best of the situation, immediately customizing the quarters. Dave Langas built a bar in one end of the officers' hootch. Everyone pitched in to paint the outside bunkers red, and Doug Lobser painted the Red Marker name on the outside. As the unit received more O-2s, the Skymaster FACs began flying from Tay Ninh. The O-1s moved to Phouc Vinh and later to Song Be as the Airborne opened operations in those areas. Neither field was authorized for use by O-2s. Having a soft nose-wheel strut, the O-2 was susceptible to dinging its front propeller when landing on a rough runway. Even taxiing on uneven surfaces (for example PSP) could cause problems. Early in 1968, the TASS conducted a review of airfields for FAC operations and published a safety classification of each. In late 1968, the TASS supplemented that classification with a survey specific to the safety of O-2 operations. The comments on FOLs visited in conjunction with the survey included the following:

- Quan Loi, 7 Nov 68, Runway Surface Marginal Not Suitable;
- Phuoc Vinh, 7 Nov 68, Runway Surface Fair, Not Suitable;
- Tay Ninh West, Runway Surface Good, Limited Operations....[12]

12 19th TASS Unit History, Oct –Dec 1968, p. 6.

Tay Ninh Bar. Dave Langas Collection.

In addition to these locations, the TASS had long restricted Song Be City even from O-1 operations. However, Red Marker O-1s used it regularly from late 1969 onward.

Dave Langas was a steadying influence on some of the younger pilots. When one of the young O-1 pilots came into the Tay Ninh hootch with a hangdog look after a mission, Dave asked what was the problem. The lieutenant answered that one of his fighters had a short round in a TIC and injured some friendlies.[13] He was afraid he would be kicked out of the service or worse. Langas calmed him down. Dave instructed him to immediately go to the ALO and explain what happened, and to write up the details. The young FAC did as instructed. He became one of the best FACs in the unit and had a successful Air Force career.

As O-2 Combat Tactics IP, Dave also helped younger pilots gain confidence and fly safely. His council and encouragement helped them pass the check rides administered by Squadron Stan/Eval. He is particularly proud of the fact that each of his charges survived the war and returned home to his family.

---

13 A "short round" was an artillery shell or bomb that fell "short" of the target and impacted friendly troops.

Sergeant Barry R. Schupp came to the Airborne already jump rated and with a year of experience in the Far East. He had been stationed at Clark AB in the Philippines with the 5th Direct Air Support Flight and had spent time in Vietnam TDY with several different units. He had also spent six months TDY in Korea with a TACP supporting the 73rd Armored Division following the Pueblo Incident. In January 1969, he transferred to Vietnam and joined the Red Markers. Schupp made a number of parachute jumps with the Vietnamese Airborne and helped schedule some of the FACs (e.g., Freeman and Dunne) and enlisted men on jumps so they could all qualify for Vietnamese jump wings.

The Airborne regularly awarded honorary jump wings to just about anyone who could generate publicity for them. On one jump, there was a small contingent of French news reporters. Barry happened to be on that jump and recalls one particularly attractive young woman whom he helped to don her parachute. Jumpers who read this vignette will appreciate the excitement of a young 20-year-old, who had already been in the Pacific Theater almost two years, hoisting the parachute onto this young woman's back and then doing the "right leg strap"... "left leg strap"... routine.

Sergeant Schupp had an arrangement with the Combat Control Team, 8th Aerial Post Squadron at Tan Son Nhut. They let him use their steerable S-11 parachutes rather than the standard T-10 if he (a) picked up and returned the parachute, (b) repacked the parachute, and (c) brought back a deployment bag for each chute borrowed. So, under the supervision of one of the CCT's riggers, he learned to pack parachutes and, as a result, had more control on his jumps. This prevent-

Enroute to Song Be Base Camp. Schupp Collection.

Song Be "Day Room." Willis Collection.

ed accidents he witnessed other jumpers make, such as, landing on a metal building or other obstacle in the drop zone.

Patches

Syndicated columnist Helen "Patches" Musgrove lived in Saigon for several years covering the war. She regularly made trips to forward units. In 1969, she visited the province chief's complex at Tay Ninh for a couple of days. During her stay, she spent a brief time inquiring about the Red Marker radio operator role in operations. Barry recalls that someone produced a bottle of Chivas Regal the night before she left, which she and the troops enjoyed immensely. When she passed away in 1989 in California, the executor of her estate found hundreds of unit patches and twenty pounds of metal pins and insignia she had collected during those days in Vietnam. No one has seen the story she wrote on the Red Markers, if indeed she ever wrote one.[14]

Song Be, Phouc Binh Province, III Corps

In late 1969, the 1st Brigade moved from Tay Ninh and opened a new operation near the Cambodian border at Song Be. The Red Marker TACP convoyed with the rest of the TOC for the several days it took to relocate. Radio operators maintained contact with FACs flying cover along the way during the daylight hours. At night, the ROMADs bivouacked with the Airborne inside hastily erected earthen berms. The MRC-108 Jeep was usually backed into a trench scraped out for its protection. However, the trench became a pond during a rainstorm one night, requiring Schupp to move the jeep quickly.

Upon arrival south of Song Be City at LZ Buttons, Red Hats and Red Markers built bunkers while still maintaining operations. The bunker walls were wooden ammunition crates filled with earth. The roofs were large timber support beams covered with PSP and sandbags. Sergeant Schupp remembers,

"When we moved into Song Be Base Camp, we had to build those bunkers. The Army gave us hundreds of shell boxes, an engineer on a small dozer to scratch up a huge dirt pile, the same engineer with a small front end loader, some steel culvert, some PSP and several chutes to help fill sand bags. It actually only took a couple of days. My hootch was in the center of the back row and I built a collapsible table

---

[14] Helen Musgrove's home newspaper was the now defunct Jacksonville (FL) Journal. The author is attempting to locate archives of the newspaper to search for this story.

Song Be bunkers. Willis Collection.

with a washbasin so I could shave each day." [15]

The Red Hats, FACs, crew chiefs and RO-MADs worked on the bunkers during their off-duty hours. They built interconnecting bunkers in a U-shape with all the doors facing the inside of the "U." In the center of the U, the Red Hats erected a large tent to serve as a "Day Room" gathering area. Red Hat officers and Red Marker FACs shared one bunker equipped with four or five cots and a desk. Enlisted men roomed together in several other bunkers.

After installing a roof with a layer of PSP and sandbags, the team placed half round metal culvert pieces on top. They laid another layer of PSP and sandbags across the culvert, which created a secondary roof and provided "stand off" protection from mortars. The theory was that a mortar round would explode upon hitting the higher layer, and the denotation might not penetrate the real roof several feet below.

The VC attacked Song Be with mortar fire on a regular basis, making the bunkers essential. During one attack, Lieutenant Byron Mayberry was wounded when a piece of shrapnel came through a gap in the bunker wall. Each ammo box had three small skids on the bottom. These skids created a small gap between the boxes when stacked on each other. A needle-sized piece of shrapnel came through one gap and struck Mayberry in the side. He pulled it out. The Red Hat in the bunker made him report to the aid station for treatment and to fill out paperwork for a Purple Heart. Mayberry was duly embarrassed.

After another attack, Red Marker crew chief A1C William F. Kaeser, III, discovered an unexploded shell beside one of the planes. In a story Bill tells in *Cleared Hot, Book Two*, he went to the flight line the morning after an attack to preflight a

---

15 Lt. Colonel Barry R. Schupp, USAR (Ret), Questionnaire 19 Jan 2011.

CHAPTER 11 - 1969 - MAJOR BILL FULTON & MAJOR MICHAEL BRANZ

Song Be City Strip. Willis Collection.

Bird Dog for the first sortie. He found that a mortar round had gone through the wing of one of the O-1s without exploding and had embedded itself in the ground. Bill dug the shell out of the ground and took it outside the revetment. Only later did it occur to him that a better course of action might have been to leave the shell in the ground and move the plane out of harms way.[16]

Since the Red Markers and their aircraft remained overnight at LZ Buttons (also known as Song Be West or Phouc Binh), they could have run their flying operation from that location. They elected instead to operate primarily from the Song Be City strip a couple of miles to the north. The City strip was the home of the Viper FACs who supported the 18th Vietnamese Division and the Rod FACs who supported some Special Forces camps. Each day, Red Markers launched two sorties from Phouc Binh, but recovered at the City strip. The crew chiefs drove from Phouc Binh to Song Be City to rearm and refuel the Bird Dogs' turnarounds. At the City strip, they refueled from a rubber fuel bladder using a gasoline-powered pump. When the pump engine failed, which it did occasionally, the crew chiefs drained avgas from the bladder into jerry cans and poured the fuel into the wing tanks manually. They created a makeshift funnel from a Number 10 can with a hole punched in the bottom. Although more reliable refueling facilities were available at Phouc Binh, that airstrip was busy with numerous helicopter, C-123 and C-130 resupply missions supporting the large allied army contingent. The Red Markers put up with the conditions at the City strip to avoid the wake turbulence from the heavy aircraft and the blowing red grit from the helicopter activity.

The Song Be City airstrip was the town's former Main Street. It led directly to the front door of the Provincial Headquarters, which stood at the north end of the street. Because the building blocked one end of the "runway," FACs always landed heading north and took off to the south regardless of prevailing winds. The dangers of operating at this field were apparent to everyone who used it. A new Viper ALO was killed in 1967 when he collided with a helicopter as he attempted to land at the City.[17] After close observation on a go-around from a bad landing approach, Lieutenant Willis swears that the bell tower of the headquarters building has a red tiled floor.

---

16 *Cleared Hot, Book Two, Forward Air Controller Stories from the Vietnam War,* published by the Forward Air Controllers Association, Inc. 2009, p. 160.

---

17 19th TASS Unit History, Jan – Mar 1967.

Jim Hoppe and Sector FAC Billy Hall refueling at Song Be City. Willis Collection.

Lt Terry Weaver. Jim Hill Collection.

As previously noted, the 504th TASG had directed each TASS in early 1968 to review the suitability of airfields from a safety standpoint.[18]

That review classified the following airfields in III Corps for unrestricted use:

a. Bien Hoa
b. Cu Chi
c. Di An
d. Hon Quan
e. Lai Khe
f. Lam Son
g. Long Giao
h. Long Than North
i. Phu Loi
j. Phuoc Vinh
k. Song Be West
l. Tan An
m. Tan Son Nhut
n. Tay Ninh West
o. Tay Ninh City
p. Vung Tau
q. Xuan Loc

The following were approved for limited operation, as indicated:

a. Baria – Day/VFR only
b. Dong Tam – Day/Dry runway – Night/Max crosswind 15 knots for takeoff, 10 knots for landing. Runway must be dry. (This was a 1500' x 50' PSP runway, which is notoriously slick when wet.)
c. Dau Tieng – Day/VFR
d. Ham Tan – Day/VFR
e. Long Hai – Day/VFR

Finally, the following airfields were restricted, requiring explicit authorization prior to use:

a. Katum
b. Luscombe
c. Tanh Ling
d. Thien Ngon
e. Vo Dat I
f. Tonle Cham
g. Song Be City

Most of the "restricted" fields other than Song Be City were dirt or grass strips scraped out of the terrain outside Special Forces camps. Putting the Song Be City strip in the same class with these makeshift, unimproved runways speaks volumes. Nonetheless, Red Markers used the City strip for months in normal operations without incident.

The typical FAC missions at Song Be were either visual reconnaissance of the Airborne's ground sweeps of the area or directing preplanned airstrikes on suspected VC camp locations. Frequently, the Airborne contacted the enemy on its sweeps and preplanned strikes turned into TIC airstrikes. Usually three or four

---

18 19th TASS Unit History, May – Jun 1968.

FACs spent several weeks at Song Be before rotating to duty at a less rustic location.

First Lieutenant Terry L. Weaver, Red Marker 07, spent a lot of time at Song Be. Occasionally, he flew from Tay Ninh and, for a brief period, from Vung Tau in IV Corps. However, most of his tour was spent at Song Be. As a new FAC in late 1969, First Lieutenant Gary N. Willis logged copilot time with Weaver, who familiarized Willis with the AO and demonstrated proper airstrike control. Night sorties for the Red Markers had become rare since the Sleepytime FACs had taken over the rocket cap mission for Saigon in 1968. On the evening of 30 December 1969, however, the battalion senior advisor came from the TOC to the bunker shared with the FACs. He indicated one of their units was being heavily engaged and asked if someone could put in some airstrikes. Weaver said he'd volunteer to fly that mission and asked if anyone would be willing to ride in back. Willis said, "Sure, let's go."

The weather was clear. A little moonlight helped the two FACs keep their bearings. Weaver flew with all external lights off to the general vicinity of the Airborne unit in the rugged country north of Song Be. The Red Hat on the ground could not see the Bird Dog, but could hear the engine. Weaver instructed the Red Hat to call out when the plane passed directly overhead, which helped the FACs pinpoint his position on the ground. Taking up a figure eight over the friendlies, Weaver checked in a flight of F-100s. Flight lead spotted the O-1 when Terry momentarily turned on the top rotating beacon. He briefed the fighters on the target, cautioned them to expect ground fire and rolled in to mark the target as the Airborne popped smoke. Weaver's Willie Pete and the friendlies' smoke were all visible in the dim moonlight as lead rolled in hot. What caught everyone's eye, however, were the VC .51 caliber tracer rounds reaching up for the Bird Dog. Terry diverted lead from the WP smoke and cleared him onto the gun location. The gun ceased firing with lead's strike. Terry cleared number two to drop twenty meters short of lead's strike and directed they both hold high and dry.

Red Hat broke in on FM to advise that contact was broken. He said he could hear Charlie withdrawing in haste. To do as much damage as possible to the withdrawing forces, Weaver called in another pass from the fighters fifty meters further away from the Airborne lines than the initial strike. He directed a final pass fifty meters beyond that. Red Hat reported the results were outstanding and promised to put Weaver in for a well-deserved award. After lingering a bit longer to make sure all remained quiet, Terry headed back to Song Be, landing an hour and a half after takeoff. Weaver exhibited courageous conduct under fire ... night TIC, no margin for error, no flare-ship, red tracers in the darkness, cool-headed FAC, mission accomplished.

Blackout Landings

Runway lighting at Phouc Vinh was provided by diesel fuel smudge pots on either side of the runway at about fifteen foot intervals. Responsibility for lighting the pots rotated among the three organizations that used the field. One night, Lieutenant Willis approached the field after a late mission to find the smudge pots unlit. After orbiting for a period of time while Red Marker control tried to find someone to light the pots, Willis told Control he needed to land before he ran out of gas. A crew chief quickly drove a jeep to the end of the runway, providing some light.

Willis approached directly over the jeep and landed on the blacked out strip. He discovered, as had every other O-1 pilot attempting this maneuver, that the Bird Dog's wing mounted landing light was only marginally useful. It provided some illumination of the runway while on final approach. However, the light pointed skyward as the pilot rounded out for touchdown, leaving the landing strip in total darkness. After he landed the tail dragging Bird Dog, the landing light continued to point to the sky, useless for taxiing. Willis brought the plane to a stop until the crew chief could pass him with the jeep and lead him from the runway to the revetment.

Casualty Minimization

As the Vietnamization program accelerated, the American command instituted steps designed to minimize casualties. One step was a change in FAC training at Hurlburt. Instead of encouraging low-level reconnaissance, instructors repeatedly cautioned FACs in training to avoid flying below 1,500 feet AGL. With armored seat panels in place, the pilot was relatively well protected from small arms fire, as long as he remained at or above 1,500 feet. Below that level, he was vulnerable.

In contrast, earlier training at Hurlburt had encouraged low altitude passes for visual recon and positive target identification. Some argued not only that low altitudes were necessary but that the FAC was safer flying at fifty to one hundred feet than at higher altitude. In April 1964, Colonel Mellish, III Corps ALO, complained about the new minimum altitude for FACs imposed by 2nd Air Division in January 1963. He stated,

"Neither my ALO/FACs nor I have ever been able to find a VC at altitudes above 500 feet over wooded areas. Indeed, 150 feet over [such] areas is a safer altitude and one from which concealed VC are more likely to be discovered." [19]

Despite such assertions, practice proved that flying higher was safer. This was especially true as the NVA brought larger antiaircraft weapons into the south.

As a result of the policy change, Bird Dog FACs learned to mark a target without going below the 1,500-foot level. The prescribed maneuver began from cruise speed with a climbing wingover. The FAC raised the nose 45 degrees while pulling the throttle to idle and simultaneously banking hard to the right or left. As the nose fell below the horizon, the FAC continued to turn, bringing the nose below the target in a 45-degree dive. Without adding power, the FAC raised the nose to the target and fired the rocket when the "crosshairs" reached the target.[20] While the rocket was on the way, the FAC added full power and raised the nose in a climbing turn off the target. The initial climbing wingover at 100 knots, combined with a power-off dive to line up and mark the target, could be accomplished without going below 1,500 feet. The training stressed never pressing to the target, which would take the FAC below the danger level. Instead, the emphasis was on getting a proper alignment and getting the shot off quickly.

In some high threat areas where the enemy had higher caliber anti-aircraft weapons, the TASS set a minimum flight altitude above 1,500 feet. Furthermore, FACs in those areas were trained to mark targets from a shallower dive, allowing them to remain at a greater lateral distance from the target.

---

19 Rowley, p. 88.

20 The "crosshairs" consisted of a vertical line from a welding rod attached to the cowling just behind the propeller and a horizontal line from a grease pencil mark on the windscreen made by the FAC. See p. 79.

FACs also learned to fly in a slight "crab" ... applying a little right or left rudder while in level flight. As a result, the nose of the aircraft did not point in the actual direction of flight. The jungles and forests that hid the enemy from the FAC flying overhead also hid the FAC from view, except for brief glimpses through the foliage. If the enemy fired at the plane, he would presumably aim where the nose was pointing rather than along the actual line of flight. At least that was the theory.

Living Conditions

Early in the war, the Airborne rotated in and out of Saigon on a frequent basis, accompanied by Red Marker teams. The families of the Airborne generally lived in the vicinity of Saigon. Likewise, the Red Markers considered Saigon their "home" during their tour in SEA. Deployments to other locations were considered temporary duty for which the Red Markers received TDY pay.

Later in the war, the Airborne deployed for longer periods of time, which created a burden for the Airborne troopers and their families. By 1969, two brigades remained at remote posts within III Corps. Later, two brigades permanently deployed to stations in I Corps and II Corps. The Red Markers extended their deployments to match the Airborne. The forward operating locations for these extended deployments provided barracks (or bunkers) for the team rather than tents. As a result, most Red Markers took their personal belongings with them to the FOLs.[21] Every few weeks, each team member rotated back to Saigon for a few days off before returning to the field. Since they could not fly from the restricted FOLs, the O-2 FACs spent more time in Saigon than the Bird Dog pilots. With fewer FACs permanently in Saigon, the officers could not fill both halves of the villa. Some of the enlisted men took the other half, while some lived in the BEQ on Plantation Road. On Yen Do Street, the ALO, assistant ALO and enlisted NCOIC each had assigned rooms. Other team members rotated into whatever rooms were available when they arrived.

These arrangements lasted until about August 1970, at which time the TASS assigned quarters for the unit on Tan Son Nhut AB.

Red Hat Major Bill Mozey, Red Marker Major Jim Leach. Freeman Collection.

---

[21] By late 1969, the Red Markers were no longer paid TDY pay for service away from Saigon. They also no longer were issued a combat ration of brandy, nor did they spend in-country R&R at Vung Tau. A few days in the Saigon villa was considered in-country rest.

RED MARKERS

Lts Ed Weiss and Art Intemann. Freeman Collection.

Ron Wessell, Bruce Freeman, Barry Schupp. Freeman Collection.

Lt Bruce Freeman and Sergeant Barry Schupp. Freeman Collection.

Sergeant Bill McAlexander. Jim Hill Collection.

Staff Sergeant Bill Mackey, Sergeants Larry Lauber and Bill McAlexander. Freeman Collection.

CHAPTER 11 - 1969 - MAJOR BILL FULTON & MAJOR MICHAEL BRANZ

Bird Dog at Song Be showing the welding rod "rocket sight." Bill Kaeser Collection.

Bill Kaeser at Song Be City. Bill Kaeser Collection.

Caution Song Be may be Hazardous to your Health. Willis Collection.

CHAPTER 12

1970 - MAJOR BOB DRAWBAUGH, LT COL ROBERT DAUGHERTY, MAJOR JACK KOPPIN

In 1970, the Vietnamization program got underway in III Corps. In January, the 19th TASS transferred the Red Markers and other FAC units supporting Vietnamese Divisions to the 22nd TASS. The 19th TASS continued controlling the units supporting American and other Free World Forces.

During 1969, the 22nd TASS had successfully completed the Vietnamization program in IV Corps. TASS personnel trained Vietnamese FACs and turned over the FAC mission and all Forward Operating Locations in IV Corps to the Vietnamese Air Force. The VNAF also took complete responsibility for operating IV DASC, which previously had been staffed with both VNAF and USAF personnel. The 22nd TASS's new responsibility was to complete the same process within III Corps. It would do so in just over a year.

In late 1969, Major Robert E. Drawbaugh joined the Red Markers and served as ALO for six months. During the year, the Airborne deployed task forces only in III Corps or the adjoining Cambodian border region. The Airborne operated near Song Be for about four months and near Phuoc Vinh for seven months. In March, a brigade moved back into operation around Tay Ninh. The Red Markers re-inhabited their old red-painted hootch. Additionally, the Division continued its role as palace guard.

With this relatively small geographic area to cover, Drawbaugh and his assistant ALO Major Gerald P. Schwalb shuttled among all the forward operating locations to oversee TACP and FAC activities. Schwalb primarily supervised O-2 operations flying from Tay Ninh or Tan Son Nhut. Those craft usually did not operate from Phouc Vinh or Song Be City because of inadequate runways.

A 1970 inventory indicates the Red Markers had a more adequate allocation of equipment than in previous years. The unit had five radio jeeps, each with a full pallet of radio gear. The inventory also lists three slick jeeps, five trailers, five generators, FM radios for the slick jeeps, and assorted power supplies, batteries and battery chargers.[1] The slick jeep count remained below the proper allotment for a division-sized operation. The Red Markers compensated for that short-

---
1 1970 Equipment Inventory, associated with the transfer from 19th to 22nd TASS naming Lt. Art Intemann as responsible party.

CHAPTER 12 - 1970 - MAJOR BOB DRAWBAUGH, LT COL ROBERT DAUGHERTY, MAJOR JACK KOPPIN

age at some locations by off-loading the pallet from the radio jeeps into the Tactical Operations Center. This freed the vehicles for on-base transportation. Also, enterprising mechanics salvaged and repaired a Vietnamese vehicle as an "off-the-books" jeep. In addition to this high-value equipment, the unit had other items needed for operation in the field, including beds and bunks for the hootches, as well as folding cots and tents for more rustic living conditions. Among the unit's prized possessions were two refrigerators and a small air conditioner.

REMFs

Every tale of wartime experiences includes encounters with less than useful rear echelon personnel. The Air Force likely has more of these encounters than other services. This may be the case because a far greater percentage of Air Force personnel serve in a support role from a relatively secure location rather than engaging in regular combat. FACs soon learned to regard highly most maintenance personnel at the main bases. They performed periodic inspections and repairs on aircraft and radio gear beyond the capabilities of field ROMADs and crew chiefs. Likewise, most supply troops were responsive in meeting the needs of the remote locations. On the other hand, some members of the rear echelon made life more difficult for FACs at forward locations. Lieutenant Willis met one such officer during his second month as a Red Marker at Phuoc Vinh. Major Drawbaugh informed Willis one morning that a Major at 19th TASS needed to see him. Willis flew to Bien Hoa, naively thinking that he was due for his first Air Medal and perhaps headquarters wanted to present it in person. He reported to the Major, possibly the Operations Officer.[2] The Major left Willis standing at attention holding a salute, without returning it, and stated, "Lieutenant, you are just the kind of person who gives the rest of us a bad name." Willis silently held his salute until the Major returned it. He continued to berate the Lieutenant before finally mentioning the reason for this ass chewing.

"You bounced a check. What do you have to say for yourself?"

"Impossible. It's only the fifth of the month. I just got paid. I can't possibly be overdrawn."

Old Red Markers 1970

Major Robert Drawbaugh 01
Major Gerald Schwalb 02
Captain Dave Langas 24
1Lt Doug Lobser
1Lt Art Intemann 09
1Lt Terry Weaver 07
1Lt/Captain Dave Blair 16
1Lt Larry Shaevitz 24
Captain Bill Dunne 25
1Lt Lloyd Prevett 26
1Lt/Captain Gary Willis 18
1Lt Byron Mayberry 19
Staff Sgt Raymond Moore
Sgt Walt Stepaniak
Sgt Greg Lockwood
Sgt Ron DeVries
Sgt Barry Schupp
Staff Sgt Bill Bradley
A1C Bob Byrnes
Sgt Charles Cude
A1C Roger Egleston
Sgt Terry Elliott
Richard Guy
A1C David Janssen
Staff Sgt Billy Johnson
A1C Bill Kaeser
Staff Sgt Bill Mackey
Sgt Orlando Metcalf
Staff Sgt Ken Poteet
A1C Henry Presswood
A1C George Smith
Sgt James Stokes
A1C Ron Wessell
Sgt Pat Williams

Sgt Tran Dinh Luong
Cpl Phuong

---

2 Author's note: I would name this officer if positive of his identity.

Major Bob Drawbaugh and Captain Bill Dunne. Stepaniak Collection.

Lt Willis at Song Be. Willis Collection.

"Did you get confirmation that your paycheck was deposited?"

"I don't need confirmation. I'm serving at an FOL and can assume that my check is deposited on the first of the month."

"Where did you ever get a cockamamie idea like that," the Major asked loudly.

"I read it in the Daily Bulletin issued by this office a couple of months ago," Willis responded even more loudly.

"Well," sniffed the Major, "first you need to get your butt over to Bank of America and see if they can straighten this out. Then, get back here and see if you can find that Daily Bulletin."

Willis did indeed go to Bank of America, where a gentleman searched the records and found that his monthly pay had been deposited by wire transfer to the wrong account. The bank apologized for its error and any inconvenience it had caused Willis.[3] The Lieutenant returned to 19th TASS headquarters and spent more than an hour leafing through clipboards of Daily Bulletins. He located the document authorizing all personnel working at FOLs to assume they had been paid on the first of the month without first receiving a deposit confirmation in the mail. Willis went to confront the Major, who was conveniently absent. The Lieutenant flew back to Phouc Vinh, convinced that the Air Force was not the right career choice for him.

Opium Smuggling

In late February, the Office of Special Investigation (OSI) arrested two VC-118 pilots at Tan Son Nhut and charged them with smuggling opium.[4] On 12 April 1970, a Court Martial acquitted one pilot of smuggling but convicted him of possessing U.S. currency. He was fined $600 and confined to base for three months.[5]

The other officer was the highly decorated former Red Marker Major Del Fleener. He had been flying the VC-118 for several years, including two years at Hickam AFB in Hawaii and, since May 1968, from Tan Son Nhut. He routinely flew from Saigon throughout Southeast Asia. Am-

---

3 To this day, Willis cringes at the thought of automatic deposits and withdrawals from his family checking account.

4 "Pacific Stars & Stripes," Sunday, 1 March 1970, p 6.
5 "Pacific Stars & Stripes," Tuesday, 14 April 1970, p 6.

bassador Ellsworth Bunker was an occasional passenger. On 20 February 1970, Fleener experienced engine trouble on a flight to Bangkok. He completed the flight without incident, but had to ground the plane in Bangkok awaiting an engine change. While stranded, Del asked a couple of other transient pilots if they would haul some boxes back to Tan Son Nhut for him. He claimed the boxes contained either books or some brass articles. The other pilots agreed to do so and to give the boxes to an officer at Tan Son Nhut, who would take them to Fleener's BOQ room.

During one such flight, the navigator became suspicious when he attempted to move one of the boxes and found it considerably heavier than expected. The navigator opened the box to discover individually wrapped bricks of a dark plaster-like substance. He kept one brick, resealed the box and took the brick to the OSI when they landed.

On 26 March, a Court Martial completed Fleener's trial. It convicted him of unlawful possession of at least 559 pounds of opium and of other specifications related to transporting and introducing drugs into a military installation. The Court sentenced him to total forfeiture of all benefits and confinement at hard labor for sixteen years. The Seventh Air Force approved both the Court's findings and the sentence on 31 May 1970. On 19 February 1971, the Court of Military Review affirmed the conviction but, in light of Fleener's previously outstanding record, reduced the sentence to twelve years.

Fleener appealed to the Court of Military Appeals on the theory that the search of his person by the OSI was illegal because the search authorization only provided for the search of his BOQ room. The opium was found in his room, but the OSI had found other incriminating evidence, such as currency, on his person. He won that appeal in 1972.[6]

---

6 Court-Martial Reports, Holdings and Decisions of the Courts of Military Review and United States Court of Military Appeal, Volume 44, 1971-1972, The Lawyers Co-operative Publishing Company, Rochester, New York, 1973, pp. 228-236, United States, Appellee v. Delbert W. Fleener, Major, U.S. Air Force, Appellant, 21 USCMA 174, 44CMR 228, 18 February 1972. The appeal apparently reduced the sentence further, although the author has not found the final result.

New Red Markers 1970

Lt Col Bob Daugherty 01
Major Jack Koppin 01
Major Joe Massa 02
Captain Jeff Peacock 11
Captain Jim Simpson 13
1Lt Terry Gruters 14
1Lt Jim Hix 15
1Lt Mike Rodriguez 17
1Lt Hugh Hill 18
2Lt Skip Pardee
1Lt Phil Lumpkin
1Lt Chad Swedberg 25
1Lt Yancy Hudson 12
1Lt Sid Conley 13
Captain Don Ward 14
Captain Billy Barrett 15
1Lt Crawford Deems 16
1Lt D Beckingham 18
1Lt Pete Stetson 25
1Lt J Cosgrave 12
1Lt Paul Williams 27
A1C Jim Hoppe
A1C Barry Silfies
Thomas Still
A1C Cary Strickbine
Joe Jergens
Sgt Al Ramirez
A1C Don Avery
A1C Steve Figuli
Airman Jeff Froh
Sgt Charles Gussman
Sgt Jerry Justice
Sgt Dennis Hull
Staff Sgt Larry Lamb
Sgt Dave Marion
A1C John Wetzler
A1C Mike Possemato
A1C Richard Ruel
Staff Sgt Miles Tyson
A1C Steve Volz
Staff Sgt Warren Wiley
Sgt Jim Yeonopolus
Sgt John Wilkins

New Quarters At Phuoc Vinh

The Red Markers at Phouc Vinh outgrew their quarters in early 1970, and the Army assigned new barracks for the unit. Prior to occupying the new quarters, the Red Markers began improving the facilities.

The quarters assigned were two open-bay, screened hootches standing about 20 feet apart. The first priority was to construct a partially underground bunker between the two for protection during mortar and rocket attacks. When the ground proved too hard to excavate by Airborne troopers under Sergeant Luong's direction, Lieutenant Willis, the Red Marker designated scrounge officer, paid an Army backhoe operator a fifth of Jim Beam to do the job. The Airborne detail filled sand bags with the excavated soil and used them to build bunker walls and to cover the PSP roof.

With safety concerns satisfied, the Red Markers turned their attention to personal comfort. Sergeant Luong requisitioned two Airborne deuce-and-a-half trucks to meet Willis at Tan Son Nhut for a shopping trip. The trucks and Willis's jeep drove to the supply depot at Long Binh. They loaded two pallets of ¾ inch plywood and two bundles of 4 x 4s. Willis had requisitioned the material for construction of revetments around the hootches. It would be put to other use, since a wall of sand bags already provided adequate protection. The convoy next drove to the storage yard of Pacific Architects & Engineers. PA&E was a contracting firm, which built and maintained virtually all the facilities at the main bases and the larger FOLs. They constructed everything from runways to office buildings. The storage yard was full of discarded and reclaimed building material. The guard at the gate said, "You can take anything you find except the prefabbed roof frames. Everything else is surplus." The Red Marker scavengers filled a truck with wiring, lumber, electrical outlets and other supplies. The convoy drove the 45 miles to Phouc Vinh that afternoon.

Major Schwalb made a discovery that contributed to the improvements being built. The Phouc Vinh garbage dump contained numerous broken bags of ready mix cement and a bundle of corrugated tin. The tin bundle had been dropped in handling, bending one corner of the material a couple of inches. Otherwise, the tin sheets were perfectly serviceable. The ripped cement bags probably were also damaged in shipping, but most of the contents were still dry. The Red Markers made several trips with their jeeps and utility trailers and seized the lot. With all this material, they built a roofed patio bar in front of the bunker between the hootches—complete with a concrete floor. Later dubbed the "C'est La Vie Bar," it became the after work gathering place for Red Markers and some of the Red Hats as well.

The construction volunteers also built small individual rooms in the officer hootch. Additionally, they created one large room at an end of the hootch with plywood walls and ceilings. They insulated this room with Styrofoam boxes used to ship WP rockets and installed the treasured air conditioner. This sealed off area became a lounge and an operations planning room—when the air conditioner worked. Wiring the hootch to provide power and light to each bedroom cubicle was a major challenge. The original power supply—two hot wires and one neutral—ran under the rafters down the center of the building. Willis cut off the power and tapped into this supply, putting a light fixture and an outlet in each room and additional outlets in the air-conditioned space. When everything powered up, the

Major Jerry Schwalb at Phuoc Vinh "C'est La Vie Bar" with Larry Lamb, Rich Ruel and Warren Wiley. Don Avery Collection

complex drew so much electricity that the Army had to increase the feed to the hootch to prevent browning out other users in the area.[7]

Captain James M. Simpson recalls that, late in 1970, a few cockroaches were seen scurrying under the refrigerator in the air-conditioned retreat. Someone produced a can of insect spray and, after properly marking the target, rolled in hot. After one pass with the spray, a swarm of roaches fled the nest, making it impossible for the rest of the night to walk across the floor without crunching some bugs.

In early 1970, 2nd Lieutenant Stuart F. "Skip" Pardee joined the Red Markers. He was only the second FAC to make it from commissioning to assignment with the Red Markers prior to being promoted to 1st Lieutenant. In March, Skip transferred from the Red Markers and the Bird Dog to OV-10s. The Air Force had determined that pilots taller than 6' 2" should not fly the O-1. Above that height, a pilot could not easily get out of the cabin if he needed to bail out. Pardee, who was taller than the magic height, completed his tour as a Covey FAC. He nonetheless managed to return to Phouc Vinh under the guise of needing to refuel, just so he could show the Bird Dog FACs what a real war plane looked like!

The Fishhook, Cambodia

On 1 May 1970, the 3rd Airborne Brigade and the Red Markers participated in the invasion of the Fishhook region of Cambodia to destroy NVA basecamps. At dawn, two C-130s each dropped a 15,000 lb. Commando Vault bomb to blast out clearings in the Cambodian jungle.[8] At

---

[7] Inadvertently bounce a check and all Hell breaks loose. Brown out several buildings with unauthorized electrical installations, no problem.

[8] Commando Vault bombs had a length of pipe attached to the nose, extending the detonator so they would explode above ground level. They were designed to blow down enough trees to create a place for helicopter insertion of troops.

Lt Skip Pardee gloating over his transfer to OV-10s. Willis Collection.

the same time, Red Marker Lieutenants Byron L. Mayberry and David G. Blair took off from Quan Loi and crossed the border between Binh Long Province and Cambodia. The two O-1 FACs met pre-arranged flights of fighters on location and began directing bombardment of tree lines around the clearings. About an hour later, the first helicopters carrying Airborne troopers began to hover into the LZs beginning the invasion.

The Red Marker Bird Dogs had relocated for this operation from Phouc Vinh to Quan Loi, about 25 miles northwest.[9] With two days notice, aircraft maintenance crews, radio technicians and operators, assisted by Sergeant Luong and Corporal Phuong, packed up enough gear to support their missions and headed overland to Quan Loi. The Red Marker enlisted men included crew chiefs Jim Hoppe and Jim Stokes, and radio operators Walter Stepaniak, Ron Wessel, and Jim Yeonopolus.

Quan Loi was a good location for the operation. It was closer to the border than Phouc Vinh, thereby reducing flight time

Sergeant Jim Stokes at Song Be. Willis Collection.

Lts Dave Blair and Byron Mayberry, Sergeant Luong at Phouc Vinh. Willis Collection.

---

9 Other detachments of Red Marker O-1s were operating at Song Be, and O-2s were at Tay Ninh and Saigon at this time.

CHAPTER 12 - 1970 - MAJOR BOB DRAWBAUGH, LT COL ROBERT DAUGHERTY, MAJOR JACK KOPPIN

Commando Vault LZ and a natural clearing used as LZ East, also known as LZ Scout. Willis Collection.

to and from the AO and increasing available time on station. Quan Loi also had a controlled, lighted runway with a VASI system.[10] On the occasions that FACs stretched missions into the evening hours, the lights were a welcome improvement over the smudge pots at Phouc Vinh.

Quan Loi was also important from the standpoint of command and control. General Robert M. Shoemaker, deputy commander of the 1st Air Cavalry Division, headed the combined forces, named Task Force Shoemaker. He established his headquarters in the TOC at Quan Loi. The Task Force included elements of 1st Air Cavalry Division, the 11th Armored Cavalry Regiment (ACR) and the 3rd Brigade of the Vietnamese Airborne Division. Locating the command elements of all these forces at Quan Loi simplified communications.

The ground operation was straightforward. The 11th ACR attacked across the southern border of the Fishhook. The 3rd Brigade of the 1st Air Cav crossed the border on the left flank of the Armored Cav. North of these units, the 3rd Brigade of the Vietnamese Airborne Division air assaulted into two landing zones about six kilometers from the southern border. On day two of the operation, the 11th ACR linked up with the Airborne, passed through their positions and headed north toward the Cambodian town of Snoul. On day three, the 2nd Brigade of the Air Cav air assaulted into a blocking position south of Snoul. The objective of the operation was to uncover and destroy the supplies at known base camps in the border area and to cut off and destroy any troops attempting to defend the camps.

---

10 Visual Approach Slope Indicator – a set of lights that show a pilot on approach that the aircraft is above, below, or on the correct glide slope for a landing.

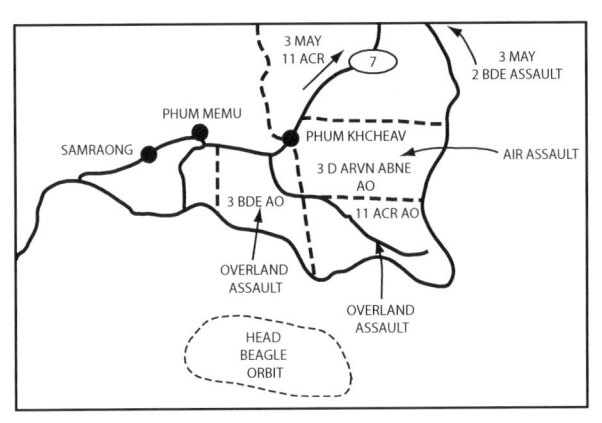

Fishhook Areas of Operation during the Cambodian Incursion, from Project CHECO Report.

The Air Plan

Lt. Colonel Robert G. "Doc" Daugherty, Jr., Air Liaison Officer for the 1st Air Cavalry Division, call sign Rash 01, served as Task Force ALO. On 26 April, the operations office at 7th Air Force notified Doc to fly to headquarters the next morning without telling anyone where he was going.[11] Headquarters briefed Doc on the incursion and instructed him to create a plan to control the TACAIR for the operation. However, they instructed him not to reveal the plan to anyone. The need for secrecy created some interesting confrontations as he drew up a plan and began to assemble the assets needed to execute it. Officers around Bien Hoa wondered why and under what authority he was relocating aircraft, FACs, radio equipment and other personnel.

Daugherty's plan created three AOs for the FAC units covering each ground force. The Rash FACs flying OV-10s from Quan Loi supported the 1st Air Cav. Nile FACs flying O-2s from Bien Hoa (because the field at Quan Loi was too rough for their use) covered the 11th Armored Cav. Red Markers covered the Vietnamese Airborne with the O-1Es moved to Quan Loi for that purpose. Rash FACs had previously located a TACP at Quan Loi, and Red Marker and Nile TACPs moved in alongside. Daugherty then established Rash ADVON as the overall air supervisor as an umbrella to the TACPs. Rash ADVON consolidated and forwarded to III DASC calls for immediate airstrikes and other communications from the TACPs.

With numerous sorties to be concentrated in a small area during the campaign, Daugherty established an airborne traffic coordinator and three rendezvous points for fighters at radials off the Bien Hoa TACAN.[12] Point Alpha was near Katum, south of the Fishhook at 320°/55 miles from Bien Hoa; Point Bravo was near Loc Ninh east of the Fishhook at 335°/55 miles; and Point Charlie was at 326°/56 miles near Fort Defiance, also south of the Fishhook. A dual piloted O-2A with the call sign "Head Beagle" performed the airborne traffic coordination. Sleepytime FACs who normally flew night watch over Saigon piloted the Head Beagle in an orbit south of the Fishhook at 8,000 feet.[13] Riding with the FACs were O-2 and OV-10 instructor pilots from the 19th TASS with copies of the day's Frag Orders. Enroute to one of the three rendevous points, each fighter aircraft contacted Head Beagle for instructions. If the assigned FAC was ready for the fighters, Head Beagle released the flight to the Fragged target. If the FAC was not ready or if the weather was adverse, Head Beagle might hold a flight at the rendezvous point. If there was a request for immediate air support in another area, Head Beagle could divert the fighters to a different target. The O-2 and OV-10 instructors who handled all these communications were, at the outset, not pleased about their desig-

---

11 Colonel Robert G. Daugherty, USAF (Ret), telephone interview, 12 Feb 2011.

12 Tactical Air Navigation system used by all fighter aircraft.

13 Head Beagle orbit from Project CHECO map (Contemporary Historical Examination of Current Operations).

nated role because they were passengers and traffic controllers rather than being "in on the action." After the first day, however, they recognized the importance of the position.[14] They were the focal point for allocating TACAIR in response to weather and conditions on the ground. The job was both demanding and critical to the success of the operation.

One part of the planning involved expected anti-aircraft fire. On the night of 30 April, Major Drawbaugh gave the Red Markers several typed pages listing the locations of more than 100 suspected anti-aircraft sites. The FACs conscientiously plotted the coordinates on their maps, marking each with a "donut," a small circle with a dot in the center. The VC and NVA often created field emplacements for anti-aircraft weapons by digging a circular trench around a center hub that was left at ground level. The view from the air resembled a donut. The weapons crew placed the tripod of the weapon on the center of the donut. Standing in the trench, the gunner could aim and fire upward in any direction by circling in the trench. When the FACs finished plotting all the sites, the border between Cambodia and Vietnam was gray with pencil marks. Thankfully, the defensive fire never materialized. Either the intelligence on these locations was outdated, the NVA were truly surprised, or despite the attempt at security, the NVA knew about the operation.

The First Day

Operations began in the predawn hours of 1 May 1970 with indirect fire support followed by air and ground assaults on the various objectives.[15] The Airborne Division's timetable was as follows:

- From 0410 to 0545, six B-52 Arc Light missions each dropped an estimated 80 tons of high explosives into the target area.[16]
- At 0600, allied artillery took over the indirect fire mission, pounding the proposed landing zones for the 3rd Brigade of the Airborne Division.
- At 0630, two C-130s each dropped a Commando Vault 15,000 lb. bomb at locations about six kilometers north of the border to create landing zones, designated LZ East and LZ Center, for the 3rd Brigade.
- At the same time, David Blair and Byron Mayberry took off from Quan Loi. Each arrived at one of the LZ locations before the first fighter-bombers checked in at 0700. For the next hour, Blair and Mayberry directed attacks into the tree line around their respective LZs to suppress any activity in the area prior to the helicopter insertion of troops.
- At 0810, the 1st Battalion, 3rd Vietnamese Airborne Brigade, combat assaulted into LZ East. The Battalion opted to use a natural clearing for its LZ rather than the Commando Vault space blasted out of the forest.
- At 0830, Red Markers Captain Simpson and Lieutenant Willis took off from Quan Loi to direct more strikes. They arrived in the AO before Blair and Mayberry departed, providing constant aerial presence above the Airborne.
- At 1005, the 5th and 9th Battalions, 3rd Airborne Brigade, combat assaulted into LZ Center.
- At 1030, Lieutenant Terence J. Gruters and another FAC, possibly Lieutenant Luis M. "Mike" Rodriquez, took off shortly

---

14 Daugherty interview.
15 Keith William Nolan, Into Cambodia, Spring Campaign, Summer Offensive, 1970, Presidio Press, Novato, CA, 1990, p. 101.
16 Arc Light missions usually involved a flight of three B-52s. Part of the venerable B-52 fleet was modified in the mid-1960s to carry 108 Mk-82 500 lb. conventional bombs internally and on under-wing pylons (54,000 lbs. or 27 tons of payload per aircraft). The ordnance was dropped from 30,000 feet so that the aircraft were neither seen nor heard by enemy personnel in the target area.

after Blair and Mayberry landed at Quan Loi.

The FAC rotation continued throughout the day. The first two pairs of FACs each flew three sorties and the others flew two each. The FACs controlled a couple of airstrikes on each sortie. Some of the strikes were preplanned, but most were in response to requests from Airborne troops in contact. Due to the pace of the activity on the first day, FACs deferred collecting Bomb Damage Assessment (BDA) after each strike. Instead, the FACs acquired BDA of the early targets during the next several days through aerial surveillance or from the ground sweeps by the Airborne. Later, the Red Markers reported the accumulated BDA to the appropriate fighter squadron.

In addition to the Red Marker's move to Quan Loi, Major Drawbaugh redeployed other personnel to support the Cambodian operation. The 1st Airborne Brigade had been operating near Song Be. It moved south near the Fishhook as a reserve for the cross-border operation. Drawbaugh moved the FACs covering the brigade, Lieutenants James H. Hix, Jr. and Chad L. Swedberg, from Song Be to Special Forces camps as Air Liaison Officers for the 1st Brigade TOCs. Hix went to Tonle Cham, a few miles southeast of the Fishhook. He was airlifted in via a C-130 to a grass strip outside the camp with a MRC-108 jeep and two radio operators, Sergeants Dennis Hull and Mike Possemato. They were quickly directed inside the berm and warned of snipers in the area. Hull climbed a forty-foot tower to mount their FM antenna. As he descended, he saw in incoming mortar round. Hull believes he set a speed record getting down that tower. Lieutenant Swedberg went to Katum, south of the Fishhook, with Airman First Class Steve Volz.

The radio operators stayed busy following the radio traffic, but both of the young pilots were bored out of their minds as other Red Marker FACs flew the missions into Cambodia.

Several days into the operation, the multiple flights per day began to take a predictable toll on the O-1 pilots. In one incident, Lieutenant Willis taxied into a runway marker on his third mission of the day, bending a prop and taking aircraft #622 out of action for a day.[17]

Drawbaugh reinforced the FACs by getting emergency approval to fly O-2s out of Phouc Vinh. He ordered some O-2 aircraft and FACs from Tan Son Nhut to pick up part of the load. These extra forces eliminated the need for three sorties per day from any of the pilots. Lieutenants Larry Shaevitz and Lloyd Prevett moved into Phouc Vinh and the luxurious C'est La Vie Bar. Prevett had taken over the O-2A Tactics IP job from Dave Langas when Dave rotated home. Following these redeployments, the Red Marker radio controllers were operating from six locations: Tan Son Nhut, Tay Ninh, Phouc Vinh, Quan Loi, Tomle Chan and Katum. FACs flew from the first four.

On 4 May, Lieutenant Willis found a major base camp. A number of large, tin-roofed buildings, barely visible below the triple canopy jungle, nestled under the trees on a low ridge. They were well hidden from directly overhead, but the slight elevation of the ridgeline allowed an angled view of the structures under the trees. A narrow stream ran parallel to the east side of the ridge, with a cleared, formerly cultivated

---

[17] Records indicate this aircraft wound up in the service of the Khmer Air Force, per Dr. Joe F. Leeker, "Khmer Air Force O-1s," O-1D tail number 622 believed to be 56-2622, had electrical problems repaired at Pochentong in June 1974, from Air America's Phnom Penh Station report.

CHAPTER 12 - 1970 - MAJOR BOB DRAWBAUGH, LT COL ROBERT DAUGHERTY, MAJOR JACK KOPPIN

Lt Chad Swedberg. Willis Collection.

Dinged Propeller on 622. Willis Collection.

area close to the stream. Willis was flying above that cleared area when he saw trails leading from the field onto the hill and first spotted the structures. It was clearly a large base camp, possibly the temporary home of the NVA unit that had been engaging the Airborne for the past several days. Willis was near the end of his time on station. He reported the find to Red Marker Control and headed to Quan Loi for fuel and rockets.

On his next sortie, Willis headed for the coordinates of a preplanned strike, but the weather had deteriorated. Rain pounded the scheduled target, and a lowering overcast covered much of the AO. However, there was a hole in the overcast near the base camp. When the fighters checked in at their scheduled rendezvous and confirmed a complete overcast in the target area, Willis gave them a general heading to the break in the overcast where he was orbiting. Within minutes they were able to put the first bombs onto what the Red Markers began to call Base Camp Willis.[18] As he finished the first strike, Control asked if Red Marker 18 had targets for any additional fighters. Throughout the region, the weather was so bad that missions were being cancelled. Head Beagle began stacking up fighters at the rendezvous points or directing them to jettison ordnance and return to base. Willis replied that Control could send every spare flight of fighters. Red Marker Control passed on the location of the base camp to Head Beagle. The radio crackled as one diverted flight after another came up on Willis's frequency looking for the hole in the clouds.

"Red Marker One Eight, this is Devil Eight

---

18 Project CHECO, Cambodian Incursion, Figures 3 and 4, prior intelligence had identified the general location of the basecamps in the Fishhook. The FACs were not told this information. The camp spotted by Willis had been designated 352, which along with 353 contained 12 camps, 3 hospitals, a storage area, a POW camp and almost 7,000 troops.

One, two F-100s with 12 Mark 82s, 4 Nape and 20 mike-mike. Have you in sight."

"Devil One Eight, copy. Two F-100s, 12 Mark 82s, 4 Nape, 20 mike-mike.[19] Target is a base camp in the trees west of my position. Nearest friendlies are five klicks south.[20] Attack heading one-niner-zero with a left break. Let's drop the bombs in pairs on three passes and then hold before we drop the Nape. I'm going in to mark the target now."

"Roger, Red Marker. One-niner-zero and break left. We'll drop in pairs and hold. I see your smoke. Devil Eight One lead rolling in. Two, get your spacing."

"Lead, I have you rolling in. Hit my smoke. You are cleared in hot."

And so it went for the next two hours. As one flight completed its mission, the next would be shuttled to the base camp by the Head Beagle controllers with instructions to monitor the strike frequency and orbit nearby, ready to check in. Within three hours, three more flights had hit the target with a variety of payloads before Willis had to call a halt and head back to Quan Loi for more avgas and smoke rockets.

Willis headed out for a third mission at about 1700, with weather conditions in the AO the same as midday, with the same remarkable break in the overcast above Base Camp Willis. He was able to put in four more strikes on the target before the lowering overcast and nightfall put an end to the day's action. In between Willis's sorties and in subsequent days, David Blair, Terry Gruters and others directed other strikes into the same area,

Sergeant Dennis Hull. Jim Hoppe Collection.

Katum Operations Office. Chad Swedberg Collection. Below – Sergeant Jim Yeonopolus at Quan Loi, Lt Byron Mayberry in the background. Jim Yeonopolus Collection.

---

19 Mark 82s (Mk-82), 500 lb. high explosive bombs. If equipped with high-drag fins to retard the bomb's trajectory and allow lower level release altitudes, it was called "Snake." Mark 117s (Mk-117) were 750 lb. bombs. Nape was napalm – jellied gasoline. "20 mike-mike" was 20 mm cannon, usually with high explosive rounds.

20 Klicks is short for kilometers.

adding to the destruction.[21] From the Airborne's later ground reports, the BDA from the combined strikes amounted to twenty-two structures and twelve bunkers, one 2½-ton truck, 6,000 lbs. of rice, several bicycles and a stack of tires destroyed.

After several days of operation, the various ground units had occupied their respective AOs and began to systematically search the base camps and weapons caches. At that point, the Head Beagle operation was discontinued, and Rash ADVON was closed down. The individual Rash, Nile and Red Marker TACPs resumed direct communication with III DASC for immediate air requests. The DASC, however, maintained the three rendezvous points for the duration of the operation to aid in separating the fighter sorties coming into the area.

On 11 May, the Airborne made contact with NVA troops about two klicks northwest of some of the heaviest strikes on the base camp. For the rest of the day, Blair, Mayberry and Willis put in strikes supporting those troopers, finishing the last strike about 1840 and remaining on station until well past dark in case of further enemy attacks. The NVA retreated under cover of darkness, and the Airborne secured the area.

Kent State

The Cambodian Incursion generated student protests on numerous college campuses in the United States. In a tragic occurrence at Kent State University, Ohio National Guardsmen opened fire at a protest on 4 May, killing four students and wounding nine. Kent State closed for the remainder of the semester.[22] Students at other schools held candlelight vigils in memory of the slain. In the following days, other student strikes shut down hundreds of colleges and universities nationwide for shorter periods of time. The killings at Kent State highlighted the division in the nation over the conflict in Vietnam. While the American withdrawal from Vietnam was well underway, the public viewed the cross-border operation into Cambodia as a widening of the war. The Nixon administration and the military viewed it as an appropriate short-term operation that would deny needed supplies to the VC and NVA. If the operation were successful, the withdrawal of forces could be completed with less danger of attack. The protests over the incursion and the killings at Kent State put a bloody exclamation point on the deep social divisions generated by the war in Vietnam.

Medal of Honor

On 24 May, the NVA shot down a MedEvac helicopter attempting to extract wounded troopers from a fierce action northeast of Katum. The Airborne controlled only one side of the clearing, subsequently known as "MedEvac Meadow." Mayberry, Blair, Gruters and Willis, directed strikes on the other three sides of the meadow to try to enable another chopper to land. The enemy, however, did not withdraw.

Late in the day, Red Hat Sergeant First Class Louis R. Rocco volunteered to accompany another medical evacuation team to extract the wounded.[23] As his helicopter came in for landing, it became the

---

21 Lt David Blair identified an extension of this base camp one klick to the northwest that the Red Markers called the Blair Annex.

22 Jerry M. Lewis and Thomas R. Hensley, "The May 4 Shootings at Kent State University: The Search for Historical Accuracy," The Ohio Council for The Social Studies Review, Vol. 34, Number 1 (Summer 1998), pp. 9-21.

23 From the Citation to accompany the Congressional Medal of Honor awarded to Warrant Officer (then Sergeant First Class) Louis Richard Rocco.

target for intense enemy automatic weapons fire. Manning the door gun, Rocco returned fire as the helicopter continued to attempt a landing. The aircraft was so badly damaged it crashed in flames. Rocco suffered a broken hip and wrist, a badly bruised back and burns. Disregarding his injuries, he pulled the other injured survivors from the burning wreckage. He carried each unconscious man to the Airborne perimeter, making multiple trips across 20 meters of exposed terrain to and from the burning chopper.

Once inside the friendly position, Sergeant Rocco administered first aid to his wounded comrades until he collapsed and lost consciousness. His brave acts were directly responsible for saving three of his fellow soldiers from certain death. All the wounded, including Sergeant Rocco, spent the night in the field. A helicopter brought them out the next morning. Sergeant Rocco was awarded the Medal of Honor for his actions on that day.

Red Marker radio operator Sergeant Jim Yeonopolus remembers that the firefight became very hectic about 1500, when the FACs called up additional airstrikes to support the troops on the ground. As it began to get dark, the fighting became more intense. At that point, Red Hat Sergeants Rocco, Brubaker and James H. Collier asked Yeonopolus if he would accompany them in a helicopter and stay on the ground in case they needed him to call in air support overnight. Jim correctly told them he could do more good with his radios at his location in the TOC. Had he gone, Jim might not have survived the trip.

Continued Action

Meanwhile, Lieutenants Hix and Swedberg remained with their radio operators

Katum. Swedberg Collection.

at Tonle Cham and Katum, where they suffered mortar attacks and occasional probing ground attacks. Sergeants Dennis Hull and Mike Possemato shared a Conex[24] container for sleeping quarters at Tonle Cham. They had reinforced the steel container with sandbags around the outside walls and 55-gallon drums on the roof. The theory was that the 55-gallon drums would trigger an incoming mortar round before it penetrated the Conex, similar to the culvert roofs on the bunkers at Song Be. One night during a particularly heavy barrage, a mortar round exploded right outside the Conex. The blast blew the heavy doors open and filled the Conex with shrapnel and dust. Sergeant Hull crept over and closed the door. He kept his M-16 at the ready, concerned that the NVA might follow the mortars with a ground attack. During a lull in the shelling, Lieutenant Hix went from his bunker to the Conex to see if the sergeants were safe. As Hix opened the door to the Con-

---

24 A standard shipping container in 1970 was an 8-foot steel cube with full opening double doors at one side. They could be padlocked from the outside. They were used at FOLs for secure storage of items such as PE gear (flying helmets, survival vests, parachutes). If a spare Conex was sitting around unused, it would be drafted into service as living quarters or buried in the ground as a bunker.

ex, Hull paused just long enough before opening fire that he did not shoot the Red Marker.

Hix escaped injury on that date, but was wounded in a later mortar attack by an embarrassingly small piece of shrapnel. It was embarrassing because the Red Hats with him put in the paperwork for a Purple Heart. (The same thing had happened to Byron Mayberry at Song Be.)

Hix eventually rotated from Tonle Chan to Quan Loi and flew missions into Cambodia. Lieutenant Yancy D. Hudson, Red Marker 12, replaced him at Tonle Chan. During NVA probing attacks, Hudson positioned himself on the berm surrounding the camp, directing Spooky gunships, helicopters and fighters. Hudson was also wounded during his time at Tonle Cham and rotated from the camp, but no one replaced him. By mid June, Hull and Possemato had transferred from Tonle Cham to another FOL.[25]

Willis's personal log for the month of May showed he flew forty-three sorties in twenty-seven days totaling 112 hours of flying time. During those missions, he directed fifty-six airstrikes that dropped ninety tons of high explosives and 144 napalm cans on NVA targets. The strikes destroyed sixty-one structures, eighty-nine bunkers, four tons of rice and one truck. The Airborne sweeps of the area reported twenty-six NVA killed attributable to his air attacks.

The Project CHECO Report on the Cambodian Incursion lists the following among the enemy assets destroyed by airstrikes in the Fishhook: 218 KBA, 1,044 structures, 1,902 bunkers, fourteen trucks, 289 fighting positions, seven bridges, and forty-one tons of rice, plus 207 secondary fires and eighty-four secondary explosions.[26]

Lloyd Prevett recalls being at Phouc Vinh when some of the captured enemy equipment began to arrive. Of particular interest was a ZPU anti-aircraft gun. The weapon traversed and elevated at an impressive speed, giving Lloyd a sobering recognition of his aircraft's vulnerability.

Lloyd also remembers one particularly nasty fight in Cambodia that lasted two days. In that engagement, the Airborne unit was practically surrounded by the NVA as Lloyd directed strike after strike. He used all his smoke rockets and resorted to smoke cans to mark the target for the last airstrike. After flying four hours, another FAC relieved him on station. Refueled and rearmed, Lloyd returned for another four hours. Still the NVA did not break contact. Only after an Arc Light mission the next day, did the NVA retreat.

The Airborne seized numerous crates of small arms from the weapons caches they overran. They awarded Chinese SKS assault rifles as trophies to Major Drawbaugh and to Lieutenants Blair, Mayberry and Willis. The officers were also authorized a trophy weapon from a storehouse of old rusted relics. Willis had been to the warehouse and selected an inoperative, bolt action Mauser. With a second weapon now in his possession, one fresh from the crate still coated in cosmoline, Willis no longer needed the Mauser. He traded it to a supply sergeant at Bien Hoa for a "surplus" O-1E propeller. The Red Marker crew chiefs attached it to the wall in the ALO's office at Tan Son Nhut in remembrance of the prop that had bitten the dust on Willis's O-1 at Quan Loi.

---

25 Major Dennis L. Hull, USAF (Ret), Red Marker Questionnaire, 28 Feb 2011.

26 Project CHECO Report, Cambodian Incursion, Figure 23.

Weapons Seized in Cambodia. Jim Yeonopolus Collection.

After Cambodia

As the Cambodian operation came to a close, Major Drawbaugh prepared to leave for a new assignment with the Raven FACs and the secret war in Laos. Lt. Colonel Robert G. "Doc" Daugherty, Jr. joined the unit as ALO. Daugherty had first served in Vietnam as Sidewinder 01, Air Liaison Officer for the U.S. 1st Division. When the 1st Division rotated back to the States, Daugherty became ALO to the 1st Air Cavalry Division, which led to his planning and command role in the Cambodian Incursion. After the first several days of that operation, TASS Headquarters summoned Daugherty to Bien Hoa. The commander congratulated Doc on putting together and executing a good operation. Doc was escorted to an air-conditioned hootch, given a drink of whiskey and asked if he would like to take over the Red Markers. The TASS explained that the Airborne Commander had complained that the ALO for every other division in the Vietnamese Army held the rank of Lt. Colonel. In contrast, the last several ALOs for the Airborne had been Majors. The Airborne felt slighted by that treatment. It took several more drinks before Doc "volunteered" to transfer from the OV-10s supporting the 1st Air Cav to the Red Markers.

After withdrawing from Cambodia, the Airborne operated from several locations in Tay Ninh Province. They maintained operations from Katum and Tonle Cham and established new TOCs at Thien Ngon, Go Dau Ha and Firebase Bruiser. Red Marker radio operators deployed with them, setting up radios in the TOC and providing the communication link for close air support. The Red Markers moved aircraft and personnel from Phouc Vinh to Tay Ninh West to cover these operations.

In August, all the O-2 FACs and O-2A aircraft in 22nd TASS transferred to 19th TASS. This included several Red Marker planes and FACs. Shaevitz and Peacock appear on the August transfer list. However, Jeff Peacock is listed in error, since he was an O-1 pilot. The order should have named Lloyd Prevett instead. Prevett continued his role as an O-2A Tactics IP. He transferred to the Spat FACs flying missions from Bien Hoa and completing his tour in November. However, he didn't leave Vietnam until early December because the Freedom Bird scheduled to take him home crashed in Alaska enroute to Vietnam. Larry Shaevitz completed his tour in IV Corps in late October or early November.

The transfer of O-2s left the 22nd TASS with all of the Bird Dogs and O-1 FACs that supported Vietnamese ground units in III Corps. The logic for this realignment was twofold. First, as the Americans withdrew from Vietnam, the USAF planned to transfer its O-1s to the VNAF (or other allied forces) under the Military Assistance Program. The Air Force also transferred enough Skymasters to the VNAF to equip one squadron of O-2 FACs, the 118th.

CHAPTER 12 - 1970 - MAJOR BOB DRAWBAUGH, LT COL ROBERT DAUGHERTY, MAJOR JACK KOPPIN

Captain Jim Simpson at Tay Ninh. Simpson Collection.

1 Lt. Byron Mayberry. Simpson Collection.

Sergeants Stepaniak and Metcalf prepare for a practice jump with the Airborne. Stepaniak Collection.

A1C Don Avery, radio operator. Avery Collection.

Building bunkers at Thien Ngon north of Tay Ninh. Yeonopolus Collection.

RED MARKERS

1970 G-3 Staff, Major Truc on the left. Truc Van Tran Collection.

Airman Jeff Froh. Avery Collection.

Lts. Yancy Hudson and Crawford Deems. Avery Collection.

Ground-looped O-1 #239. Hoppe Collection.

Sergeant Dennis Hull, Lt. Sid Conley. Hull Collection.

165

However, the U.S. planned to send most O-2s either back to the States, to Korea or to the American "out-country" FAC mission in Thailand. As a practical matter, the O-2s could not operate from rough runways at the FOLs to be operated by the VNAF. The fleet realignment therefore reflected both that operational constraint and the future ownership of the aircraft. Most of the O-2s were to remain at large bases and under USAF control. Most of the O-1s would remain at forward locations and ultimately under VNAF control.

By mid-August, the U.S. 1st Cavalry Division left Tay Ninh. Part of the division returned to the States, while part remained in country. The Cav compound was located on the west side of the runway at Tay Ninh; the ARVN compound was on the east side. To house their increased manpower at Tay Ninh, the Red Markers were assigned a bunker and a hootch on the east, adjacent to the runway but outside the ARVN perimeter. Under the direction of NCOIC Staff Sergeant Larry Lamb, the team demolished the back wall of the hootch and built an expansion that almost doubled the size of the building to accommodate the number of FACs.

In addition, the enterprising enlisted men created a compound surrounded by concertina wire. It had a guard tower acquired from the 1st Air Cav by Staff Sergeant Lamb and A1C Jim Hoppe, who traded some booze for the used tower. The Cav pitched in a .50 caliber machine gun. A sign above the gate to the compound announced "Red Markers, Nam's Finest FACs." The enlisted crew made another sign that they displayed from time to time, depending on who was in the compound. That sign read, "Camp Massa, R & R Center, Tay Ninh." It listed the officers of the camp: Executive Director – Bobby Daugherty; Camp Director – Joey Massa;

Safety Director – Jimmy Hix; Accidents and Claims – Terry Gruters; Athletic Director – Louie Rodriguez; Entertainment – Buzzy Mayberry; and Grounds Keeper – Chip Deems.

Lamb and his troops also attached a lean-to roof to the side of the expanded hootch to shelter a radio jeep and serve as a radio shack, since there was no Airborne TOC at Tay Ninh. Finally, they created a sundeck by adding a floor above the flat roof of the enlisted bunker and erecting a flare parachute for shade. FACs and enlisted men relaxed together off duty with cold beer and card games and a panoramic view of the O-1 revetments next door.

Sundogs and Ravens

Shortly thereafter, the TASS began to increase support for the loyalist Cambodian forces. To that end, they sought FACs with experience flying on the other side of the border. Lieutenants Hix and Swedberg volunteered and became the original Sundog FACs. They flew from Tay Ninh East using their Red Marker call signs notwithstanding that the Sundog TACP controlled their missions. The Lieutenants' participation in the Sundog program was short lived, however. It ended when the TASS formed a new O-2 unit that took over, using the Sundog call sign. Hix and Swedberg flew a few more visual recon missions for the Sundogs. They were instructed to stay close to the border. Hix, nevertheless, went all the way to Phnom Penh.

In September, Hix and Swedberg transferred from the Red Markers to the Raven FACs in Laos. The two lieutenants had been in the same class at the Air Force Academy and had gone to pilot training together. Both were assigned to O-1s at the end of pilot training. They joined the

Red Markers within a month of each other. Given this history, going to the Ravens at the same time seemed natural. Swedberg was motivated by the secrecy of the program and a desire for something more exciting. The men were also under the impression they would be in line for better follow-on assignments, which did not turn out to be the case. As a Raven, Hix was shot down over Laos flying a T-28 and was rescued. He refused an award of the Purple Heart because he had already received one for the trivial wound he got at Tonle Cham.

Personnel Changes

As FACs rotated home at the end of their tours—sometimes shortened by two weeks to a month—new pilots replaced them. Major Joseph V. Massa came in as Red Marker 02, replacing Major Jerry Schwalb. Jerry rotated to the States as head of the ROTC unit at Kent State University, where a new building was needed to replace the wooden structure burned during demonstrations. Lieutenant Dave Blair and newly-promoted Captain Gary Willis both went home in early July. Blair returned for another tour in SEA, flying F-4C missions over North Vietnam with the Night Owls. Captain Jim Simpson went back to the States in October.

A dozen new FACs joined the unit during 1970 including Lieutenant Luis M. "Mike" Rodriguez, Red Marker 17; Lieutenant Yancy D. Hudson, Red Marker 12; and Captain Paul J. "Jeff" Peacock, Red Marker 11. All arrived in time to participate in the Cambodian Incursion. In July, Lieutenant Hugh T. Hill transferred from IV Corps, where he had been a Spat FAC. He served one month as Red Marker 18. FACs assigned later in the year included Captain Donald R. Ward, Red Marker 14; Captain Billy R. Barrett, Red Marker

Lt Col Doc Daugherty presents 'Airman of the Month Award' to A1C Jim Hoppe in June 1970. Hoppe Collection.

Tay Ninh Compound guard tower. Jim Hoppe Collection.

15; Lieutenant Crawford R. Deems, Red Marker 16; Lieutenant D. C. Beckingham, Red Marker 18; Lieutenant Peter W. Stetson, Red Marker 25; Lieutenant James B. Cosgrave, Red Marker 12; Lieutenant Sidney E. Conley, Red Marker 13; and Lieutenant Paul E. Williams, Red Marker 27. Williams transferred to the Ravens after about six months with the Red Markers.

During the next several months, Doc Daugherty got to know his young cadre of FACs. He flew in the back seat with each on at least one mission. After one such sortie, Terry Gruters, a young but veteran FAC, ground looped the Bird Dog. The accident was violent enough that the fuselage bent and the skin split. Luckily, there were no injuries other than Terry's ego. Terry rotated home in November. His brother Guy was a POW, and one of Terry's wishes was to come back in B-52s so that he could carry the fight to North Vietnam. He got his wish, flying over the north during Linebacker II. On one mission, after being hit by a SAM, he helped get the crippled aircraft to friendly territory, where the entire crew bailed out safely.

Late in 1970, headquarters issued a directive requiring that all pilots wear fire-retardant Nomex flight suits. That order ended the Red Marker tradition of dressing for battle like the Airborne it supported. The camouflage fatigues with the distinctive insignia were thereafter worn only on the ground. Red Marker Lieutenants Conley and Deems took on the monikers Neil and Norman Nomex in laughing protest of the new policy. Nomex suits were considerably warmer than the relatively thin fatigue uniforms. After a mission, Doc Daugherty would strip off his sweat-drenched Nomex almost before he got back to the officer hootch. Leaving the flight suit in the hootch, he would climb to the sundeck in his boxer shorts for a beer.

Radio Operations

The ALO assigned two radio operators to each remote location. The ROs manned the radios from sunrise to sunset, or longer if needed. Each usually worked the radios for six or seven hours. They alternated the duty of opening and closing the shop. Periodically, the Red Marker generator man would visit each FOL to perform preventive maintenance. During Jim Yeonopolus's tour, Sergeant Billy Johnson served in that position. Jim usually drew duty at remote locations exposed to mortar fire or ground attacks. To entice Billy to come to these locations, Jim kept on hand a supply of Cherry and Grape Kool-Aid, Billy's favorite flavors.

Living conditions varied from location to location. At Fire Base Bruiser, Steve Volz and Walter Stepaniak shared quarters that consisted of two cots in a hole in the ground covered with PSP and sand bags. At Katum, the ROs slept in a Conex. At Thien Ngon and Tonle Cham, they slept on cots in the TOC. The operators rotated in and out of locations every three weeks. They served two rotations at a field location, followed by one rotation in Saigon.

Conditions at the FOLs did not suit everyone. A1C Cary Strickbine served as an RO for a few months during 1970. Strickbine came to Vietnam from an assignment at Langley AFB where he did everything "by the book." The relatively loose atmosphere among the Red Markers, the lack of specific training and instruction, and the rustic living conditions did not match his view of a rear echelon job. Cary was probably not alone in these feelings. Despite the loose atmosphere, old hands like Pat Williams and David Janssen got him situated and taught him what he needed to know to become a good combat operator during his short tour of duty. After the death of his father, he went home early and separated from the service under the sole surviving son rule.

A radio operator at each Red Marker FOL started the day by contacting III DASC (Pawnee Target) and Red Marker Control at Saigon on the HF radio. Pawnee Target confirmed flight information on all the pre-planned strikes for the day. As each FAC took off from Tay Ninh, he reported that he was airborne to the Tay Ninh TACP. The FAC remained in contact with Tay Ninh until approaching the AO of one of the remote TOCs. He then reported in to the radio operator at that location and remained in contact until ready to return to Tay Ninh. The RO periodically recorded a position report to track the FAC's location.

When the Airborne made contact with hostile forces, the FAC on station typically requested an immediate airstrike. If there was no FAC in the AO, the Red Hats or the Airborne operations officer usually asked the radio operator to launch a FAC and request an immediate strike. The RO radioed that request to the Tay Ninh FACs and to Pawnee Target with pertinent information: target coordinates, type of target, ordnance requested, weather and location of friendlies. After receiving confirmation of incoming air support, the RO relayed the fighter call sign and flight information to the FAC. The ROs monitored the strike frequency, ready to call for additional help if needed. After the strikes, the operators received after action reports from both the FACs and the troops on the ground, which they passed on to Pawnee Target.

While off duty at the FOLs, the ROs found ways to entertain themselves. On one occasion at Song Be, Sergeant Yeonopolus was sitting outside shooting at rats with a BB gun as night began to fall. He caught a glimpse of a man sneaking behind a bunker. Jim called out to him to halt. The man raised his hands over his head as Jim pointed the gun at him. In the gathering dusk, the man evidently believed the gun was a lethal weapon. Jim held him at gunpoint and called for help. Until help arrived, Yeonopolus carefully held the BB gun steady, afraid that any movement would cause the BBs to roll around in the magazine. That telltale rattle would give away the subterfuge. Some soldiers arrived and took the Vietnamese into custody. Under questioning, the captive admitted he was a VC officer who had infiltrated the base to mark off targets for an upcoming mortar attack.[27]

Red Marker Down

On 23 September, Lieutenant Byron Mayberry, Red Marker 19, took off from Tay Ninh with a new FAC in the backseat on an orientation ride that was supposed to include a preplanned airstrike. The weather in the AO was miserable, so Mayberry cancelled the strike and turned for home. On the way back, he smelled the odor of hot oil in the cockpit. Mayberry declared an emergency, gave his coordinates and set the Bird Dog down in a dry lake bed as his oil pressure dropped to zero.[28]

AIC Donald G. Avery was manning the radios at Thien Ngon when Mayberry called. Staff Sergeant Miles E. Tyson, Red Marker RO supervisor was also on duty. Avery

---
27 Drahn Diary, 4 July 1968, the Red Hats acquired several BB guns in 1968. They held quick shot classes teaching instinctive aiming. Pete Drahn was good, hitting a 4" disc in midair. On 24 Jul, he killed a mouse with the BB gun.
28 22 TASS History, Jul – Sep 1970, p. 18.

Sergeant Jerry Justice at Downed Aircraft. Jim Hoppe Collection.

Lt Mayberry and Recovery Crew. Jim Hoppe Collection. Below – 648 Ready for Extraction. Jim Hoppe Collection.

maintained contact with Mayberry while Tyson notified the Red Hats and Airborne duty personnel in the TOC. The Airborne quickly summoned a security team of troopers and a Huey to fly to the downed Bird Dog immediately. Sergeant Jerry Justice and A1C Jim Hoppe, Red Marker crew chiefs, accompanied the security detail to assess the situation and prepare the plane for extraction. Sergeant Justice was an experienced crew chief who had transferred to the Red Markers from IV Corps when the Spat FAC mission was turned over to the VNAF. The Huey flew Mayberry and his backseater to Tay Ninh and returned later for Justice and Hoppe. The Airborne guards remained overnight to protect the plane. Justice and Hoppe returned the next day. They removed the propeller, wings, rudder, elevators and encryption equipment and waited as the plane was lifted out by helicopter.[29] Subsequent investigation determined that the line to the oil pressure gauge had ruptured at a point where it was routed near the exhaust manifold. The TASS modified its preflight inspection program to check the oil line for deterioration in that critical location before every mission.[30]

Winding Down

On 7 November, Lt. Colonel Robert Daugherty rotated home. In his place, Major John A. (Jack) Koppin Jr. became ALO for the Airborne. Jack had previously served as ALO for the Vietnamese 25th Division with the Allen FACs at Tay Ninh.[31]

Near the end of the year, many of the Airborne units returned to Saigon. The Red

---

29 The standard procedure for hoisting the O-1 included removal of the wings to prevent the type of accident described by Ed Fairchild. According to Ed, a Bird Dog being salvaged with the wings still on flew into the transporting helicopter, causing a fatal crash.
30 22 TASS History, Jul – Sep 1970, p. 19.
31 See Attachment to 22 TASS History for Oct-Dec 1970.

RED MARKERS

Red Markers Last Qtr 1970
Lt Col Bob Daugherty 01
Major Jack Koppin 01
Major Joe Massa 02
Captain Jeff Peacock 11
Lt Yancy Hudson 12
Lt J Cosgrave 12
Lt Sid Conley 13
1Lt Terry Gruters 14
Captain Don Ward 14
Captain Billy Barrett 15
1Lt Crawford Deems 16
1Lt Mike Rodriguez 17
1Lt D Beckingham 18
1Lt Byron Mayberry 19
1Lt Pete Stetson 25
1Lt Paul Williams 27
Staff Sgt Bill Mackey*
A1C Jim Hoppe
A1C Barry Silfies
Thomas Still
Joe Jergens
Sgt Al Ramirez
A1C Don Avery
A1C Steve Figuli
Airman Jeff Froh
Sgt Charles Gussman
Sgt Jerry Justice
Sgt Dennis Hull
Staff Sgt Larry Lamb
Terry Hill
Sgt Dave Marion
A1C John Wetzler
A1C Mike Possemato
A1C Richard Ruel
Staff Sgt Miles Tyson
A1C Steve Volz
Staff Sgt Warren Wiley
Sgt Jim Yeonopolus
Sgt John Wilkins
Sgt Tran Dinh Luong
Cpl Phuong

Markers departed Tay Ninh for Tan Son Nhut. By December 1970, the 22nd TASS had nearly completed its Vietnamization mission in III Corps. It had transferred all but two FOLs and TACPs to the VNAF, leaving only Red Marker Control TACP at Tan Son Nhut and Sundog Control TACP at Tay Ninh.[32]

Jack Koppin wound down the Red Marker unit, overseeing the reassignment of FACs, crew chiefs and ROs, as well as the transfer of equipment. Jeff Peacock, for example, remained a Red Marker until December 1970. After that, he served in various capacities through the end of his tour in May 1971. In one assignment, he was Air Liaison Officer for one of the Vietnamese units during Lam Son 719 in February 1971. In another, he flew several night missions in the right seat of Rustic FAC night missions. The Rustics flew from Bien Hoa in support of Royal Khmer ground forces in Cambodia.

After the U.S. forces left Tay Ninh, ARVN forces began dismantling some of the abandoned structures. Jim Yeonopolus and some Red Hats were sent back to Tay Ninh with orders to secure the area and prevent "looting." Presumably, headquarters was concerned that the lumber, tin and PSP would be sold on the black market and either the materials or the profits would find their way into the hands of the VC. Having no viable option to secure the area, the detachment destroyed many structures by placing flares inside and igniting the flares by firing tracer rounds into them. The Red Markers' former compound went up in flames.

---

[32] See 22 TASS History for Oct-Dec 1970. FOLs/TACPs closed during the quarter were Lai Khe, Song Be and Hon Quan, all related to support of the 5th ARVN Division (Bruce Control), Duc Hoa supporting the 25th ARVN Division and the Bien Hoa operation supporting the 18th ARVN Division. Additionally, the stand down of the 11th Armored Cavalry Regiment and the 1st Australian Task Force resulted in closing the Bien Hoa sector operation and the Vung Tau TACP.

CHAPTER 12 - 1970 - MAJOR BOB DRAWBAUGH, LT COL ROBERT DAUGHERTY, MAJOR JACK KOPPIN

Jim Yeonopolus Hwy 1 in Cambodia. Yeonopolus Collection.

Sergeant Terry Elliot. Hoppe Collection.

Dennis Hull. Yeonopolus Collection.

Jim Figuli, Jim Yeonopolus, Dave Marion, Alberto Ramirez. Hoppe Collection.

Staff Sergeant Larry Lamb. Hoppe Collection.

RED MARKERS

Sergeants Jerry Justice and his Dad, WWII. Justice Collection.

Jim Hoppe at Christmas 1970. Yeonopolus Collection.

Major Jack Koppin decorating the Christmas tree on the hootch bar. Yeonopolus Collection.

Fire Base Scout. Swedberg Collection.

173

CHAPTER 12 - 1970 - MAJOR BOB DRAWBAUGH, LT COL ROBERT DAUGHERTY, MAJOR JACK KOPPIN

Bob Drawbaugh and Byron Mayberry v. General Dong and other troopers. Simpson Collection.

Lt. Sid Conley, unidentified crew chiefs. Hoppe Collection.

Major Massa in background, Cpl Phuong, SSgt. Billy Johnson, Lt Hugh Hill. Avery Collection.

O-2 in a ditch after a hot brakes taxiing event. Hoppe Collection.

Lamb, Justice and Hoppe loading 239's wings onto a C-130. Hoppe Collection.

174

The expanded officers' hootch at Tay Ninh with radio shack attached. Near the end of 1970, the Red Markers operated from a radio jeep parked under this shelter rather than a TOC. This photo was taken from the "sun deck" built atop the adjacent enlisted bunker. Avery Collection.

648 at Song Be. Willis Collection.

A1C Mike Possemato and Sergeant Dennis Hull. Hull Collection.

Low-Flying Bird Dog Turns Tiger, Seizes 3 Red Troops

BIEN HOA AB, Vietnam (Special) — First Lt. Byron L. Mayberry, a forward air controller (FAC) with the 22nd Tactical Air Support Sq., recently played cowboy in Cambodia as he rounded up three enemy soldiers and herded them to captivity.

Mayberry received a call from an allied ground commander in the Fishhook area of Cambodia that enemy movement had been spotted near his location. The lieutenant radioed for another flight of fighter-bombers and set out toward the enemy position.

"When I arrived at the area," explained Mayberry, "I spotted a fortified complex and four enemy soldiers running toward a bunker. They must have seen me and had a pretty good idea of what was to come."

The fighter pilots arrived, and the lieutenant directed them against the target.

"After the fighters left," Mayberry said, "I went down as low as I could to check out the area. My engine noise must have frightened the three enemy soldiers hiding in the rubble because they immediately came running into the clearing with their hands up."

At this point the FAC began his rodeo-fashion roundup. Keeping his O1 Bird Dog aircraft at slow speed and as low as possible, he herded the soldiers through the jungle toward the Allied position and a very surprised ground commander.

During the Cambodian Incursion, Lt Byron Mayberry happened to have a "Stars and Stripes" reporter in the back seat on one sortie. The story published from that mission brought Mayberry a lot of good natured grief from the other Red Markers. It also brought some unwanted attention from the TASS Safety Officer for flying dangerously low. Byron had to explain to the authorities that he never went below 1,500 feet ... that the reporter was just exercising poetic license in his description of the flight.

*Major Jack Koppin with his wife, Georgie.
Permission to print by Georgie Koppin.*

SECTION V
RETURN TO ADVISORY STATUS

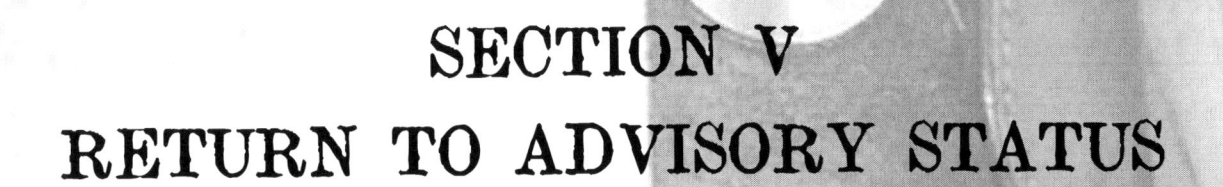

- 1971 - Major Dean Haeusler, Major Chuck Waterman
- 1972 - Major Bob Johnson, Lt Col Jack Bryant

1971–72 AIRBORNE OPERATIONS – EASTER OFFENSIVE

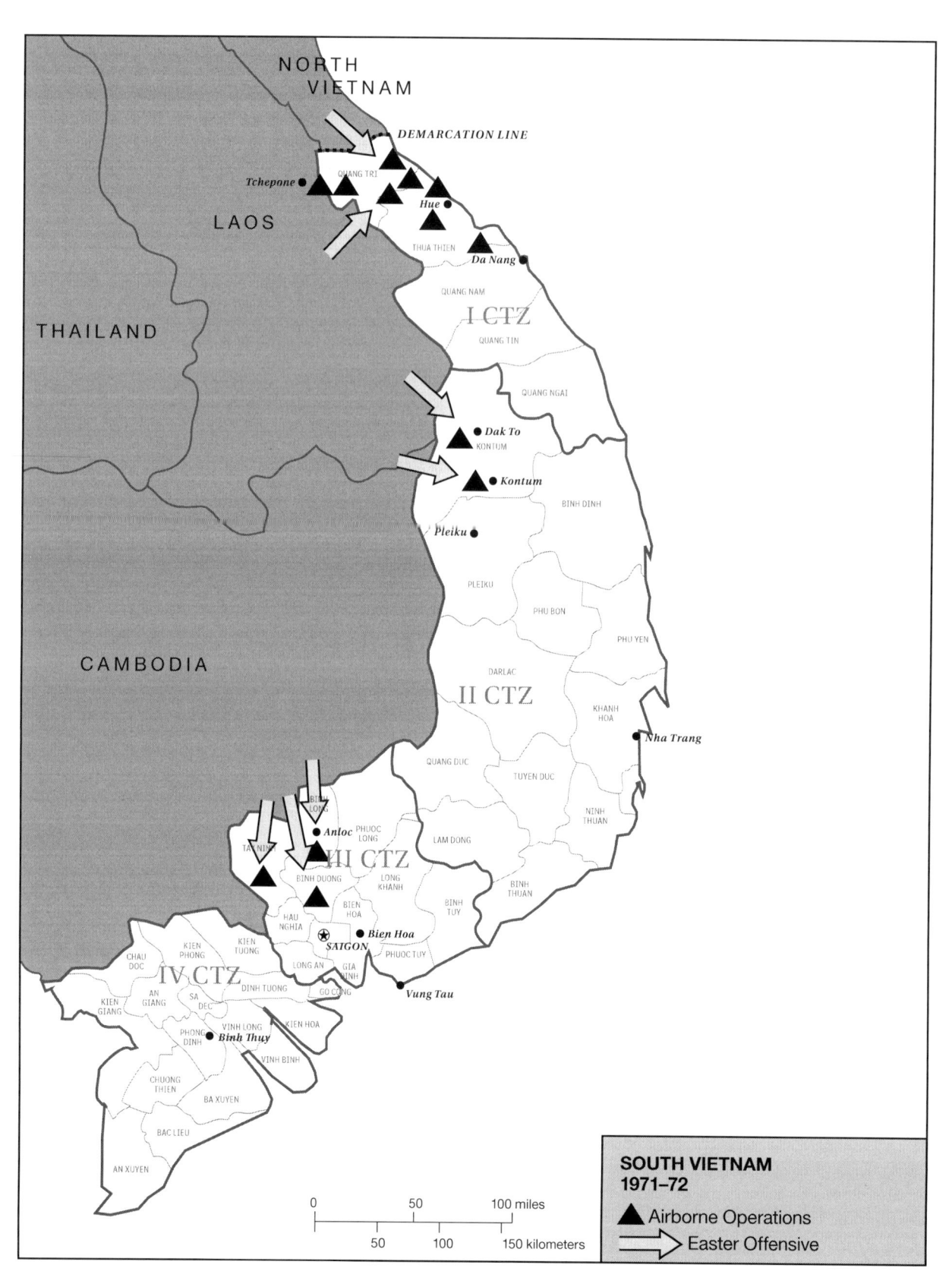

CHAPTER 13

1971 - MAJOR DEAN HAEUSLER
MAJOR CHUCK WATERMAN

Reorganization

On 15 January 1971, 22nd TASS merged the remaining units of its command into 19th TASS. Two weeks later, 19th TASS closed the last two TACPs from the 22nd: Red Marker Control at Tan Son Nhut and Sundog Control at Tay Ninh.[1] As the Red Marker TACP closed its doors, FACs, radio operators and crew chiefs transferred elsewhere. The ALO remained as an advisor. It was almost a return to the status of 1962. The ALO for the Airborne served alone, as Major Gene McCutchan had done nine years earlier. Major Jack Koppin served in that lone position for just a short time before moving to the Rustic FACs. Major Dean Haeusler replaced Koppin as Red Marker ALO in the first quarter of 1971.

In another organizational change, the ALOs assigned to Vietnamese divisions transferred from the TASS to the Air Force Advisory Team (AFAT). This organization fell under the direction of the Air Force Advisory Group (AFGP) rather than 7th Air Force. The Air Force provided one Corps ALO attached to the DASC in each Military Region (MR) plus one Division ALO for each Vietnamese unit.[2] In the

> **New Red Markers 1971**
>
> Major Dean Haeusler 01
> Major Chuck Waterman 01

case of MR 3, the staffing consisted of a Corps ALO and four Division ALOs, one of whom was assigned to the Vietnamese Airborne. This staffing conformed to the planned approach to Vietnamization of the FAC function.

Reassignment

As the Vietnamization process continued, the TASS reassigned many O-1 FACs whose duties were taken over by the VNAF. Those with enough time remaining in their tours upgraded into O-2s or OV-10s. Short timers either flew right seat in O-2s or maintained their status in the O-1.

A surplus of company grade O-1 FACs had existed within the 504th TASG since

---

1 "Sundog 20" based at Bien Hoa was renamed Sundog Control. This TACP took over the Sundog Cambodian mission and remained part of 19th TASS.

2 Military Regions 1, 2, 3 and 4 became the new nomenclature for I, II, III and IV Corps.

179

CHAPTER 13 - 1971 - MAJOR DEAN HAEUSLER & MAJOR CHUCK WATERMAN

1969. As Vietnamization became a reality, many Red Marker Captains and Lieutenants received curtailed or shortene tours. Others, like Bill Barrett, upgraded to the O-2A. He finished his tour in July 1971, flying missions from Saigon into Tay Ninh Province and the adjacent area of Cambodia. Barrett kept his Red Marker 15 callsign but flew under the direction of Sundog Control. In 1972 and 1973, Barrett returned to Southeast Asia for three 90-day TDYs as an aircraft commander flying KC-135s.

Some enlisted personnel also received curtailed tours. However, the 19th TASS continued to need crew chiefs, mechanics and radio operators. A1C Jim Hoppe served his complete tour, leaving in January before the unit shut down. He attended a "disbanding" party in Saigon arranged by Staff Sergeant Larry Lamb and Sergeant Luong for many of the enlisted crew. Sergeant Jerry Justice, a crew chief having experience with both O-1s and O-2As, transferred in February to Bien Hoa for the last thirty days of his scheduled tour. Similarly, A1C Steve Volz, a radio operator whose DEROS was not until May 1971, transferred to the U.S. 1st Air Cavalry Division. A1C Don Avery also finished his tour with the 1st Air Cav at Phouc Vinh.

> **Old Red Markers 1971**
>
> Major Jack Koppin 01
> Major Joe Massa 02
> Jeff Peacock 11
> 1Lt Jim Cosgrave 12
> 1Lt Sid Conley 13
> Captain Don Ward 14
> Captain Billy Barrett 15
> 1Lt Crawford Deems 16
> 1Lt D Beckingham 18
> 1Lt Phil Lumpkin
> 1Lt Pete Stetson 25
> 1Lt Paul Williams 27
> Staff Sgt Larry Lamb
> A1C Jim Hoppe
> A1C Barry Silfies
> Thomas Still
> Joe Jergens
> Sgt Al Ramirez
> A1C Don Avery
> A1C Steve Figuli
> Airman Jeff Froh
> Sgt Charles Gussman
> Sgt Jerry Justice
> Sgt Dennis Hull
> Sgt Dave Marion
> A1C John (M/W)etzler
> A1C Mike Possemato
> A1C Richard Ruel
> Staff Sgt Miles Tyson
> A1C Steve Volz
> Staff Sgt Warren Wiley
> Sgt Jim Yeonopolus
> Sgt John Wilkins
>
> Sgt Tran Dinh Luong
> Cpl Phuong

A1C Richard Ruel finished his tour as a crew chief for a unit flying into Cambodia. He recalls some former Red Marker FACs moved to the unit, but does not remember their names. Radio operator Jim Yeonopolus left the unit in late February, close to his scheduled departure. He came from the field not feeling well. Jim went from his last deployment, a Special Forces "A Camp," to Saigon to gather a few personal belongings enroute to Bien Hoa for out-processing. He noted there was very little activity at the headquarters, however, no one told him, an E-4, much of anything. As it turned out, Jim had contracted a mild form of malaria and was hospitalized at Bien Hoa before he could leave the country. He finally left in the first week of March 1971, having never learned that the Red Markers had shut down. Jim's next assignment was with the 100th Special Reconnaissance Wing at Tucson, Arizona. Part of his duties involved reviewing U-2 aerial photos of parts of III Corps where he had operated as a Red Marker. His task was to identify changes from his time on the ground. He also returned to Southeast Asia for a six month TDY at Utapao, Thailand.

Lam Son 719

In February 1971, the ARVN launched

180

Sergeant Jim Yeonopolus at Special Forces Camp. Yeonopolus Collection.

A1C Steve Volz at the BEQ in Saigon. Yeonopolus Collection.

Operation Delaware, also known as Lam Son 719. The plan was to drive westward on Route 9 from Khe San in MR 1 in order to cut the Ho Chi Minh Trail in Laos near Tchepone. President Nixon prohibited American ground units from participating in this operation. For the first time since American units had deployed to Vietnam, the Vietnamese Army undertook a major offensive without allied ground support. Further, the Airborne went into battle without its Red Marker FAC arm for the first time since 1962.

For the operation, other American and Vietnamese FACs directed close air support from both USAF and VNAF fighter aircraft. The American FACs came from the 20th TASS flying out of Quang Tri, supplemented by personnel and aircraft from the 19th and 21st TASS. The 19th TASS sent eleven FACs with O-2A and OV-10 aircraft and four radio operators with MRC-108 radio jeeps for thirty days.[3] The 21st TASS sent seven FACs and seventeen radio operators with equipment.[4] The VNAF provided a number of FACs from their liaison squadrons.

Unlike the Red Markers, however, none of these FACs was attached to the Airborne unit, and none had a relationship with the Airborne commanders or the Red Hats.

The rationale for excluding American ground forces from this operation was to minimize casualties during the transition period leading up to complete withdrawal of American forces. That concern about losses dictated a minimum flying altitude of 5,000 feet AGL for some of the American FACs due to expected antiaircraft fire. That restriction dated back to an earlier restriction issued by 23rd TASS for slow FAC missions in Laos. However, the Covey FACs

A1C Richard Ruel. Ruel Collection.

---
3 21st TASS History, Jan – Mar 1971. These personnel were sent PCS without PCA which meant no one was entitled to the TDY pay enjoyed by Lt. Rennick back in 1965.

4 21st TASS History, Jan – Mar 1971, p. vii.

from DaNang who supported the operation used 1,500 feet as a minimum.[5] The VNAF operated under no restriction and consequently lost several FACs during the operation. Furthermore, despite the restriction, the USAF lost one O-2 and its crew, Captain Douglas M. Seeley and Lieutenant Stephen R. Scrivener, who were from the 19th TASS.[6]

The Airborne Division was hampered in this operation by a battle plan that required it to maintain security at several firebases, while other Vietnamese units pressed the attack down Route 9 toward Tchepone. Instead of being mobile and aggressive—its principal military strength—the three Airborne brigades were relegated to stationary defense. As a result, they became easy targets for NVA artillery and ground forces. Having no organic FAC organization also impacted the success of the operation. The NVA overran one of the Airborne positions, Firebase 31, capturing the 3rd Brigade commander and his staff. Following that debacle, the Airborne reverted to form and went on the offense. Attacking from their base locations at the suggestion of the new senior advisor, Colonel James Vaught, the remaining battalions wreaked havoc on the NVA and fought their way back into Vietnam. Once the battalions became mobile and went on the attack, they did not lose another piece of major equipment.[7]

Major Charles R. (Chuck) Waterman, Jr. became the new ALO in mid 1971. He had previously served as assistant ALO at II Field Force, arriving there during the first quarter 1971. The principal responsibility of the ALO II FFV was to advise the Commanding General as to the capabilities and availability of tactical airpower. The ALO had supervisory responsibility for the American Air Force personnel at the TACPs supporting Free World Forces.[8] Waterman's new assignment was significantly more front-line.

Mike Anderson served with the U.S. 173rd Airborne Brigade in 1967 and as a Red Hat advisor to the Airborne 6th Battalion in 1970-71. He recalls,

"I left the Viet Nam countryside and places like Dak To behind me years ago, but I will never forget the U.S. and Vietnamese men of all ranks with whom I served. Some did brave deeds and some rose to high positions of authority. Most of us just did our jobs - we watched our buddies' backs as they watched ours. We flew in their helicopters, we called for their artillery rounds, we called for bombs and munitions from their fast movers and gunships, and some of us were extracted from some hell hole and taken to them to stop our bleeding. I'm proud to say that they all, even the ones I've never met, are my brothers and sisters whom I will always love and respect."[9]

Mike's sentiments reflect the views of many who served with the Red Markers as well as the Red Hats.

---

5 Lt. Colonel Anthony V. Lolas, USAF (Ret), Covey FAC during the operation.
6 19th TASS History, Jan – Mar 1971, p. 31, 20th TASS History, Jan – Mar 1971, p. v.
7 See Martin, p. 141.

8 19th TASS History, Jan – Mar 1971, p. 43.
9 Lt. Colonel Mike Anderson, USA (Ret), email Nov 2011.

CHAPTER 14

1972 - MAJOR BOB JOHNSON
LT COL JACK BRYANT

As withdrawal of American ground units continued, the U.S. also withdrew advisors to many Vietnamese divisions. The Red Hats, although reduced somewhat in numbers, remained as active advisors to the Airborne. In addition, as the advisors for the Vietnamese Ranger battalions withdrew, the Red Hats began staffing those positions. Subsequently, the Rangers deployed with the Airborne in more frequent combined operations. At its peak staffing, Team 162 had provided advisors down to the company level in maneuver battalions, with additional advisors at staff functions and with artillery battalions. The maximum number of Red Hats at any one time was about 120. By 1972, Red Hats staffed positions only down to the battalion level, a reduction to about seventy advisors, with more reductions to come.

Major Charles R. Waterman completed his tour as Red Marker ALO in December 1971. Major Robert W. Johnson replaced him in January 1972.[1] Bob's original orders assigned him to a staff position at the 504th TASG in October 1971. When he reported for duty, the Group Commander advised that he could probably find a better job. He asked to be assigned as Raven 01, but the position was already filled. Instead, he located an operations job at 21st TASS and worked from Da Nang for several months, then moved to II DASC at Phan Rang. When he learned about the ALO opening with the Vietnamese Airborne, he arranged another transfer.

Bob went through the Vietnamese Jump School to gain credibility with the Airborne and with the Red Hat advisors. He subsequently developed a rapport with the Red Hat senior non-coms.[2] He also worked closely with Captain Jeff Johnson, G-3 Air (no relationship). The divi-

> Red Markers 1972
>
> Major Bob Johnson 01
> Lt Col Jack Bryant 01
> Lt Chuck Provini (USMC ANGLO)

---
[1] Major Robert W. Johnson, USAF (Ret), 2 Nov 2010, telephone interview, Bob confirmed that when he took over, there was no longer any Red Marker staff.
[2] Per interview, Sergeant Luong was no longer the Red Marker ALO driver.

183

sion of three brigades often operated with other attached elements including the 81st Airborne Ranger Group and the 7th Ranger Group. The 81st was a single battalion; the 7th was four battalions. As the only USAF representative, Bob spent a lot of time visiting deployed locations to determine if things were working properly. His reviews uncovered many problems.

Close Air Support System

The Vietnamese Air Force operated a close air support system that paralleled the system installed by the Americans. The Vietnamese operated a DASC in each Military Region. The VNAF assigned an ALO to the Airborne Division and operated a TACP at each deployed task force or brigade. VNAF FACs and liaison pilots flew from forward locations to support deployments. The elements of the system were identical to the American system. However, there were significant differences. For example, Johnson's counterpart, the Vietnamese Air Force ALO to the Airborne Division, never left Saigon. Instead, he sent a captain to head each TACP with a couple of radio operators. Further, the ALO and the TACPs had no assigned aircraft, pilots or FACs. Rather, all the planes and flying personnel belonged to one of eight liaison squadrons and only deployed to forward locations for short periods. Furthermore, the ALO had risen through the VNAF observer program and was not a rated pilot.

In practice, this system did not work well for a number of reasons. First, keeping the Vietnamese Air Force ALO in Saigon was a mistake. His captains were not comfortable communicating with Airborne staff officers, all of whom were superior in rank. The captains should have been involved in operational planning and in advising the Airborne colonels about the use of air assets, but tended to remain silent.

The second problem was the centralized nature of FAC assets and their brief deployment to the FOLs. The pilots and FACs from liaison squadrons might operate from a forward location supporting the Airborne for one or two weeks before returning to their home base. Their next rotation to the field would likely be to a different area and in support of a unit other than the Airborne. This practice prevented development of a unit identity with the Airborne, creation of any operational continuity or familiarity with hostile positions in the area of operations.

Additionally, Bob observed that FACs who came to the AO for pre-planned strikes did not exercise any initiative. Instead, they merely directed the scheduled strike on the scheduled target and then returned to the FOL. They did not look for targets of opportunity, nor did they conduct useful visual reconnaissance for the Airborne. Bob suspected that they were sent to forward locations as punishment. If they made a mistake, they opened themselves to criticism and further punishment. If this were the case, it would make sense to put in the preplanned strikes and not exercise any initiative, such as moving a strike location to a better target.

Major Johnson advised the Red Hats to instruct their counterparts to call upon VNAF assets and to demand more of them. However, when they needed immediate air support, Red Hats usually asked Bob to get U.S. assets. Sometimes he was able to get U.S. Marine A-4s from Bien Hoa, but not always.

Finally, the inexperience of the Vietnamese FACs was a more pervasive problem. Many of the most experienced Observer/FACs and liaison pilots had long since moved into other roles. Many jumped at the chance to advance into a more prestigious job, such as becoming a fighter pilot or an Air Operations officer like Lieutenant Truc with the Airborne.[3] The American withdrawal of its FACs from support of the Vietnamese Army had created a gap not easily filled.

Another observation, more speculative than fact-based, is that the Vietnamese FACs (like the entire South Vietnamese population) had been at war most of their lives. By 1972, the Vietnamese on both sides of the DMZ had been in armed conflict for more than a generation. American and other allied forces, on the other hand, arrived in country for a limited tour of duty. These soldiers left their families behind, hoping that they would return in a year to resume their lives. The South Vietnamese soldiers and airmen attempted to accommodate family lives and military careers simultaneously, while surviving the battles. Consequently, the South Vietnamese certainly had different motivations than their American counterparts, and sometimes approached the mission with different actions.

Although, Major Johnson did not have an assigned aircraft, he had carte blanche to fly any VNAF O-1 or U-17 for transportation around the country. Sometimes he flew Airborne command or staff officers to view the terrain when there was no helicopter available. Thus, on a limited basis he filled a gap in the VNAF performance.

Easter Offensive

On 30 March 1972, the NVA launched an attack across the DMZ, followed by assaults into MR 2 from Laos and into MR 3 from the Fishhook region of Cambodia. The USAF had been sending its fighter squadrons back to the States as the Vietnamization program continued. As the extent of the invasion became apparent, the Air Force recalled many units to bolster the South Vietnamese defense. Within a week, Air Force fighter squadrons rotated into Vietnam from Korea and the States. Two aircraft carriers joined the two already on station offshore South Vietnam. The U.S. Marines sent two squadrons of F-4s from Japan. Additional B-52s and two more aircraft carriers deployed within a month. By mid-May, two Marine A-4 squadrons from Japan were flying sorties from Bien Hoa.[4] The U.S. also brought in FAC support from the 23rd TASS in Thailand. Pilots and OV-10s moved from NKP into Da Nang to direct the increased TACAIR.[5] This rapid deployment of assets more than doubled allied air power in the theater. It eventually broke the back of the attack.

As the invasion began, the Airborne had a brigade operating near Kontum in MR 2. This brigade and two reserve brigades at Saigon would each be involved in ferocious battles during the next several months.

Military Region 1

The NVA invasion had initial success on all fronts. In MR 1, the South Vietnamese defenders included the 1st Division, the newly activated 3rd Division, several Ranger Battalions, the Vietnamese Marines and an armored battalion. At the outset of the invasion, the allies could

---

3 Rowley, p. 18.

4 Lt. Colonel Matthew C. Brant, USAF, "Air Power and the 1972 Easter Offensive," Fort Leavenworth, KS, 2007, p. 82-84.

5 Colonel Darrel D. Whitcomb, USAFR (Ret), Nail 25, "During the Easter Offensive we flew direct support for the ARVN Airborne, Marines, Rangers and 1st Division," email 24 Nov 2010.

employ only limited air power. The NVA timed the assault to coincide with the spring monsoon season specifically to limit TACAIR operations.[6] VNAF A-1s frequently flew under the low ceilings to help the MR 1 defenders. However, the larger, faster jets could not operate effectively until the weather improved.[7] The allies, therefore, substituted Combat Skyspot or LORAN guided F-4 missions and B-52 Arc Light sorties in lieu of closer, more precise air support.[8]

On 2 April, much of this air support was interrupted after an RB-66 was shot down on a reconnaissance mission. A Search and Rescue (SAR) operation began for the surviving crewmember, Bat 21B. The SAR created a no-fire zone having a 17-mile radius, which halted the B-52 and F-4 bombing sorties. The no-fire zone sat astride the main invasion route. Although the size of the zone decreased over time, it arguably deprived the defenders of needed air support until the rescue was accomplished on 13 April.[9]

While some of the South Vietnamese ground forces fought well even with limited air support, the NVA beat the 3rd Division badly. The South Vietnamese lost a number of outlying fire bases within the first week, and ultimately lost Quang Tri City on 1 May. The loss of the city led to a disorganized retreat of civilian and infantry personnel and vehicles down Highway 1 with no flank protection. Enemy artillery fired repeatedly on the retreating mass, inflicting an estimated 2,000 casualties.[10] The Marines, Rangers and armor, in contrast, maintained unit cohesion and fought southward toward a new defensive line north of Hue. The new line held at the river on the border of Quang Tri and Thua Thien Provinces.

The loss of Quang Tri Province led to the sacking of the I Corps commander. President Thieu replaced him with Lieutenant General Ngo Quang Truong, IV Corps commander, formerly of the Airborne. Truong had been the Airborne commander who assaulted Hue during TET 1968, leading the way to recapture the historic capital. In the present battle, Truong organized his defense rapidly and decisively. Two brigades of Vietnamese Marines supplemented with regional forces held the northern approaches at the river. A third Marine brigade controlled the Hue Citadel. Meanwhile, the 1st Division had responsibility for all the western and southwestern routes of attack. Truong set up headquarters in Hue and demanded that the DASC be relocated to Hue from Da Nang. After some consultation, 7th Air Force agreed. Truong located the DASC with the Fire Control Center, which directed artillery and naval gunfire support. The various armed services established discrete sectors for employing VNAF, USAF and artillery fire support. The system worked. The impact on the enemy was devastating.[11] Airpower and artillery stymied NVA attempts to resupply and organize a continued attack southward. Repeatedly, allied airstrikes bombed columns of trucks and tanks attempting to reinforce the NVA front lines.

Throughout the campaign, tactical air strikes from all services were excellent. However, the VNAF FACs did not dis-

---

6 Captain David K. Mann, Project CHECO Report, "The 1972 Invasion of Military Region 1: The Fall of Quang Tri and the Defense of Hue," HQ PACAF, 15 March 1973, p. 13.

7 *Id.* at 35.

8 Combat Skyspot sorties were radar directed. LORAN missions used Long Range Navigation for guidance. Both allowed the F-4C with its load of 24 Mk-82, 500 lb. bombs to operate with a degree of accuracy in inclement weather.

9 Mann at 23, "arguable" because the SAR effort included as many as ninety airstrikes in one day against targets inside the "zone."

10 *Id.* at 48.

11 *Id.* at 54-56.

tinguish themselves. The DASC established three operating zones during the attempt to hold Quang Tri. It directed Arc Light and Combat Skyspot missions to targets in the zone farthest from the friendly lines. USAF FACs controlled airstrikes in the middle zone, closer to the lines. The DASC directed VNAF FACs to control all strikes immediately in front of the ARVN troops. However, VNAF FACs rarely flew close to the front, usually orbiting at 6,000 feet well behind the embattled ARVN. On numerous occasions, VNAF A-1s contacted ground commanders directly and conducted strikes at targets identified by the ground forces, with no FAC involved. As a result, the DASC directed that USAF FACs take over the frontline zone.[12] In addition to the "Nail" FACs from 23rd TASS, FACs from 20th TASS covered MR 1. These included FACs flying OV-10s, call sign "Trail," and O-2s, call signs "Bilk" and "Helix."[13]

On 8 May, Truong requested the 2nd Brigade of the Airborne airlifted to Hue from Saigon. On 24 May, he requested the 3rd Brigade to join them.[14] Elements of the 2nd Brigade joined the 1st Division in extended sweeps west and southwest of Hue. U.S. FAC-controlled TACAIR and B-52 strikes supported those sweeps. Within a week, the operation had forced the NVA 29th Regiment out of battle due to losses sustained in combat with the Airborne and 1st Division.[15]

The northern defense line withstood two major attacks near the end of May. By the end of June, Truong was ready to counter-attack in force. He positioned the two Airborne Brigades to attack directly up Route 1. Their front extended from the highlands in the west to east of the high-

Lt Colonel Jack Bryant north of Quang Tri with an NVA T-54 tank destroyed during the Easter Offensive. Paul DeVries Collection.

way. The Marines were on the Airborne's right flank with a front that extended to the coast. This operation was one of few during the war that was similar to a conventional World War II battle with an identifiable front line, a FEBA and coordinated combined arms operations. The Airborne faced three main force North Vietnamese divisions, the 304th, 308th and 312th with combat records dating to the First Indochina war against the French. The Airborne and Marine force drove north, pushing the NVA back from the river and toward Quang Tri City, where dogged NVA units defended in the Quang Tri Citadel.

Before this offensive began, Major Johnson returned to the States on emergency leave. On 12 June, Lt. Colonel Jack Bryant replaced him as Red Marker 01.[16] Bryant stepped in immediately to coordinate the air support for the Airborne advance to Quang Tri City and a line along the Thach Han River. Jack worked closely with Colonel Tuong, Division Artillery Commander, and Lt. Colonel Nha, Divi-

---

12 *Id.* at 34-35.
13 *Id.* at 32.
14 *Id.* at 60.
15 *Id.* at 61.

16 Colonel Paul T. DeVries, USA (Ret), emails 21 Jun 2012.

sion G-3 to integrate tactical air into the overall fire support plan complementing the ground scheme of maneuver. Red Hat Major Michael J. Flynn was G-2 Advisor to Lt. Colonel Pham Van Be, Airborne Division G-2. Mike was the Team 162 focal point for B-52 strikes. Bryant advised him on target selection to successfully fit the Arc Light strikes into the fire support operation.[17]

Truong initially restricted airstrikes during the counter-offensive to targets outside the city in an effort to preserve Quang Tri. However, the Airborne and Marines suffered severe casualties attempting to retake the Citadel without air support. Ultimately, Truong approved B-52 and TACAIR strikes against targets within the city. In one mission, Captain Darrel Whitcomb, Nail 25, directed a strike of two 2,000 lb. Laser Guided Bombs (LGBs) against the main gate of the Citadel.[18] The LGB guidance system provided pinpoint accuracy. Usually, a FAC illuminated the target with a laser, and the bomb sensors tracked the laser to hit individual tanks, trucks or bridges. In this strike, the Citadel gates disappeared in a cloud of smoke. On 16 September, after bloody weeks of fighting, the Marines secured the Citadel, which by then was little more than a pile of rubble.[19]

The boundary between the Airborne and the Marines became Highway 1 with the Airborne to the west and the Marines to the east. The Marines threw five battalions against the NVA troops entrenched in the Citadel and suffered four hundred killed in their assault. West of the highway, the Airborne faced three American-built compounds now occupied by the NVA. The Airborne assault began with B-52 strikes directly on the compounds. The strikes wounded the opposing forces, but they only dug in deeper and continued to fight. Finally, the first compound fell under an attack led by tracked flame throwers. The other two compounds fell in like manner.[20]

Military Region 2

The NVA invasion from Laos into MR 2 coincided with main force VC attacks within the region. These forces successfully gained control of coastal Binh Dinh Province. The NVA then turned its attention to isolating the western provinces by cutting Highway 19, the only route connecting Qui Nhon and Pleiku. If successful, the NVA would split South Vietnam in two. The ARVN 22nd and 23rd Infantry Divisions, reinforced by an Airborne brigade and several Ranger battalions, defended the western region. These defenders were positioned generally along Highway 14, which ran north from Pleiku to Dak To and Tan Canh. The 22nd Division was headquartered at Tan Canh and the 23rd at Pleiku. In between, the 9th Airborne Battalion held positions near Dak To; the 11th Airborne Battalion manned Fire Support Base (FSB) Charlie. Charlie was one of several FSBs on a ridgeline west of the highway. Since early 1972, patrols from the FSBs had experienced contact with hostile forces almost daily.[21]

On 11 and 12 April, the 11th Airborne Battalion withstood a major ground at-

---

17 Colonel Michael J. Flynn, USA (Ret), emails 3 Jun 2012.
18 Colonel Darrel D. Whitcomb, USAFR (Ret), emails 28 April 2012. Whitcomb flew support missions during the counteroffensive to retake Quang Tri Province. He praises the esprit and fighting capability of the Airborne and Marines. In 2005, Whitcomb met retired Colonel Trien Tho, commander of the NVA 36th Regiment, which had occupied the Citadel during the battle.
19 Mann at 70.
20 Colonel Paul T. DeVries, USA (Ret), interview 19 Jul 2012.
21 Captain Peter A. W. Liebchen, CHECO Report, "Kontum: Battle for the Central Highlands, 30 March – 10 June 1972," HQ PACAF, 27 October 1972, p.5.

tack at FSB Charlie by the 48th NVA Regiment. With the aid of TACAIR, the battalion killed 200 NVA while holding their ground.[22] VNAF FACs probably controlled some of this action, although Covey FACs flying from Tan Canh and Pleiku undoubtedly directed some of the strikes. Rustic FACs from Bien Hoa and Nail FACs from 23rd TASS reinforced the Coveys.[23] On 14 and 15 April, having not been resupplied for four days, the 11th Battalion withdrew from FSB Charlie and moved south. The 48th NVA Regiment was so battered from the attacks against FSB Charlie, that it withdrew from action to refit and replace its losses.[24]

On 23 April, the NVA cut Highway 14 north and south of Dak To and south of Kontum City, isolating both towns so that neither could receive overland resupply and reinforcement. At the same time, NVA tanks pressed an attack against Tan Canh, destroying the 22nd Division TOC. Some regiments of the 22nd fought well. Others fled before the armored forces, which they had never before faced in combat. Although TACAIR and Spectre gunships came to the aid of the ARVN infantry, the NVA overran the 22nd Division position.[25]

Stragglers from the 22nd linked up with the 9th Airborne Battalion and several battalions of Rangers. This formation moved from the Dak To area to create a defensive line south of FSB Charlie and near the town of Vo Dinh on Highway 14. They held this line until 29 April when they withdrew toward the defenses of Kontum City that were being organized by the 23rd Division.[26]

The allies employed B-52 strikes along with tactical fighters and Spectre gunships to bolster the defenses. FACs also directed F-4Cs armed with LGBs. Sometimes, Spectre gunships with laser equipment acted as FACs and directed LGB strikes. A significant number of airstrikes had to be diverted from attacking the enemy to destroying arms and equipment abandoned by the 22nd Division.[27] The NVA nevertheless suffered significant losses while moving south from Tan Cahn to Vo Dinh and toward the approaches to Kontum City. On about 2 May, the South Vietnamese Joint General Staff ordered the Airborne brigade with its three battalions to leave Kontum City and return to reserve in Saigon.[28]

The remaining allied forces at Kontum withstood concerted attacks during the following two weeks. Airpower decimated enemy forces approaching the friendly lines and prevented easy resupply and replacement of enemy losses. By June, II DASC reported that 1,000 B-52 sorties had been flown in MR 2 since the first of the year.[29] In mid June, it was clear that Kontum would not fall.

Under the Vietnamization program, the VNAF had been scheduled to assume full control of II DASC on 1 June 1972. The Easter Offensive delayed that turnover. However, USAF staffing had already been reduced significantly. The remaining American personnel acted in an advisory role only. The VNAF staff performed well, and the coordination among the ARVN, VNAF and USAF was remarkable during this

---

22 *Id.* at 13.
23 *Id.* at 36.
24 *Id.* at 14.
25 *Id.* at 20. "Spectre" gunships were AC-130 aircraft equipped with rapid-fire 20mm and 40mm cannons. Some carried a 105mm howitzer.

26 *Id.* at 21, 31.
27 *Id.* at 27.
28 *Id.* at 36.
29 *Id.* at 68.

operation. The senior USAF officer at II DASC noted that the ultimate in cooperation occurred when a VNAF FAC had expended all his Willie Petes and asked a USAF FAC on the scene to mark the target. The VNAF FAC then directed VNAF TACAIR for a very successful airstrike using the USAF FAC's mark.[30]

After successfully holding Kontum City, further operations by the South Vietnamese forces in MR 2 broke the VC hold on the eastern provinces. The Airborne did not participate in the final victory, but their tenacious defense throughout the month of April had helped make that victory possible.

Military Region 3

The third major element of the Easter Offensive involved an invasion into MR 3 from the Fishhook region of Cambodia. On 30 March, two independent NVA regiments struck targets in Tay Ninh Province. However, this was a diversion. The real objective of the offensive was An Loc, the province capital of neighboring Binh Long Province. An Loc was on Highway 13 forty-seven miles north of Saigon.[31] On 5 April, the real offensive began with three enemy infantry divisions supported by tanks and artillery. The 5th VC Division assaulted Loc Ninh north of An Loc, while the 9th VC Division began advancing on An Loc. At the same time, the NVA 7th Division moved to cut the highway south of An Loc to prevent relief forces from reaching the town.[32] The South Vietnamese 5th Division defended the province along with RF/PFs and a task force (TF 52) from the 18th Division.[33]

Supported by tanks and artillery, the 5th VC Division overwhelmed the few hundred defenders at Loc Ninh on the third day of the battle. Only airpower had prevented an earlier VC victory. TACAIR, AC-130 Spectre gunships and Cobra attack helicopters repeatedly struck the VC. When the remaining defenders could no longer hold, they escaped into the surrounding rubber plantations and headed south. About fifty survivors joined the ARVN forces inside An Loc.[34]

Meanwhile, elements of the 9th VC Division attacked TF 52 at two fire support base camps northwest of An Loc. Within days, part of TF 52 surrendered. The remainder retreated, abandoning all its artillery, trucks and mechanized equipment. About 600 of the original 1,000-man task force made it to An Loc to help man the perimeter.[35] Ironically, the speed of the Communist forces' success created logistics issues. It took another week before the NVA could bring up additional forces and supplies to complete the encirclement of An Loc and fortify the highway to prevent relief from the south.

The ARVN responded to the invasion by reinforcing MR 3 forces with the 1st Airborne Brigade from reserve in Saigon and the 21st Infantry Division from MR 4. By 9 April, the 1st Brigade, composed of the 5th, 6th and 8th Airborne Battalions and the 81st Airborne Ranger Battalion, headed north on Route 13. The unit, commanded by Colonel Le Quang Luong, got within fifteen klicks of An Loc before

---

30 Id. at 44.
31 Major Paul T. Ringenbach and Captain Peter J. Kelly, CHECO Report, "The Battle for An Loc, 5 April – 26 June 1972 (U)," HQ PACAF, 31 January 1973, p. xii.
32 James H. Willbanks, The Battle of An Loc, Indiana University Press, Bloomington, IN, 2005, p. 34.

33 RF/PFs were Regional Forces and Popular Forces. Some units were of dubious quality. Those at An Loc were well-armed, well-lead, and fought bravely.
34 Id. at 54.
35 Id. at 61.

running into the NVA fortified blockade.[36] Trailing the Airborne up the highway, ARVN 21st Division set up its own defensive line as a precaution against the NVA breaking through and heading toward Saigon.

On 13 April, while these relief forces were on the highway, the NVA pounded An Loc with artillery and attacked the town with infantry and twenty-four tanks.[37] The NVA succeeded in occupying the northern part of An Loc, but could go no further. Determined resistance by the 5th ARVN Division and RF/PFs, supported by B-52s and TACAIR, stopped every attempt to overrun the defenders. The South Vietnamese ground forces became particularly adept at stopping the NVA tanks with LAW (Light Antitank Weapon) missiles.

III DASC, which had been an all-VNAF operation since 1971, directed the air support. The DASC divided the AO into sectors for VNAF and USAF FACs and their respective tactical fighters. Additionally, B-52 and almost constant Spectre missions supported the defenders. Cobra gunships from the US 1st Air Cavalry Division became an especially important close support weapon after the NVA seized the northern part of the town. Gunships armed with HEAT (High Explosive Anti-Tank) missiles worked with precision extremely close to friendly troops. Sundog, Rash and Chico FACs of the 21st TASS were the USAF contingent of on-site control. Through much of the operation, the Sundogs kept three FACs airborne. One, known as the King FAC, orbited high above the battle. He stayed abreast of the tactical situation, communicating directly with the senior ground advisor and III DASC. The King FAC allocated the air resources to the other FACs as the situation dictated.[38]

On 14 April, the Airborne was ordered to disengage from the blocking force on Highway 13 and reinforce the defenders inside An Loc. The unit helicoptered to positions three kilometers east and southeast of the town. A battery of six 105 mm howitzers helicoptered in with the brigade to replace artillery lost by the NVA's relentless destruction of ARVN firebases and the guns inside An Loc.[39] On 16 April, the 5th and 8th Airborne Battalions and the 81st Rangers attacked from those positions toward An Loc. The 6th Battalion remained behind to defend the artillery. The 8th reached the southeast corner of town with little opposition. The 5th ran into heavy contact and reached the eastern edge of town after a six-hour battle. The 81st occupied the northeast perimeter and began clearing house to house that night.[40]

On 19 April, the NVA launched its second major attack on An Loc and responded to the threat created by the Airborne firebase southeast of the city. The NVA attacked the firebase with two regiments, overwhelming the defenders and obliterating the 6th Battalion. The two regiments overran one company and forced the other two to retreat. Red Hat Deputy Senior Advisor Major Jack Todd arranged additional B-52 strikes to cover a breakout and retreat of about eighty troopers. Red Hat Advisor First Lieutenant Ross Kelly was awarded the Distinguished Service Cross for his role in the breakout, leading the escapees to a helicopter evacuation. For several weeks, other survivors

---

36 *Id.* at 67.
37 Ringenbach at 16.
38 Ringenbach at 19.
39 Willbanks at 87.
40 *Id.* at 89.

escaped southward or straggled into An Loc.[41]

Meanwhile, the NVA attack against An Loc was not as successful. Massive air strikes decimated its forces with TACAIR hitting within 200 meters of the friendly lines. Spectres with see-in-the-dark capability flew constant cover at night, keeping the NVA at bay.

During the succeeding three weeks, the NVA continued to shell An Loc, and the ARVN 21st Division was unable to make headway against the blockade on Highway 13. Cut off by land, An Loc's defenders were resupplied by air. As the NVA air defense weaponry increased, helicopters could no longer land. Therefore, C-119s and C-123s began airdropping supplies. As the environment became even more hostile, C-130s began high altitude airdrops. The NVA supplemented its antiaircraft guns with SA-7 Strela missiles, which were especially effective on slow moving targets. In response, the Air Force imposed new minimum altitude restrictions. FACs began operating at 7,000 feet, A-1s at 6,000 feet, and AC-130s at 10,000 feet. Helicopter gunships and AC-119s were removed from the fight because their miniguns were not effective from the higher, safe altitudes.[42]

On 11 May, the NVA made a final concerted attempt to overrun An Loc. The attack created a major salient into the ARVN lines from the west and another from the north. The ARVN commander ordered the 5th Airborne Battalion into the gap between the two intrusions. The 5th reinforced the defenders on both fronts and prevented the ARVN forces from being split. Although desperate fighting and relentless artillery bombardment continued for weeks, the defenders at An Loc were never again threatened with being overrun. The NVA began shifting more of its infantry south of the city to battle the 21st ARVN on the highway to prevent it reaching An Loc.

The turning point in the battle for Highway 13 came on 4 June, when the reconstituted 6th Airborne Battalion airlifted beyond the blockade into a new firebase near Tan Khai and attacked north toward An Loc. The new 6th Battalion fought well. On 8 June, it linked up with the 8th Airborne's position south of An Loc.[43] By 18 June, the situation had so improved that the 1st Brigade was no longer needed. It was ordered to move south down Highway 13 to a Pickup Zone near Tan Khai. The troopers were helicoptered from the PZ to waiting trucks and convoyed back to Saigon. After a short period for rest and refitting, the 1st Brigade moved to north as a reserve for the offensive to retake Quang Tri Province.

In the defense of An Loc, the the brigade suffered casualties of 346 killed, 1,093 wounded and 66 missing. Additionally, nine Red Hat advisors were wounded.[44]

Military Region 4

The NVA did not target any South Vietnamese strongholds in MR 4. However, the local VC took advantage of the vacuum created by the redeployment of the ARVN 21st Division into MR 3 for the Battle of An Loc. The VC extended their influence by seizing more than 100 abandoned government positions. These territorial gains would prove important in the years to come.[45]

---

41 *Id.* at 95-96.
42 *Id.* at 48.
43 *Id.* at 140.
44 *Id.* at 143.
45 Stanley Karnow, "Vietnam, A History," The Viking Press, New York, NY, 1983, p. 642.

Johnson's Return

When former Red Marker Major Johnson returned from emergency leave in September, he became advisor to several VNAF FAC squadrons at Bien Hoa. From that position, he continued to encourage the Vietnamese TACPs to use VNAF A-1Es and A-37s, rather than USAF air, for tactical air support.

Bob learned a few things from his new perspective inside the VNAF. He discovered one instance of the squadron "selling" airstrikes. Bob often flew FAC missions with a VNAF controller in the backseat. On this particular occasion, he had the aircraft alone and landed in a town square (possibly Song Be City) to find a couple of VNAF helicopters parked. He recognized an operations officer from his FAC outfit, and wondered what he was doing there. A few inquiries back at Bien Hoa revealed that the squadron needed some beef for an upcoming holiday feast. The officer was offering airstrikes in exchange for cattle.

Another thing he learned was that excess fuel costs were the funding source for certain social programs. VNAF aircraft could be refueled at any base. However, the squadron had to buy an entire 55-gallon drum of avgas from the local base supply organization, regardless of the quantity needed. An O-1's maximum fuel capacity was 41 gallons. Most fill-ups only used 30 to 35 gallons of the 55-gallon drum. The excess was sold in the black market for cash, which was used to fund support for widows and orphans of lost pilots, with a cut for the organizers.

Johnson also found another market existed for survival gear. Some of the U.S. equipment, such as pencil flares, had expiration dates. When the U.S. discarded these items, they found their way into the VNAF survival kits, because the discards were the most reliable supply the Vietnamese had. Bob carefully checked the survival bag of every VNAF FAC he flew with. If the only thing in the bag was a pair of black pajamas, Bob knew which side the guy would be on if they were ever forced down, and knew he would have to act accordingly. Thankfully, he never had to do so.

LZ Sally

After the successful operation that retook Quang Tri City in September, the Airborne stationed the division command post at LZ Sally, a major army base located north of DaNang on the coast. The Division stationed the 1st and 2nd Airborne Brigades on the Thach Han River and the 3rd Brigade in reserve at Camp Evan Smith. The Division also commanded the 81st Airborne Ranger Group (one battalion), the 7th Ranger Group (four battalions), thirteen artillery battalions, two tank battalions and two APC squadrons. As the Airborne staged sweep operations from LZ Sally, Lt. Colonel Bryant helped coordinate TACAIR to support each of these operations. Major Paul DeVries convinced Colonel Tuong to employ offshore naval forces for additional support and drafted U.S. Marine Lieutenant Charles R. Provini into service at LZ Sally. Provini served the Team as an Air and Naval Gunnery Liaison Officer (or ANGLO), directing naval gunfire.

Beyond his duties as Red Marker 01, Jack Bryant developed excellent rapport with the Vietnamese division staff and command group. He became not just an advisor but was accepted as a trusted professional. As a consequence, he served as an important intermediary between the division command group and other members of the advisory team. He contributed greatly to the success of the Vietnamese Airborne Division.[46]

---
[46] Colonel Michael J. Flynn, USA (Ret).

SECTION VI - GOING IT ALONE

- 1973-1975—VNAF FACs, B-130s, Xuan Loc, Newport Bridge

1974–75 AIRBORNE OPERATIONS – FINAL OFFENSIVE

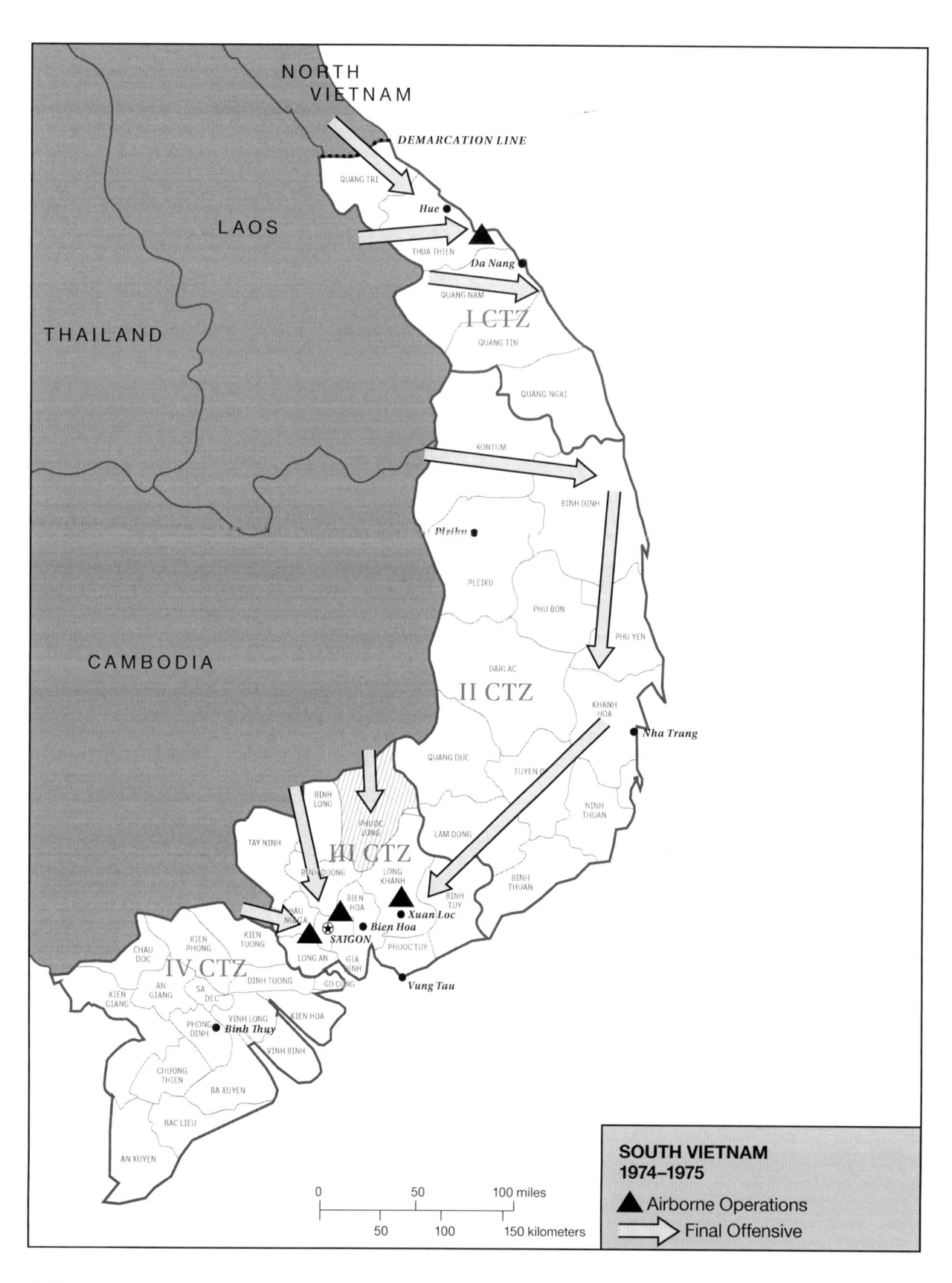

CHAPTER 15

1973-1975 - VNAF FACs, B-130s, XUAN LOC, NEWPORT BRIDGE

The Paris peace negotiations produced an agreement that American forces would leave South Vietnam and North Vietnam would free American prisoners of war. On 27 January 1973, the day before the ceasefire, both sides conducted local attacks attempting to gain territory. Lt. Colonel Bryant coordinated airstrikes up to the end. Red Hat Paul DeVries remembers the U.S. lost an F-4 that day.[1]

In February 1973, the order came for the American advisors to stand down. In a brief ceremony in Saigon, the remaining forty-two Red Hats were dismissed from duty as advisors to the Vietnamese Airborne Division. The Red Hats stood in formation on the grounds of their Tan Son Nhut headquarters dressed in khaki uniforms and low quarter shoes rather than combat uniforms. Each received a Bronze Star for his service. It was an abrupt and incongruous ending to a valiant story. No camouflage fatigues, no bloused trousers, no combat boots. I do not know whether Lt. Colonel Bryant, Red Marker ALO, attended the ceremony. He transferred to Thailand for the completion of his tour.

However, the American withdrawal was not the end of operations for the Airborne, nor was it the end of efforts to provide and improve close air support.

Red Marker 1973

Lt Colonel Jack Bryant 01
Stand Down - February 1973

There were eventually eight VNAF Liaison Squadrons, two in each Military Region. Seven of these were equipped with O-1 Bird Dog and U-17 Skywagon aircraft.[2] The eighth flew O-2A Skymasters.

During final negotiations of the peace agreement, the U.S. military received advance notice regarding one provision. The U.S. would be allowed to support the South Vietnamese by replacing any equipment or supplies on hand as of the treaty date. The U.S. could not, however, introduce any new technology or increase stockpiles beyond those on hand at the

---

[1] Colonel Paul T. DeVries, USA (Ret), emails. Per http//:taskforceomega.org/h168.htm, the F-4 lost was a Navy plane from the Enterprise, piloted by Commander H.H. Hall, weapons officer Lt Commander P.A. Kientzer. Nail 89, with Lt. Mark Peterson and Captain George Morris was also shot down. Only Kientzer was returned from captivity.

[2] The VNAF continued to use the Army designation of L-19 for the Bird Dog.

date of the agreement. As a result, the military scrambled to stock the Vietnamese with as many aircraft, munitions and equipment as possible before the treaty date.[3] Giant C-5As loaded with materiel began arriving. Pilots shuttled numerous USAF F-5s and A-37s to Vietnamese bases. In fact, the USAF transferred more jets to the VNAF than there were qualified pilots to fly them. Similarly, ammunition stockpiles were soon three times the rated containment capacity of the armored revetments. At the same time, the Military Assistance Program shuffled assets to other allies in Southeast Asia. One of the last duties of former Red Marker Major Bob Johnson was flying O-1s to the Khmer AF.[4]

The peace accords also provided that both sides would hold positions already occupied in South Vietnam. Consequently, the United States encouraged the South Vietnamese to occupy as much territory as possible before the treaty date.[5] A ceasefire applied to both sides. However, violations of the ceasefire began shortly after American POWs returned to the United States. Furthermore, after August 1973, the U.S. no longer attacked the Ho Chi Minh trail and movement of men and materiel along that route increased without hindrance. The "trail" was eventually improved into a highway, with a petroleum pipeline along the route. The NVA methodically replaced the losses suffered during the 1972 Easter Offensive and prepared for another major operation to subdue South Vietnam. In the interim, through late 1973 and into 1974, the NVA and VC avoided large assaults. Instead they hit small airfields, remote outposts and storage facilities.[6]

Review of VNAF FACs

After the U.S. withdrawal, the only American Tactical Air Support Squadron in the theater was 23rd TASS, based at Nakhon Phanom Royal Thai AB, Thailand. On 17 December 1973, the commander of the 23rd, Lt. Colonel Howard J. Pierson, visited South Vietnam to study VNAF Forward Air Controller capabilities. His report echoed some of the criticisms voiced early in 1972 by Red Marker Major Johnson and noted a number of other areas of weakness that needed to be addressed.[7] Principal shortcomings included the following:

- <u>FAC Experience.</u> Due to the rapid expansion of the Vietnamese Air Force, seasoned combat FACs had advanced into supervisory positions. Younger pilots were weak in target coverage, strike control and airmanship. Many were not able to fly in marginal weather conditions. Further, the FACs acquired little if any BDA to submit to Intelligence. Clearly, they needed more training. Pierson suggested that experienced fighter pilots be assigned to each Liaison Squadron to both train and supervise the young FACs.

- <u>Training Program.</u> Squadrons lacked maps and other training aids. FACs generally did not know fighter tactics and ordnance delivery parameters, or differing requirements between slow and fast movers. Pierson reiterated his suggestion to assign fighter pilots to the FAC units to conduct an active training program. Pierson noted that fighter pilots held a prestigious position in the VNAF. Relegating experienced fighter pilots to work with the FACs would therefore meet resistance, although it needed to be done.

- <u>Vulnerability to Ground Fire.</u> The SA-7/AAA threat in the major enemy

---

3 Karnow at p. 649.
4 Major Robert Johnson, interview.
5 Karnow at p. 648.
6 Id. at p. 660.

---

7 23rd TASS History, Oct – Dec 1973, Attachment #18, "VNAF Forward Air Controller."

complexes was significant. Consequently, missions in those areas without Infrared/Radar Homing and Warning (IR/RHAW) defense and with O-1, O-2 and U-17 aircraft would be extremely hazardous. These slow FACs were vulnerable and could not survive in this environment. Pierson recommended continuing to develop A-37 Fast-FACs for such high threat complexes, similar to what had been started at DaNang. The A-37 fast-FAC could precede the strike flight by 2-5 minutes and could survive with IR flares and evasive maneuvers. Pierson observed that new FAC aircraft with the latest IR/RHAW gear might be available if permitted by the peace accords.[8]

• Misuse of TACAIR. The South Vietnamese Army's knowledge of ordnance was weak in many instances, resulting in the misuse of TACAIR. The relatively limited resources of the VNAF needed to be directed efficiently at good targets. Pierson recommended that a local Air-Ground Operation School (AGOS) be developed for the combined ARVN-VNAF and that the VNAF conduct operations briefings for ARVN units in the field. He further noted that FACs needed to fly ground commanders over their own operations when possible.

• Low Visual Reconnaissance. An individual FAC was seldom dedicated to any particular sector for consecutive weeks or months. Pierson recommended keeping FACs at the same location for extended periods to increase their knowledge of the area and ability to spot likely enemy activity. Further, he suggested flying the maximum possible visual recon flights for training and intelligence gathering.

• Slow Response of TACAIR. The VNAF was often slow to validate requests for air support and launch strikes. Apparently, approval authorities at each communication level delayed decisions, echoing similar problems in the earliest operation of DASCs and the TACC. Pierson observed that the delays could only be resolved with open "cross-talk" among all elements of the ARVN and VNAF. The services needed a follow-up critique of each delayed action in order to determine who did not respond timely.

Lt. Colonel Pierson did not include in his report that the Vietnamese Air Force had fought long and hard for independence from the Vietnamese Army. The VNAF command would likely view permanently stationing FACs with Army units as losing some of that independence. Regardless of the reasoning, assigning FACs on a temporary basis resulted in less effective support for the ARVN.

By 1975, the VNAF had reorganized into four groups, each dedicated to a single Military Region. This geographic focus should theoretically have created better support for the ground troops. The fact that it was less than adequate was due at least in part to the lack of resources. By 1975, the VNAF experienced shortages of parts, fuel, ammunition and ordnance, largely because Congress cut funding. This rendered meaningless the peace accord provision allowing the United States to replace anything on hand at the time of the accord. Aid appropriations declined from $2.3 billion in 1972, to $1 billion in 1973 and $700 million in 1974. Lt. Colonel Pierson's review of the VNAF FACs concluded that the reduced resources available to South Vietnam made efficient employment of TACAIR even more imperative.

The Final Invasion

On 13 December 1974, the NVA began

---

[8] However, such new technology probably would not have been permitted.

what would become the final invasion of the south. The NVA attacked ARVN positions in Phuoc Long Province in MR 3 with overwhelming artillery, tanks and mechanized personnel carriers. By 6 January 1975, the NVA had seized control of the province. The invasion was a test of the resolve of the United States under the leadership of new President Gerald Ford. When the U.S. did not retaliate, the North Vietnamese ordered a cross-border offensive on several fronts, similar to the Easter Offensive. The general offensive began in early March.

Just as in 1972, NVA forces invaded across the DMZ and Laos into MR 1, from Laos into MR 2, and from Cambodia into MR 3. The lack of American response contracted starkly with its action in 1972 when the U.S. doubled the allied air power within a few weeks, deployed USAF and Marine fighter squadrons to South Vietnamese air bases, launched strikes from Navy carriers offshore, transferred OV-10 FACs from Thailand to help control airstrikes, attacked the NVA's advancing armor using Army Cobra gunships armed with HEAT missiles, covered beleaguered defenders at night with AC-130 Spectre gunships, and attacked massed NVA troop formations with B-52 Arc Light missions and F-4C Combat Skyspot flights. Instead, on 21 January, President Ford announced that the United States was unwilling to reenter the war.

B-130s

The VNAF did the best they could with the F-5, A-37 and A-1 fighters at hand. However, inadequate supplies of fuel and munitions limited their effectiveness. Other shortcomings limited the VNAF response. Specifically, the VNAF's O-1 and O-2 FAC aircraft were particularly vulnerable to NVA anti aircraft fire. The AC-119 gunships in the VNAF inventory were also vulnerable and did not have the firepower of the AC-130 Spectres. Most importantly, the South Vietnamese sorely missed the support of B-52s, whose massive striking power had been decisive in blunting the Easter Offensive. In an attempt to replicate some of the B-52 firepower, the Vietnamese fitted bomb racks to some of their C-130s with good results. However, the "B-130s" could not cruise high enough to be unheard by ground observers. Furthermore, the Herky's lower flight altitude and slower speed made the craft susceptible to the enhanced anti-aircraft armament being sent south by the NVA. Even as losses mounted, the VNAF continued use of the lumbering transport as a bomber.

Without the massive close air support that responded to the Easter Offensive, the South Vietnamese suffered loss after loss. On 14 March, President Thieu ordered a retreat from the central highlands and the two northernmost provinces to consolidate the ARVN further south. He then partially reversed that order, declaring that Hue must be held. The defense at Hue nevertheless collapsed after five days, and the NVA columns moved south. The NVA thrust through MR 2 to the coast effectively isolated major South Vietnamese forces, including Airborne units.

Battle of Xuan Loc

On 9 April 1975, three divisions of the 4th NVA Corps, supported by a fourth infantry division, T-54 tanks and artillery, launched an attack on heavily outnumbered ARVN defenders in the area around Xuan Loc, only 38 miles from Saigon. The 18th ARVN Division and the Long Khanh Regional Forces took up positions reinforced by the 82nd Ranger Battalion. On 12 April, the 1st Airborne Brigade (three maneuver battalions and one Artillery battalion) from Saigon joined the defenders.

For ten days, the NVA forces pounded headlong into the ARVN defenders, ultimately leaving an estimated 5,000 dead. Although the defenders suffered about 30% casualties, they held. The VNAF supported the defense with numerous airstrikes. The proximity to Tan Son Nhut and Bien Hoa air bases contributed to the VNAF's ability to support these defenders.

For nearly two weeks, the ARVN held Xuan Loc, and then counterattacked against impossible odds. The NVA offensive up to this point had rolled over every ARVN unit it faced. In contrast, Xuan Loc was one of the few places where the ARVN, though outnumbered, stood and fought with a tenacity that stunned their opponents. News reporters were flown in from around the world to witness the battlefield, which was strewn with NVA casualties who died in the repeated assaults. After twelve days and nights of ferocious combat against the North Vietnamese forces, the defensive line at Xuan Loc still held.[9]

ARVN Military Region 3 Headquarters ordered the 18th Infantry Division, the 1st Airborne Brigade and other units in the Xuan Loc battle to retreat to Bien Hoa to establish a new line defending the outer approaches to Saigon. The retreat back to Bien Hoa to assume the new mission took place during the night of 20 April 1975.

On 25 April, President Thieu resigned and departed Saigon for Taiwan. On 28 April, Vice President Tran Van Huong transferred power to General Duong Van Minh.[10]

Newport Bridge

On 28 April, the 12th Airborne Battalion deployed to the Saigon River at the Newport Bridge on the highway to Bien Hoa. The enemy was trying to capture and occupy the entire bridge, and all traffic on the freeway between Saigon and Bien Hoa was blocked. After crossing the river in boats, the 12th Battalion cleared the eastern end of the bridge of VC and awaited an onslaught of NVA armor.[11]

Shortly, the NVA began shelling Tan Son Nhut AB. The VNAF ordered many pilots to fly their aircraft to Thailand. F-5s, A-37s, Caribous and other aircraft flew to Ubon and Utapao, where aircraft parked on the grass between the runways anywhere space could be found. Ground crews painted USAF emblems over the VNAF insignia as rapidly as possible. Many of the VNAF pilots were surprised to learn they could not return home. They were, in effect, exiled and would have to find a way in the future to bring their families out of Vietnam. Other pilots, especially of large transport aircraft, sometimes were ordered to land at remote fields in Vietnam where senior officers' families waited to board. However, the first C-130 to escape Vietnam landed at Singapore on 3 April 1975, commandeered by a junior officer. Lieutenant Pham Quang Khiem assisted by his friend Major Nguyen Huu Canh, flew more than fifty of Khiem's family from an abandoned strip south of Saigon to Singapore.[12]

Other VNAF officers kept fighting. An AC-119 Shadow gunship flew missions de-

---

9 Karnow, p. 668.
10 Id. at 685.

11 www.truclamyentu.info/tlls_lichsuvietnamcandai/12thairbornebattalion.html
12 Robert C. Mikesh, "The Labors of Hercules," Air & Space Magazine, August/September 1989. The author met Khiem in 2000 at a VNAF Reunion. Khiem told his story first hand and provided a detailed account published in "Air War Over S.E. Asia" Magazine. The aircraft now belongs to the Smithsonian Institution and is in mothballs at the Dulles Smithsonian annex.

fending Tan Son Nhut until shot down on 30 April. The same day, a VNAF O-1 crashed in downtown Saigon after being hit by NVA anti-aircraft fire. One of the last flights of a VNAF O-1 was by Major Buong Ly, who flew a Bird Dog to the USS Midway with his wife and five children in the rear cabin. He orbited over the aircraft carrier for almost an hour, dropping written messages asking for permission to land. After numerous Huey helicopters were pushed over the side, Major Ly landed safely on the cleared deck.

On 30 April 1975 at approximately 1000 hours, General Duong Van Minh issued an order for all troops to lay down their weapons. The 12th Airborne Battalion headquarters called a meeting of company commanders to inform them of this order and instructed them to act at will. Years of combat ended in Vietnam, but the suffering continued for more than a decade.

VNAF Major Buong Ly landing on the deck of the USS Midway. This aircraft is now in the National Naval Aviation Museum in Pensacola, FL.

SECTION VII
BACK IN THE WORLD

- Red Markers Revisited

CHAPTER 16

RED MARKERS REVISITED

With their tours in Vietnam completed, the men who served with the Red Markers and Red Hats came home. Some completed a career in the armed services, while some pursued higher education or a civilian career. All whom I have contacted remember vividly their time in Vietnam.

For the Vietnamese who served with the Airborne or in any other capacity in the service of their country, the defeat in April 1975 led to a far different path. Many were subjected to re-education camps. Some died or were executed there. Almost all suffered. A lucky and resourceful percentage escaped with their families. Many others who escaped spent years working to relocate their families to the States.

Here are the stories of a few, with the Red Marker ALOs listed first. The rest are in approximate chronological order of their service with the Airborne.

Gene McCutchan, the original Red Marker, 1962-63 and 1965-67, retired as a Lt. Colonel in his hometown of Phoenix, Arizona. He celebrated his 92nd birthday in 2011 by renewing his driver's license. He was active in the FAC Association and attended annual reunions of the Vietnamese Airborne in California. Gene reviewed and commented on the final draft of this history. He died 24 June 2012 about a month before its publication.

Jim Martin, Red Marker 01, 1963-64, retired from the Air Force in Hawaii as a Colonel. He passed away at age 82 in June 2005.

Cas Casteel, Red Marker 01, 1964-65, retired as a Colonel in Florida. At age 90, he contributed his memories and photos to this history.

Pete Almquist, Red Marker 01, 1967-68, retired as a Lt. Colonel and passed away in August 1997.

Don Glenn, Red Marker 01, 1968, retired in Florida as a Colonel.

Bill Fulton, Red Marker 01, 1968-69, retired as a Lt. Colonel and currently lives in Florida. His Airborne fatigue uniform and *beret rouge* are on display at the Air Force Museum in Dayton, Ohio.

Bob Drawbaugh, Red Marker 01, 1969-70, retired as a Colonel in Vermont. He served as a consultant to Martin Marietta

CHAPTER 16 - RED MARKERS REVISITED

in California and as an instructor at Vermont College. He died in December 2010 at age 77.

Doc Daugherty, Red Marker 01, 1970, retired as a Colonel and lives in Texas. He contributed his Air Plan for the Cambodian Incursion, as well as other memories, for this history.

Jack Koppin, Red Marker 01, 1970-71, retired in Florida as a Colonel. He died in May 2009. His widow provided a picture and her memories to this history.

Bob Johnson, Red Marker 01, 1972, retired in New Mexico and Texas. He shared his experience as the lone ALO near the end of the Red Marker existence in Vietnam.

Jack Bryant, Red Marker 01, 1972-73, was assigned to Elmendorf AFB, Alaska in 1974. He retired in Texas and died at age 55 in October 1984.

Jack Cebe-Habersky, Red Marker 02, 1963-64, the first Brigade FAC, died in 1977 at age 43 of cancer while on active duty as a Lt. Colonel. His station at the time was ALO for the 82nd Airborne at Ft. Bragg. His widow shared his scrapbook for this history.

Bob Paradis, Red Marker 02, 1964-65, returned to CONUS as head of ROTC at Texas Tech where he earned a Masters and PhD in Education. He retired as a Lt. Colonel and worked for Northrop and McDonnell-Douglas. Bob died in Houston in 2006.

Buck Rennick, TDY Red Marker and hotshot A-1E pilot, 1965, left the service and flew for Continental Airlines for many years. He retired from Continental and from the Air National Guard. In 2011, he confirmed the stories about him related by the Red Hats.

Bob Losik, Red Hat 06, retired as a Lt. Colonel in New Hampshire. He shared his memory of actions involving Red Markers Rennick, Henneberry and Windle.

Bob Webb, Red Hat, retired as a Colonel in Colorado. He shared his personal memoir and action involving Red Marker Buck Rennick.

Mike Bartelme, Red Hat, 1965, retired as a Lt. Colonel in Iowa and was killed in an airplane crash while taking flying lessons.

Joe "Duke" Granducci, Red Marker 02, 1965-66, retired as a Major in Utah. He began this history project in 2000, contacting and soliciting input from many Red Markers. Duke passed away in March 2005 before completing the project. His widow and son, Joe III, graciously pulled together his research and passed it on to be used here.

Del Fleener, Red Marker 07, 1965-66, and recipient of the Air Force Cross, went home to Indiana. He continued to fly locally and lived to age 81, passing away in May 2010.

Herb Lloyd, Red Hat, retired as a Brigadier General in Arkansas. Herb provided information on an action involving Red Marker Cebe-Habersky.

Gene Parker, Red Marker 04, 1966, passed away in Sarasota, Florida at age 71 in January 2003.

Bud Fisher, Red Marker 02, 1966-67, retired in California and contributed his stories to this history.

Wayne Kanouse, Red Marker 03, 1966-67, survived a civilian aircraft accident in November 1978. He passed away in September 1994.

Mike Morea, Red Marker 04, 1966-67, became active in the FAC Association. He served as the editor of the 19th TASS articles written for *Cleared Hot*. Mike provided his personal memoir as background material for this history.

Bill Stewart, Red Marker 05, 1966-67, retired from the service as a Colonel and resides in Virginia. Bill provided several stories for *Cleared Hot* and contributed more for this history.

Voung Dinh Thuyet, Airborne trooper, 1966-75, rose to the rank of Lt. Colonel in command of the Engineering Battalion. He lives in California.

Rip Blaisdell, Red Marker FAC, 1967, retired as a Colonel in Colorado. He shared his stories for this history.

Gary Blake, TDY Red Marker FAC, 1967-68, shared his stories for this history.

Laurie Kivisto, Red Marker O-2, 1967-68, retired in Michigan and contributed to this history.

Doug Hedensten, Red Marker crew chief, 1967-68, was medically discharged due to his wounds during TET. He lives in Washington and shared his memories for this history.

Walter Stepaniak, Red Marker ROMAD, 1967-68 and 1968-70, left the service and works for AIG overseeing contract installation of computer and communications systems. Walter is active in The Society of the Vietnamese Airborne and contributed his photos and memories to this history.

Pete Drahn, Red Marker 07, 1967-68, is the only Red Marker to wear a star. In 1994, he retired from the Air National Guard as a Brigadier General in Wisconsin. Pete transcribed the diary he kept during his year in Vietnam and made it available for this history.

Joe Kinzer, Red Hat, 1967-68, retired as a Lt. General in North Carolina. He provided memories of John Giles' service as a Red Marker. As of 2012, Joe is president of the Society of the Vietnamese Airborne.

Jack McKessy, Red Marker 08, 1968-69, retired at the end of 1988 as a Colonel. He shared his stories for this history.

Dick Blair, Red Hat, 1968, retired as a Colonel in Virginia. He shared his stories as advisor of the 9th Battalion during TET and memories of his brother, Red Marker FAC Dave Blair.

Don Spooner, Red Marker 07, 1968-69, retired as a Colonel. As of 2011, he had taught high school for seventeen years.

Ed Fairchild, Red Marker 06, 1968-69, retired from the service as a Lt. Colonel. He shared his memories and stories for this history.

Bruce Freeman, Red Marker 08, 1969, retired as a Colonel in 1995 and currently lives in North Carolina. He shared his stories and photos.

Truc Van Tran, VNAF FAC and Airborne Division G-3 Air, 1962-75, escaped by boat with his family. His older son went to the U.S. Air Force Academy, his younger son to the U.S. Naval Academy. His older daughter earned an MBA from the University of Virginia, his younger an MBA from George Mason. Truc shared his sto-

CHAPTER 16 - RED MARKERS REVISITED

ries for this history. He and his wife are retired in Virginia.

Jim Hill, Red Marker 05, 1969, shared his photographs and stories for this history.

Barry Schupp, Red Marker ROMAD, 1969-70, crossed over to the dark side and was commissioned in the US Army Reserves. He retired as a Lt. Colonel in Florida and Rhode Island, and is active in The Society of Vietnamese Airborne. He shared numerous photos and stories for this history.

Dave Langas, Red Marker 04, 14 and 24, 1969-70, one of the original O-2A FACs with the unit, flew for Delta for 31 years. He retired in Georgia and moved to San Antonio. He shared his scrapbook and memories for this history.

Gerald Schwalb, Red Marker 02, 1969-70, retired in Texas as a Lt. Colonel. He contributed his memories to this history.

Fred Bishopp, Red Marker 05, 1969, contributed to this history.

Art Intemann, Red Marker 09, 1969-70, retired as a Colonel in California.

Lloyd Prevett, Red Marker 26, 1969-70, retired as a Colonel. He contributed memories to this history.

David Blair, Red Marker 16, 1969-70, retired as a Colonel in 1987 and died of a brain tumor in 1989. He is buried at Arlington.

Byron Mayberry, Red Marker 19, 1969-70, returned home to Oklahoma and died of cancer in 1985.

Gary Willis, Red Marker 18, 1969-70, became an instructor pilot teaching Vietnamese student pilots at Keesler AFB, Mississippi. He left the service in 1973 and had a career in the energy industry, retiring in Houston, Texas.

Gam Van Tran, Willis's first student at Keesler, flew his Caribou to Thailand one day before the fall of South Vietnam. Knowing that the end was near, he sent his family to live close to his wife's parents in IV Corps before getting the order to evacuate his aircraft. It took Gam 15 years and the payment of many "fees" to reunite his family. He earned two degrees and now works for General Motors in Texas while his children attend college.

Bill Kaeser, Red Marker crew chief, 1969-70, shared his stories for this history.

Jim Simpson, Red Marker 13, 1969-70 retired from the Air Force as a Lt. Colonel. He became president of the Air Force Association before retiring in Virginia.

Terry Gruters, Red Marker 14, 1970, left the service in 1973 after his second tour and became a CPA in Florida.

Chad Swedberg, Red Marker 25 and Raven 15, and Jim Hix, Red Marker 15 and Raven 25, 1970, remain close friends. Each retired as a Lt. Colonel and each pulls the other's leg every chance he gets.

Cary Strickbine, Red Marker RO, 1970, lives in a small town in Oklahoma and works at a corrections facility.

Louis R. Rocco, Red Hat, 1970, recipient of the Congressional Medal of Honor, retired in San Antonio. He passed away on 31 October 2002 at the age of 63 of lung cancer.

Jim Hoppe, Red Marker crew chief, 1970-71, left the service in 1972. He obtained electrical and plumbing licenses in California and later built homes in the Sacramento area. He contributed his memories and photos to this history.

Jim Yeonopolus, Red Marker ROMAD, 1970-71, left the service and became a professor at Central Texas College after graduate school. He runs a program offering college courses aboard Navy ships and overseas Army and Air Force bases. He is a past president of the Society of the Vietnamese Airborne.

Dennis Hull, Red Marker Bravo, 1970-71, was commissioned through the ROTC and retired as a Major. He became a doctor and ultimately retired in North Carolina. Dennis contributed his memories and photos to this history.

Steve Volz, Red Marker ROMAD, 1970, lives in Wisconsin and is active in The Society of the Vietnamese Airborne. He chaired a committee in his hometown to create a 13-acre sports facility named Memorial Park honoring Vietnam veterans.

Steve shared his stories for this history.

Jerry Justice, 1970-71, Red Marker crew chief, continued working in aviation as a civilian. He represents Dassault Aircraft in sales.

Dave Marion, Red Marker crew chief, 1970-71, contributed to this history.

Richard Ruel, Red Marker crew chief, 1970-71, retired from the Coast Guard in Michigan. He contributed stories and pictures to this history.

Mike Flynn, Red Hat at LZ Sally, retired as a Colonel and is Secretary of The Society of the Vietnamese Airborne. Mike shared his recollections of Jack Bryant, the last Red Marker ALO, and of the stand down in February 1973.

Paul DeVries, Red Hat G-3 at LZ Sally, retired as a Colonel and is a past president of the Society of the Vietnamese Airborne. Paul shared his memories of Jack Bryant.

Sergeant Tran Dinh Luong and Corporal Phuong, Airborne troopers, aides, drivers, body guards and assistants to Red Markers, 1962-70, status is unknown. Presumably, neither escaped Vietnam.

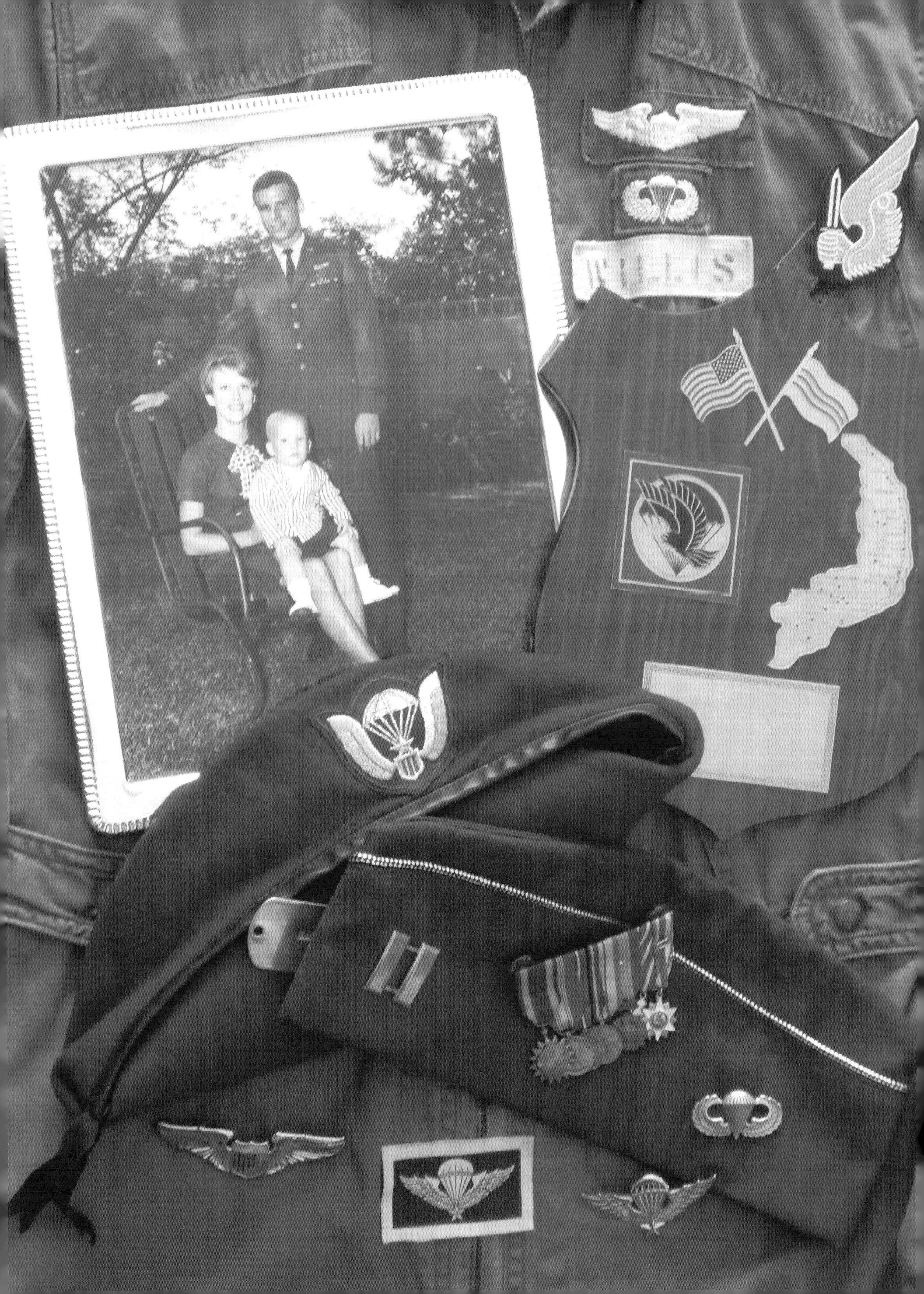

EPILOGUE

The war in Vietnam always translates into personal loss for those it touched. I did not know any of the Red Markers, Red Hats or Vietnamese killed in the war. However, I knew two friends from high school and two classmates from my squadron at the Air Force Academy who were casualties of the war.

Douglass T. Wheless was my wife's best friend in high school. In Vietnam, he was a platoon leader with the 11th Armored Cavalry Regiment when it invaded Cambodia. As the Cambodian Incursion was coming to a close in late June 1970, Captain Wheless located me at Quan Loi. Doug knew I was flying in support of the Vietnamese Airborne and that the Airborne was also involved in that operation. Doug had graduated from West Point on 6 June 1968, almost a year after my graduation from the U.S. Air Force Academy on 7 June 1967. The Army promoted a Second Lieutenant to First Lieutenant after one year of service and to Captain after another year. In contrast, the Air Force schedule was a year and a half for each of those promotions. It therefore took three years in the Air Force to make Captain, versus two years in the Army. As of 6 June 1970, Doug outranked me by one day. One reason he looked for me at Quan Loi was to gloat a little and have me salute him, which I did gladly. We also talked a long time about home and friends. It was the last time I saw him alive.

I went to my next assignment in the States on 4 July 1970. In late November, my wife received a phone call from Doug's mother asking if I would be a pallbearer at his funeral. He died in Vietnam on 22 November 1970 from wounds suffered in an explosion.

The second person the war brings to mind was my closest friend in high school. He went to Vietnam as an artillery officer and flew many missions in the backseat of an L-19 controlling artillery fire missions. He also spent a lot of time at remote firebases. One night in 1968, the NVA overran his firebase. My friend saved an injured artilleryman, dragging him into a trench during the assault. He survived and came home, apparently in one piece.

For fifteen years after Vietnam, he had a successful career as a marketing manager for a sportswear manufacturer. He ultimately was responsible for the southeastern region of the United States, from Texas to the Atlantic Coast.

The horror of the war finally caught up with him. He became unable to leave his house or function in public. He told me that it took many sessions with the PTSD counselors for him to manage to talk through the first thirty seconds after the NVA came through the wire ... a big breakthrough for him. I asked, "How about what happened after that?" His response: "Oh, the next hour or so was about the same as the first thirty seconds."

He said that the terror of that night will be with him forever. However, another burning memory of his is the devastation wreaked on the NVA ... the enemy. His unit registered guns from several firebases on NVA infiltration routes seeded with electronic sensors. Every night for weeks, when the sensors indicated movement on the trails, the firebases bombarded the predetermined coordinates. The day after each nightly barrage, my friend and his troops would find hundreds of dead NVA soldiers in the kill zone. Each night was a repeat of the previous until the night they were overrun. It is clear to me that the slaughter of those soldiers is a part of the nightmare contributing to his post-traumatic stress.

Last, I had two classmates from the Air Force Academy's 23rd Squadron who died in Southeast Asia. Both were FACs. First Lieutenant Kennard E. Svanoe, a Covey FAC piloting an O-2A, was shot down and killed 2 June 1969. Captain Samuel L. James was in the back seat of an F-4C on a Fast-FAC mission in Cambodia when shot down and killed 18 April 1973. Sam's remains and the remains of his pilot were recovered decades later and returned for burial at the Academy.

I believe wars are sometimes inevitable, but should always be the last resort. I also think most people sent into combat believe the same. I am uncertain that those responsible for committing their countries to conflict always have that understanding. Thousands of Free World allies, more than 58,000 Americans, and millions of Vietnamese died in this war, and many times that number were wounded. My friends are lost in those numbers. I cannot help wondering if there was not another way.

APPENDIX I

GLOSSARY

ADF	Automatic Direction Finder, a low frequency navigation aid.
AGE	Aerospace Ground Equipment.
ALO	Air Liaison Officer.
AO	Area of Operation.
ARVN	Army, Republic of Vietnam.
Arc Light	A B-52 bombing mission usually composed of three aircraft each carrying 108 Mk-82 and/or Mk-117 bombs.
CAS	Close Air Support.
CEMS	Communication Electronic Maintenance Section.
Class A FAC	Forward air controller previously qualified as a fighter pilot.
Class B FAC	Forward air controller not previously qualified as a fighter pilot.
Combat Skyspot	An F-4C bombing mission controlled by radar or LORAN allowing bombing in marginal weather conditions. Each F-4C carried 24 Mk-82 bombs. Missions involved from one to three aircraft.
COMM/NAV	Communications and Navigation Aids.
CONUS	Continental United States.
CTZ	Corps Tactical Zone (I, II, III, and IV Corps, and the Capital Military Zone or District).
DASC	Direct Air Support Center.
DEROS	Date of Estimated Return from Overseas Service.
Deuce-and-a-half	Two-and-a-half ton truck.
DMZ	Demilitarized Zone.
DZ	Drop Zone, target landing location for parachuting Airborne troopers.
EMO	Equipment Management Office.
FAC	Forward Air Controller.
FAN	Forward Air Navigator.
FEBA	Forward Edge of the Battle Area.
FOL	Forward Operating Location, small airfields where most FACs and support staff lived.
LZ	Landing Zone, location for helicopter insertion of troops.

APPENDIX I - GLOSSARY

Mk-82	500-pound bomb.
Mk-117	750-pound bomb.
MOB	Main Operating Base.
MRC-108	Jeep with a radio pallet containing HF, UHF, VHF and FM radios.
NVA	Army, North Vietnam (see PAVN).
PAVN	Army, Peoples Republic of Vietnam.
PSP	Perforated Steel Planking, each plank is 10 feet long by 15 inches wide with circular holes punched through its entire length. The holes reduce the weight of the plank and allow water to run through. Slots on one long edge and hooks on the other allow planks to interlock. PSP was used for runways, taxiways, ramp space and as roofs for bunkers.
PZ	Pickup Zone, location for helicopter extraction of troops.
RMS	Resources Management System.
RO or ROMAD	Radio Operator or Radio Operator, Maintainer and Driver, enlisted personnel who operated and maintained the radio equipment and jeep assigned to the Tactical Air Control Party.
Sector FAC	Forward air controller assigned to support one of the Vietnamese army divisions that had responsibility for a given geographic area or sector. The FACs attached to such a division generally lived at one FOL and flew patrols over the same sector during their entire tour of duty.
Spectre	AC-130 aircraft armed with rapid-fire 20 mm and 40 mm cannon and night vision aiming devices. Some carried a 105 mm howitzer.
TACAIR	Tactical Air.
TACC	Tactical Air Control Center, the agency responsible for day-to-day operation of the tactical air war in Vietnam. It issued orders to fighter squadrons and FAC units setting out target location, ordnance, and timing for each preplanned tactical bombing mission.
TACP	Tactical Air Control Party, a team made up of FACs, ROs and crew chiefs with aircraft and radio equipment usually supporting a battalion or larger unit of ground forces.
TASG	Tactical Air Support Group.
TASS	Tactical Air Support Squadron.
TCTO	Time Charge Technical Order.
TFS	Tactical Fighter Squadron.
VC	Viet Cong.
VNAF	Air Force, Republic of Vietnam.
WP	White Phosphorus Rocket or "Willie Pete."

APPENDIX II

RECONSTRUCTED RED MARKER ROSTER – CHRONOLOGICAL

* Killed In Action. **Deceased.

First Name	MI	Name	Rank	Call Sign	Period
AIR LIAISON OFFICERS					
Eugene "Gene"	R	McCutchan**	Major	Red Marker	1962 - Jun 63
James	F	Martin**	LTC	RM 01	Jul 63 - Jun 64
Carleton	N	Casteel	LTC	RM 01	Jul 64 - Apr 65
Eugene "Gene"	R	McCutchan**	Maj/LTC	RM 01	May 65 -1967
Peter	W	Almquist**	LTC	RM 01	1967 - Jan 68
Donald	T	Glenn	LTC	RM 01	Jan 68 - Dec 68
William	H	Fulton, Jr.	Major	RM 01	Dec 68- Jun 69
Michael	H	Branz**	Major	RM 01	Jun 69 - Dec 69
Robert "Bob"	E	Drawbaugh**	Major	RM 01	Dec 69 - Jun 70
Robert "Doc"	G	Daugherty, Jr.	LTC	RM 01	Jun 70 - Nov 70
John "Jack"	A	Koppin, Jr.**	Major	RM 01	Nov 70 - Jan 71
Dean	R	Haeusler	Major	RM 01	Jan 71 - Apr 71
Charles	R	Waterman, Jr.	Major	RM 01	May 71 - Dec 71
Robert	W	Johnson	Major	RM 01	Jan 72 - Jul 72
Jack		Bryant**	LTC	RM 01	Aug 72 - Feb 73
Charles	R	Provini	Marine LT	ANGLO	1972
ASSISTANT ALOs AND FACs					
Jack	V	Cebe-Habersky**	Capt	RM 02	May 63 - Apr 64
Robert "Bob"	L	Paradis**	Capt	RM 02	May 64 - Apr 65
Alan "Buck"	L	Rennick	Capt	RM 02	Feb 65 - Mar 65
Paul	R	Windle*	Capt	RM 02	Mar 65 - Jun 65
Robert "Bob"	M	Carn, Jr.*	1 LT	RM 03	May 65 - Aug 65
Joseph "Duke"	S	Granducci, II**	Capt	RM 02	Jul 65 - Jun 66
Richard	V	McGill	Capt	RM 05	mid 65 - mid 66

APPENDIX II - RED MARKER ROSTER - CHRONOLOGICAL

First Name	MI	Last Name	Rank	Call Sign	Period
Donald "Don"	R	Hawley*	Capt	RM 06	mid 65 - Dec 65
Delbert "Del"	W	Fleener**	Capt	RM 07	Sep 65 - Mar 66
Alfred "Gene"	E	Parker	Capt	RM 04	Jan 66 - May 66
William "Bill"	P	Stewart	Capt	RM 05	Apr 66 - Mar 67
Oliver "Bud"	P	Fisher, Jr.	Major	RM 02	May 66 - May 67
Truc	V	Tran	1 LT/Maj	DO(Red)	1966 - 1971
Wayne	E	Kanouse**	Capt/Maj	RM 03	1966 - 1967
Michael "Mike"	J	Morea	1 LT/Capt	RM 04	May 66 - Jan 67
William "Bill"	D	Jenkins	Capt	RM 09	Feb 67 - Jan 68
John	K	Giles	Major	RM 02	Mar 67 - Mar 68
Michael "Rip"	P	Blaisdell	Capt	FAC	Jun 67 - Jul 67
Duane	P	Andrews	Capt	FAC	mid 67 - mid 68
James "Jim"		Frail	Capt	TALO	late 67 - Jun 68
Gary		Blake	Capt	FAC	Dec 67 - Feb 68
Arthur "Art"	E	Greiner	Capt	FAC	Dec 67 - Feb 68
George	L	Varner	Capt	FAC	Dec 67 - Feb 68
Lawrence "Laurie"	E	Kivisto	Major	RM 02	May 67 - May 68
John "Jack"	C	Taylor	Major	FAC	April 67 - Mar 68
Peter "Pete"	L	Drahn	Capt	RM 07	Nov 67 - Nov 68
Roy	E	Moore	Capt	RM 09	Jan 68 - Apr 68
Kenneth	W	Kreger**	Major	FAC	Feb 68 - Jan 69
Bruce	C	Bechtel	Capt	RM 03	Feb 68 - Aug 69
Harold	R	Magnuson	Capt/Maj	RM 02	Feb 68 - Jan 69
John "Jack"	D	McKessy	Capt	RM 08	Mar 68 - Mar 69
Stuart	K	Wheeler	1 LT	RM 09	Apr 68 - Mar 69
William	F	Marlin	Capt	RM 04	Apr 68 - Apr 69
Freddie "Dale"	D	Dickens*	Major	RM 07	Jun 68
Donald "Don"	A	Spooner	2 LT/1 LT	RM 07	Jul 68 - Jun 69
Kenneth "Ken"	E	Munson	Capt	RM 03	Aug 68 - Nov 68
James	A	Leach**	Major	RM 02	Oct 68 - Jun 69
Edward	A	Fairchild	Capt	RM 06	Oct 68 - Jul 69
James	A	Hill	Capt	FAC	Jan 69 - Aug 69
Edward	D	Weiss	1 LT	RM 03	Nov 68 - Nov 69
Bruce	M	Freeman	1 LT	RM 08	Jan 69 - Dec 69
Arthur	J	Intemann	1 LT	RM 09	Jan 69 - Jan 70
William	E	Dunne	Capt	RM 25	69 - 70
Warren	K	Paxton	Capt	RM 03	69 - 70
Carl "Dave"	D	Langas	Capt	RM 04/14/24	Feb 69 - Feb 70
Fred	T	Bishopp, Jr.	Capt	RM 05	May 69 - Sep 69
Terry	L	Weaver	1 LT	RM 07/17	Jun 69 - May 70
Douglas	B	Lobser	Capt	RM 2X	69 - 70
Lawrence "Larry"	H	Shaevitz	1 LT	RM 24	Oct 69 - Jul 70
Lloyd	L	Prevett, Jr.	1 LT	RM 26	Nov 69 - Jul 70
David	G	Blair**	1 LT	RM 16	Aug 69 - Jul 70
Gerald	P	Schwalb	Major	RM 02	Sep 69 - Jun 70
Byron	L	Mayberry**	1 LT	RM 19	Nov 69 - Oct 70

First Name	MI	Last Name	Rank	Call Sign	Period
James "Jim"	M	Simpson	Capt	RM 13	Nov 69 - Oct 70
Gary	N	Willis	1 LT/Capt	RM 18	Dec 69 - Jun 70
Terence "Terry"	J	Gruters	1 LT	RM 14	Jan 70 - Nov 70
Yancy	D	Hudson**	1 LT	RM 12	Jan 70 - Nov 70
Stuart "Skip"	F	Pardee	1 LT	Covey 555	Mar 1970
James "Jim"	H	Hix, Jr.	1 LT	RM 15	Apr 70 - Sep 70
Chad	L	Swedberg	1 LT	RM 25	Apr 70 - Sep 70
Herbert	W	Smallman	1 LT	FAC	70
Phillip "Phil"	R	Lumpkin	1 LT	FAC	70 - 71
Paul "Jeff"	J	Peacock	Capt	RM 11	70 - 71
Luis "Mike"	M	Rodriguez	1 LT	RM 17	Apr 70 - Oct 70
Joseph	V	Massa	Major	RM 02	Jul 70 - Feb 71
Hugh	T	Hill	1 LT	RM 18	Jul 1970
Billy	R	Barrett	1 LT/Capt	RM 15	Jul 70 - Jul 71
D	C	Beckingham	1 LT	RM 18	Aug 70 - 71
Sidney	E	Conley, II	1 LT	RM 13	70 - 71
Donald	R	Ward	Capt	RM 14	70 - 71
Crawford	R	Deems, III	1 LT	RM 16	70 - 71
Peter	W	Stetson	1 LT	RM 25	70 - 71
J	B	Cosgrave	1 LT	RM 12	70 - 71
Paul	E	Williams	1 LT	RM 27	70 - 71

RADIO OPERATORS, CREW CHIEFS AND MAINTENANCE PERSONNEL

First Name	MI	Last Name	Rank	Call Sign	Period
Tran Dinh		Luong	Sgt ARVN	ABN	1962 - 1971
-		Phoung	Cpl ARVN	ABN	1965 - 1971
-		Cotton		CC	1965
James	C	Henneberry*	A2C	RO	TDY Jun 65
Robbie		Robinson		RO	1966
-		Smith	A1C		1966
Helmut		Knaup	TSGT	NCOIC	66 - 67
Art		Skillman	SGT	CC	66 - 67
John		Balasco	SSGT	RO	66 - 67
-		Humphries	A1C	RO	66 - 67
Kenneth	W	Karnes	A1C	RO	67 - 68
Walter		Stepaniak	SGT	RO	Jan 67 - Jun 68
Raymond	L	Moore	SSGT	NCOIC RO	1967 - 1969
-		Garza		CC	67 - 68
-		Funk		CC	67 - 68
-		Valliant		RO	67 - 68
-		Reguera		RO	67 - 68
Bob		Eyer	SGT	RO	67 - 68
Douglas	J	Hedensten	SGT	CC	Mid 67 - Feb 68
Pat		Lind	SGT	RO	Late 67 - Jun 68
"Chico"		Hernandez		CC	68
Bob		Jones	SSGT	NCOIC	Early 68 - Early 69

217

APPENDIX II - RED MARKER ROSTER - CHRONOLOGICAL

First Name	MI	Last Name	Rank	Call Sign	Period
Jerry	W	Marsh		Radio Maint	Feb 68 - Oct 68
John		O'Brien	SGT	RO	Jan 68 - Jun 69
Ralph "Greg"	G	Lockwood, II	SGT	Radio Maint	Jan 69 - Jul 69
John		Carpenter		RO	Apr 68 - Jan 69
John	E	Kokowski	SGT	RO	68 - 69
James	L	Fuller	SGT	RO	68 - 69
-		Coppage	SGT	RO	May 68
-		Brown	SGT	RO	Mid 68 - Mid 69
-		Pressley	SGT	RO	Mid 68 - Mid 69
Ronald		Devries	SGT	CC	Mid 68 - Mid 69
Larry		Lauber	SGT	Generator	Sep 68 - Sep 69
Bill		McAlexander	SGT	CC	68
Perry	M	Timpson		RO	68 - 69
Mathew		Fischer**	SGT	CC	68 - 69
Michael		Roberts		CC	68 - 69
Walter		Stepaniak	SGT	RO	Sep 68 - May 70
William	C	Mackey**	SSGT	NCOIC	Late 68 - Mid 70
Barry	R	Schupp	SGT	RO	Jan 69 - Jan 70
David	A	Janssen	A1C	RO	Feb 69 - Feb 70
William	F	Kaeser III	A1C	CC	Mar 69 - Mar 70
George	F	Smith	A1C	CC	Apr 69 - Mar 70
William	F	Brandley**	SSGT	RO	Mid 69 - Mid 70
Ronald	J	Wessell	A1C	RO	Mid 69 - Mid 70
Patrick	L	Williams	SGT	RO	Jun 69 - May 70
Billy	T	Johnson**	SSGT	Generator	69 - 70
Joe		Jergens		RO	69 - 70
Kenneth		Poteet**	SGT	RO	69 - 70
Orlando	P	Metcalf III	SGT	Radio Maint	69 - 70
Henry		Presswood	A1C	RO	69 - 70
Cary	W	Strickbine	A1C	RO	Dec 69 - Mar 70
Alberto		Ramirez	SGT	RO	Late 69 - Late 70
Thomas		Still			69 - 70
Robert	W	Byrnes	A1C	CC	69 - 70
Charles	D	Cude	SGT	CC	69 - 70
Roger	E	Egleston	A1C	CC	69 - 70
James	D	Stokes	SGT	CC	69 - 70
James	D	Hoppe	A1C	CC	Jan 70 - Jan 71
Jim	M	Yeonopolus	SGT	RO	Jan 70 - Feb 71
Larry	E	Lamb	SSGT	NCOIC	Feb 70 - Feb 71
Terry	O	Elliott	SGT		Early 70 - Early 71
Richard	E	Ruel	A1C	RO	Mar 70 - Mar 71
Warren	K	Wiley	SSGT		70 - 71
David	B	Marion	SGT	CC	Mar 70 - Mar 71
Donald	G	Avery	A1C	RO	Apr 70 - Dec 70
Stephen		Figuli, Jr	A1C		70 - 71
Jeffrey	D	Froh	AMN		Apr 70 - Apr 71

218

First Name	MI	Last Name	Rank	Call Sign	Period
Charles	E	Gussman	SGT		70 - 71
John	R	Wetzler	A1C		70 - 71
Barry	L	Silfies	A1C		70 - 71
Michael	A	Possemato	A1C	RO	70 - 71
Miles	E	Tyson	SSGT	RO	70 - 71
Steven	S	Volz	A1C	RO	Apr 70 - Mar 71
John	A	Wilkins	SGT		70 - 71
Richard	L	Guy		CC	70 - 71
Dennis	L	Hull	SGT	RO	Apr 70 - Apr 71
Jerry	L	Justice	SGT	CC	Jun 70 - Mar 71

APPENDIX III

RECONSTRUCTED RED MARKER ROSTER – ALPHABETICAL

* Killed In Action.   ** Deceased.

First Name	MI	Name	Rank	Call Sign	Period
Peter	W	Almquist**	LTC	RM 01	1967 - Jan 68
Duane	P	Andrews	Capt	FAC	mid 67 - mid 68
Donald	G	Avery	A1C	RO	Apr 70 - Dec 70
John		Balasco	SSGT	RO	66 - 67
Billy	R	Barrett	1 LT/Capt	RM 15	Jul 70 - Jul 71
Bruce	C	Bechtel	Capt	RM 03	Feb 68 - Aug 69
D	C	Beckingham	1 LT	RM 18	Aug 70 - 71
Fred	T	Bishopp, Jr.	Capt	RM 05	May 69 - Sep 69
David	G	Blair**	1 LT	RM 16	Aug 69 - Jul 70
Michael "Rip"	P	Blaisdell	Capt	FAC	Jun 67 - Jul 67
Gary		Blake	Capt	FAC	Dec 67 - Feb 68
William	F	Brandley**	SSGT	RO	Mid 69 - Mid 70
Michael	H	Branz**	Major	RM 01	Jun 69 - Dec 69
-		Brown	SGT	RO	Mid 68 - Mid 69
Jack		Bryant**	LTC	RM 01	Aug 72 - Feb 73
Robert	W	Byrnes	A1C	CC	69 - 70
Robert "Bob"	M	Carn, Jr.*	1 LT	RM 03	May 65 - Aug 65
John		Carpenter		RO	Apr 68 - Jan 69
Carleton	N	Casteel	LTC	RM 01	Jul 64 - Apr 65
Jack	V	Cebe-Habersky**	Capt	RM 02	May 63 - Apr 64
Sidney	E	Conley, II	1 LT	RM 13	70 - 71
-		Coppage	SGT	RO	May 68
J	B	Cosgrave	1 LT	RM 12	70 - 71
-		Cotton		CC	1965
Charles	D	Cude	SGT	CC	69 - 70
Robert "Doc"	G	Daugherty, Jr.	LTC	RM 01	Jun 70 - Nov 70
Crawford	R	Deems, III	1 LT	RM 16	70 - 71

APPENDIX III - RED MARKER ROSTER - ALPHABETICAL

First Name	MI	Last Name	Rank	Call Sign	Period
Ronald		Devries	SGT	CC	Mid 68 - Mid 69
Freddie "Dale"	D	Dickens*	Major	RM 07	Jun 68
Peter "Pete"	L	Drahn	Capt	RM 07	Nov 67 - Nov 68
Robert "Bob"	E	Drawbaugh**	Major	RM 01	Dec 69 - Jun 70
William	E	Dunne	Capt	RM 25	69 - 70
Roger	E	Egleston	A1C	CC	69 - 70
Terry	O	Elliott	SGT		Early 70 - Early 71
Bob		Eyer	SGT	RO	67 - 68
Edward	A	Fairchild	Capt	RM 06	Oct 68 - Jul 69
Stephen		Figuli, Jr.	A1C		70 - 71
Mathew		Fischer**	SGT	CC	68 - 69
Oliver "Bud"	P	Fisher, Jr.	Major	RM 02	May 66 - May 67
Delbert "Del"	W	Fleener**	Capt	RM 07	Sep 65 - Mar 66
James "Jim"		Frail	Capt	TALO	late 67 - Jun 68
Bruce	M	Freeman	1 LT	RM 08	Jan 69 - Dec 69
Jeffrey	D	Froh	AMN		Apr 70 - Apr 71
James	L	Fuller	SGT	RO	68 - 69
William	H	Fulton, Jr.	Major	RM 01	Dec 68 - Jun 69
-		Funk		CC	67 - 68
-		Garza		CC	67 - 68
John	K	Giles	Major	RM 02	Mar 67 - Mar 68
Donald	T	Glenn	LTC	RM 01	Jan 68 - Dec 68
Joseph "Duke"	S	Granducci, II**	Capt	RM 02	Jul 65 - Jun 66
Arthur "Art"	E	Greiner	Capt	FAC	Dec 67 - Feb 68
Terence "Terry"	J	Gruters	1 LT	RM 14	Jan 70 - Nov 70
Charles	E	Gussman	SGT		70 - 71
Richard	L	Guy		CC	70 - 71
Dean	R	Haeusler	Major	RM 01	Jan 71 - Apr 71
Donald "Don"	R	Hawley*	Capt	RM 06	mid 65 - 17 Dec 65
Douglas	J	Hedensten	SGT	CC	Mid 67 - Feb 68
James	C	Henneberry*	A2C	RO	TDY Jun 65
"Chico"		Hernandez		CC	68
James	A	Hill	Capt	FAC	Jan 69 - Aug 69
Hugh	T	Hill	1 LT	RM 18	Jul 1970
James "Jim"	H	Hix, Jr.	1 LT	RM 15	Apr 70 - Sep 70
James	D	Hoppe	A1C	CC	Jan 70 - Jan 71
Yancy	D	Hudson**	1 LT	RM 12	Jan 70 - Nov 70
Dennis	L	Hull	SGT	RO	Apr 70 - Apr 71
-		Humphries	A1C	RO	66 - 67
Arthur	J	Intemann	1 LT	RM 09	Jan 69 - Jan 70
David	A	Janssen	A1C	RO	Feb 69 - Feb 70
William "Bill"	D	Jenkins	Capt	RM 09	Feb 67 - Jan 68
Joe		Jergens		RO	69 - 70
Robert	W	Johnson	Major	RM 01	Jan 72 - Jul 72
Billy	T	Johnson**	SSGT	Generator	69 - 70
Bob		Jones	SSGT	NCOIC	Early 68 - Early 69

RED MARKERS

First Name	MI	Last Name	Rank	Call Sign	Period
Jerry	L	Justice	SGT	CC	Jun 70 - Mar 71
William	F	Kaeser III	A1C	CC	Mar 69 - Mar 70
Wayne	E	Kanouse**	Cpt/Maj	RM 03	66 - 67
Kenneth	W	Karnes	A1C	RO	67 - 68
Lawrence "Laurie"	E	Kivisto	Major	RM 02	May 67 - May 68
Helmut		Knaup	TSGT	NCOIC	66 - 67
John	E	Kokowski	SGT	RO	68 - 69
John "Jack"	A	Koppin, Jr.**	Major	RM 01	Nov 70 - Jan 71
Kenneth	W	Kreger**	Major	FAC	Feb 68 - Jan 69
Larry	E	Lamb	SSGT	NCOIC	Feb 70 - Feb 71
Carl "Dave"	D	Langas	Capt	RM 04/14/24	Feb 69 - Feb 70
Larry		Lauber	SGT	Generator	Sep 68 - Sep 69
James	A	Leach**	Major	RM 02	Oct 68 - Jun 69
Pat		Lind	SGT	RO	Late 67 - Jun 68
Douglas	B	Lobser	Capt	RM 2X	69 - 70
Ralph "Greg"	G	Lockwood, II	SGT	Radio Maint	Jan 69 - Jul 69
Phillip "Phil"	R	Lumpkin	1 LT	FAC	70 - 71
Tran Dinh		Luong	Sgt ARVN	ABN	1962 - 1971
William	C	Mackey**	SSGT	NCOIC	Late 68 - Mid 70
Harold	R	Magnuson	Capt/Maj	RM 02	Feb 68 - Jan 69
David	B	Marion	SGT	CC	Mar 70 - Mar 71
William	F	Marlin	Capt	RM 04	Apr 68 - Apr 69
Jerry	W	Marsh		Radio Maint	Feb 68 - Oct 68
James	F	Martin**	LTC	RM 01	Jul 63 - Jun 64
Joseph	V	Massa	Major	RM 02	Jul 70 - Feb 71
Byron	L	Mayberry**	1 LT	RM 19	Nov 69 - Oct 70
Bill		McAlexander	SGT	CC	68
Eugene "Gene"	R	McCutchan**	Major	Red Marker	1962 - Jun 63
Eugene "Gene"	R	McCutchan**	Maj/LTC	RM 01	May 65 - 1967
Richard	V	McGill	Capt	RM 05	mid 65 - mid 66
John "Jack"	D	McKessy	Capt	RM 08	Mar 68 - Mar 69
Orlando	P	Metcalf III	SGT	Radio Maint	69 - 70
Roy	E	Moore	Capt	RM 09	Jan 68 - Apr 68
Raymond	L	Moore	SSGT	NCOIC RO	1967 - 1969
Michael "Mike"	J	Morea	1 LT/Capt	RM 04	May 66 - Jan 67
Kenneth "Ken"	E	Munson	Capt	RM 03	Aug 68 - Nov 68
John		O'Brien	SGT	RO	Jan 68 - Jun 69
Robert "Bob"	L	Paradis**	Capt	RM 02	May 64 - Apr 65
Stuart "Skip"	F	Pardee	1 LT	Covey 555	Mar 1970
Alfred "Gene"	E	Parker	Capt	RM 04	Jan 66 - May 66
Warren	K	Paxton	Capt	RM 03	69 - 70
Paul "Jeff"	J	Peacock	Capt	RM 11	70 - 71
-		Phoung	Cpl ARVN	ABN	1965 - 1971
Michael	A	Possemato	A1C	RO	70 - 71
Kenneth		Poteet**	SGT	RO	69 - 70
-		Pressley	SGT	RO	Mid 68 - Mid 69

APPENDIX III - RED MARKER ROSTER - ALPHABETICAL

First Name	MI	Last Name	Rank	Call Sign	Period
Henry		Presswood	A1C	RO	69 - 70
Lloyd	L	Prevett, Jr.	1 LT	RM 26	Nov 69 - Jul 70
Charles	R	Provini	Marine LT	ANGLO	1972
Alberto		Ramirez	SGT	RO	Late 69 - Late 70
-		Reguera		RO	67 - 68
Alan "Buck"	L	Rennick	Capt	RM 02	Feb 65 - Mar 65
Michael		Roberts		CC	68 - 69
Robbie		Robinson		RO	1966
Luis "Mike"	M	Rodriguez	1 LT	RM 17	Apr 70 - Oct 70
Richard	E	Ruel	A1C	RO	Mar 70 - Mar 71
Barry	R	Schupp	SGT	RO	Jan 69 - Jan 70
Gerald	P	Schwalb	Major	RM 02	Sep 69 - Jun 70
Lawrence "Larry"	H	Shaevitz	1 LT	RM 24	Oct 69 - Jul 70
Barry	L	Silfies	A1C		70 - 71
James "Jim"	M	Simpson	Capt	RM 13	Nov 69 - Oct 70
Art		Skillman	SGT	CC	66 - 67
Herbert	W	Smallman	1 LT	FAC	70
-		Smith	A1C		1966
George	F	Smith	A1C	CC	Apr 69 - Mar 70
Donald "Don"	A	Spooner	2 LT/1 LT	RM 07	Jul 68 - Jun 69
Walter		Stepaniak	SGT	RO	Jan 67 - Jun 68
Walter		Stepaniak	SGT	RO	Sep 68 - May 70
Peter	W	Stetson	1 LT	RM 25	70 - 71
William "Bill"	P	Stewart	Capt	RM 05	Apr 66 - Mar 67
Thomas		Still			69 - 70
James	D	Stokes	SGT	CC	69 - 70
Cary	W	Strickbine	A1C	RO	Dec 69 - Mar 70
Chad	L	Swedberg	1 LT	RM 25	Apr 70 - Sep 70
John "Jack"	C	Taylor	Major	FAC	April 67 - Mar 68
Perry	M	Timpson		RO	68 - 69
Truc	V	Tran	1 LT/Maj	DO(Red)	1966 - 1971
Miles	E	Tyson	SSGT	RO	70 - 71
-		Valliant		RO	67 - 68
George	L	Varner	Capt	FAC	Dec 67 - Feb 68
Steven	S	Volz	A1C	RO	Apr 70 - Mar 71
Donald	R	Ward	Capt	RM 14	70 - 71
Charles	R	Waterman, Jr.	Major	RM 01	May 71 - Dec 71
Terry	L	Weaver	1 LT	RM 07/17	Jun 69 - May 70
Edward	D	Weiss	1 LT	RM 03	Nov 68 - Nov 69
Ronald	J	Wessell	A1C	RO	Mid 69 - Mid 70
John	R	Wetzler	A1C		70 - 71
Stuart	K	Wheeler	1 LT	RM 09	Apr 68 - Mar 69
Warren	K	Wiley	SSGT		70 - 71
John	A	Wilkins	SGT		70 - 71
Paul	E	Williams	1 LT	RM 27	70 - 71
Patrick	L	Williams	SGT	RO	Jun 69 - May 70

RED MARKERS

First Name	MI	Last Name	Rank	Call Sign	Period
Gary	N	Willis	1 LT/Capt	RM 18	Dec 69 - Jun 70
Paul	R	Windle*	Capt	RM 02	Mar 65 - Jun 65
Jim	M	Yeonopolus	SGT	RO	Jan 70 - Feb 71

APPENDIX IV

RED HATS WHO MADE GENERAL

LTG Bill Carpenter advised the 8th ABN BN in 1963-64.
MG Edward Crowley advised the 5th ABN BN in 1963-64.
LTG Michael Davison advised the 2nd ABN BN in 1971-72.
BG Pete Dawkins advised the 1s ABN BN in 1966-67.
BG Allen Goodson was an advisor in 1964-64.
MG David Grange was an advisor to the 81st ABN Ranger Group.[1]
MG John Herrling advised the 2nd BN BDE in 1969-70.
BG John Howard advised the 6th and 11th ABN BNs in 1972-73.
LTG Joe Kinzer advised the 7th ABN BN and the 3rd ABN BDE in 1967-68.
LTG John Lemoyne advised the 6th ABN BN in 1969.
GEN James Lindsay advised the 1st VN ABN BN in 1964-65.
BG Herb Lloyd was an NCO and advised to the 6th ABN BN in 1962-63, went to OCS and as a 1LT/CPT again advised the 6th ABN BN in 1966-68.
BG James Mace advised the 5th and 6th ABN BNs in 1965-66.
MG Guy Meloy advised the 1st ABN Task Force (aka BDE) in 1966.
GEN Barry McCaffery advised the 2nd ABN BN in 1966-67.
BG Dale Nelson advised the 3rd ABN BDE in 1972.
BG Jack Nicholson was the Deputy Senior Advisor in 1969-70.
MG Richard Scholtes advised the 7th ABN BN in 1964-65.
GEN Norman Schwarzkopf advised the 1st ABN Task Force (aka BDE) 1965-66.
MG Leroy Suddath advised the 8th ABN BN in 1964-65.
BG Wesley Taylor advised the 3rd and 8th BNs in 1967-68.
LTG James Vaught was the Senior Advisor in 1970-71.
BG Arvid West advised the 5th ABN BN in 1963-64.

---

1 Grange was an advisor but not technically a Red Hat. Red Hat advisors were assigned to the 81st ABN Rangers when their Special Forces advisors and the other SF units were removed from RVN.

APPENDIX V

INDIVIDUAL MEDALS AWARDED TO RED MARKERS

U.S. Medals

Air Force Cross
Silver Star
Distinguished Flying Cross
Bronze Star with V
Bronze Star
Purple Heart
Army Air Medal with V
Air Medal
Army Commendation Medal with V
Air Force Commendation Medal
National Defense Service Medal
Vietnam Service Medal

Vietnamese Medals

National Order of Vietnam Knight
Military Merit Medal
Cross of Gallantry with Palm (Armed Forces Level Award)
Cross of Gallantry with Gold Star (Corps Level)
Cross of Gallantry with Silver Star (Division Level)
Cross of Gallantry with Bronze Star (Brigade Level)
Air Force Cross of Gallantry with Silver Wings
Honor Staff Service Medal
Vietnam Campaign Medal

BIBLIOGRAPHY

Books, Articles, Publications:

Air Force Museum, "A Dangerous Business: Forward Air Control in SEA," online article at http://nationalmuseum.af.mil.factsheets.html, 2010.

"Airborne Brigade Newsletter(s)," Headquarters Airborne Brigade Advisory Detachment, APO San Francisco, 18 Dec 1963 and 10 Apr 1965.

"Airborne Division Newsletter," Headquarters Airborne Division Advisory Detachment, APO San Francisco, 5 April 1966.

Brant, Lt. Colonel Matthew C., USAF, "Air Power and the 1972 Easter Offensive," Fort Leavenworth, KS, 2007.

Campbell, Douglas Norman, B.A, M.A., *Plane in the Middle: A History of the U.S. Air Force's Dedicated Close Air Support Plane,* Texas Tech University, May 1999.

CHECO Reports (Contemporary Historical Examination of Current Operations), Headquarters Pacific Air Force, various dates as indicated below:

- "The Cambodian Campaign, 29 Apr – 30 Jun 1970," by Major D. I. Folkman and Major P. D. Caine, 1 Sep 1970.
- "Kontum: Battle for the Central Highlands, 30 March – 10 June 1972," by Captain Peter A. W. Liebchen, 27 October 1972.
- "Tactical Control Squadron Operations in SEASIA (U)," by Melvin Porter, 15 Oct 1969.
- "The 1972 Invasion of Military Region 1: The Fall of Quang Tri and the Defense of Hue," by Captain David Mann, 15 March 1973.
- "The Battle for An Loc, 5 April – 26 June 1972 (U)," by Captain Paul T. Ringenbach and Captain Peter J. Kelley, 31 January 1973.

BIBLIOGRAPHY

Chien Su, Su Doan Nhay Du, (War History, Airborne Division), published by Veterans of the Airborne Division, 2010.

Cleared Hot, Forward Air Controller Stories from the Vietnam War, published by the Forward Air Controller Association, Inc., 2008.

Cleared Hot, Book Two, Forward Air Controller Stories from the Vietnam War, published by the Forward Air Controller Association, Inc., 2009.

Correll, John T., "The Air Force in the Vietnam War," Aerospace Education Foundation, Arlington, VA, 2004.

Court-Martial Reports, Holdings and Decisions of the Courts of Military Review and United States Court of Military Appeal, Volume 44, 1971–1972, The Lawyers Co-operative Publishing Company, Rochester, NY, 1973

Granducci, Major Joseph S., II, USAF (Ret), commemoration of Captain Paul R. Windle, KIA, on the Virtual Wall, http://www.VirtualWall.org/dw/WindlePR01a.htm.

Jobe, Major R. Scott, "Snake, 'Nape and Rockets at Dawn! Modern Close Air Support and the Vietnam War," Air Command and Staff College, Air University, Maxwell AFB, AL, April 2006.

Johnson, President Lyndon B., Presidential Executive Orders, 7 February 1965 and 24 April 1965.

Johnson, Captain Marshall B., Battalion Senior Advisor, "Operations of the 9th Battalion, Airborne Division (ARVN), in a Search and Destroy Operation 27-28 March 1967, in Thua Thien Province, Republic of Vietnam," United States Infantry School, Fort Benning, GA, 2 April 1968

Karnow, Stanley, *Vietnam, A History*, The Viking Press, New York, NY, 1983

Leeker, Dr. Joe F., "Khmer Air Force O-1s," online http://www.utdallas.edu/library/collections/speccoll/Leeker/index3.html.

Lewis, Jerry M. and Hensley, Thomas R., "The May 4 Shootings at Kent State University: The Search for Historical Accuracy," The Ohio Council for The Social Studies Review, Vol. 34, Number 1 (Summer 1998).

Little, Donald D. and Spink, Barry L., "USAF Personnel Rotation in Southeast Asia (A Chronology)," Air Force Historical Research Agency, Maxwell AFB< AL, April 2008.

Martin, Command Sergeant Major Michael, USA (Ret), *Angels in Red Hats, Paratroopers of the Second Indochina War*, Harmony House, Louisville, KY, 1995.

McCutchan, Lt. Colonel Eugene R., USAF (Ret), *A Mark Too High*, published by Colonel Alva L. Matheson on behalf of the Forward Air Controllers Association, Inc., 2004.

Mikesh, Robert C., "The Labors of Hercules," Air & Space Magazine, August/September 1989, p. 21.

Nolan, Keith William, *Into Cambodia, Spring Campaign, Summer Offensive*, 1970, Presidio Press, Novato, CA, 1990.

"Observer, The," newspaper published by Military Assistance Command – Vietnam, 7 November 1964.

"Pacific Stars and Stripes," various dates.

"Phoenix Gazette," published by Phoenix Newspapers, Inc., 22 December 1964.

"Report of Special Committee on Tactical Air Support of the Committee on Armed Services," House of Representatives Eighty-Ninth Congress, Second Session, No. 44, 1 February 1966.

Rossel, Eugene D., Air Commando website, http://home.earthlink.net/~aircommando1/windle2.html.

Rowley, Major Ralph A., "USAF FAC Operations in Southeast Asia, 1961-1965," Office of Air Force History, 1972.

Rowley, Lt. Colonel Ralph A., "The Air Force in Southeast Asia, FAC Operations, 1965-1970," Office of Air Force History, 1975.

"Seventh Air Force News," published by Seventh Air Force, article by Sergeant Bob Palmer, photos by Staff Sergeant Ron Smith, 3 September 1969.

Stewart, Captain William P., Air Liaison Officer, ARVN Airborne Division, "End of Tour Report," 23 April 1966–15 March 1967, to Commander 504th Tactical Air Support Group.

"Twelfth Air Force History," online http://www.globalsecurity.org/military/agency/usaf/12af.html.

12th Airborne Battalion History, online http://www.truclayentu.info/tlls_lichsuvietnamcandai/12thairbornbattalion.html.

Unit Histories, Air Force Historical Research Agency, Maxwell AFB, AL:

    19th Tactical Air Support Squadron, various dates.
    20th Tactical Air Support Squadron, various dates.
    21st Tactical Air Support Squadron, various dates.
    22nd Tactical Air Support Squadron, various dates.
    23rd Tactical Air Support Squadron, various dates.
    504th Tactical Air Support Group, various dates.

BIBLIOGRAPHY

Whitcomb, Colonel Darrel D., USAFR (Ret), *The Rescue of Bat 21*, Naval Institute Press, Annapolis, MD, 1998.

Willbanks, James H., *The Battle of An Loc*, Indiana University Press, Bloomington, IN, 2005.

Willick, George C., "482nd Fighter Interceptor Squadron Scrapbook," online http://www.gcwillick.com/482ndFIS/Scrapbook/MartinSStar.html.

Individual interviews, surveys, diaries, scrapbooks, emails, telephone conferences:

Anderson, Lt. Colonel Michael, USA (Ret).
Avery, Donald G., former USAF Sergeant.
Barrett, Billy R., former USAF Captain.
Bishopp, Fred T., Jr., former USAFR Major.
Blair, Colonel, Richard, USA (Ret).
Blaisdell, Colonel Michael P., USAF (Ret).
Blake, Gary, former USAF Captain.
Campbell, Colonel John G., USA (Ret).
Casteel, Colonel Carleton N. USAF (Ret).
Cebe-Habersky, Lt. Colonel Jack V., USAF (Dec'd), photo scrapbook from his widow.
Ciccolo, Colonel William N., USA (Ret).
Condon, Wing Commander Peter D., RAAF (Ret).
Conklin, Captain Ralph R., USA (Ret).
Crowley, Major General Edward M., USA (Ret).
Daugherty, Colonel Robert G., USAF (Ret).
DeVries, Colonel Paul T., USA (Ret).
Drahn, Brig. General Peter L., USAFR (Ret), Diary of Vietnam Tour.
Fairchild, Lt. Colonel Edward A., USAF (Ret).
Findley, Donald T., former USAF Technical Sergeant.
Fisher, Lt. Colonel Oliver P., USAF (Ret).
Flynn, Colonel Michael J., USA (Ret).
Freeman, Colonel Bruce M., USAF (Ret).
Giles, Colonel John K., USAF (Ret).
Glenn, Colonel Donald T., USAF (Ret).
Granducci, Major Joseph S., II, USAF (Ret) (Dec'd), prior research provided by his widow and son.
Green, Robert B., former USAF Sergeant.
Gruters, Terence J., former USAF Captain.
Hedensten, Douglas J., former USAF Sergeant.
Henneberry, A2C James C., USAF KIA, material provided by his nephews.
Hill, James A., former USAF Captain.
Hix, Lt. Colonel James H., USAF (Ret).
Hoppe, James D., former USAF Staff Sergeant.
Hull, Major Dennis L., USAF (Ret).

Intemann, Lt. Colonel Arthur J., USAFR (Ret).
Johnson, Major Robert W., USAF (Ret).
Justice, Jerry L., former USAF Staff Sergeant.
Kaeser, Master Sergeant William F., III, USAF (Ret).
Kimminau, Major Leo F., USAF (Ret).
Kinzer, Lt. General Joseph W., USA (Ret).
Kivisto, Lt. Colonel Lawrence E., USAF (Ret), Diary of Vietnam Tour.
Lamb, Technical Sergeant Larry E., USAF (Ret).
Langas, Carl D., former USAF Captain.
Lauber, Larry, former USAF Sergeant.
Lenti, Colonel John M., USA (Ret).
Lindsay, General James J., USA (Ret).
Lolas, Lt. Colonel Anthony V., USAF (Ret).
Losik, Lt. Colonel Robert C., USA (Ret).
Marion, David B., former USAF Sergeant.
Marlin, William F., former USAF Captain.
Martin, Major John J., USA (Ret).
McCutchan, Lt. Colonel Eugene R., USAF (Ret).
McKessy, Colonel John D., USAF (Ret).
Moore, Lt. Colonel Roy E., USAF (Ret).
Morea, Colonel Michael J., USAF (Ret).
Murphy, Colonel Robert, USA (Ret).
Painschab, Timothy, former USAF Sergeant.
Pardee, Stuart F., former USAF Captain.
Prevett, Colonel Lloyd L., Jr., USAF (Ret).
Rennick, Lt. Colonel Alan L., USAFR (Ret).
Rodriguez, Colonel Luis M., USAF (Ret).
Ruel, Machinist Technician Richard E., USCG (Ret), former USAF Sergeant.
Schupp, Lt. Colonel Barry R., USAR (Ret).
Schwalb, Lt. Colonel Gerald P., USAF (Ret).
Sciacchitano, David, former USAF Staff Sergeant.
Simpson, Lt. Colonel James M., USAF (Ret).
Spooner, Colonel Donald A., USAF (Ret).
Stepaniak, Walter, former USAF Sergeant.
Stewart, Lt. Colonel William P., USAF (Ret).
Strickbine, Cary W., former USAF A1C.
Swedberg, Lt. Colonel Chad L., USAF (Ret).
Tran, Major Truc Van, VNAF.
Volz, Steven S., former USAF Staff Sergeant.
Weaver, Terry L., former USAF Captain.
Weiss, Edward D., former USAF Captain.
Webb, Colonel Robert H., USA (Ret).
Whitcomb, Colonel Darrel D., USAFR (Ret).
Yeonopolus, Jim M., former USAF Sergeant.

Made in the USA
Middletown, DE
05 February 2015